THE GENERATIONAL EQUITY DEBATE

I0085509

THE GENERATIONAL EQUITY DEBATE

Edited by John B. Williamson, Diane M. Watts-Roy, and Eric R. Kingson

COLUMBIA UNIVERSITY PRESS   NEW YORK

COLUMBIA UNIVERSITY PRESS

Publishers Since 1893

New York   Chichester, West Sussex

Copyright © 1999 Columbia University Press

All rights reserved

Library of Congress Cataloging-in-Publication Data

The generational equity debate / edited by John B. Williamson, Diane M. Watts-Roy,
and Eric R. Kingson.

   p.   cm.

   Includes index.

   ISBN 978-0-231-11284-0 (cloth : alk. paper)-ISBN 978-0-231-11285-7 (pbk. : alk. paper)

   1. Fiscal policy—United States. 2. Generational accounting—United States. 3. Social
security—United States. I. Williamson, John. II. Watts-Roy, Diane M. III. Kingson, Eric R.

   HJ2051.G36 1999

   336.3'0973—dc21   98–45318

∞

Casebound editions of Columbia University Press books are printed on
permanent and durable acid-free paper.

For my uncles, Blaine R. Butler Jr. and Charles B. Butler —J.B.W.

For my grandmother, Mary Catherine Blakeman —D.M.W-R

For my uncle, William R. Meyer —E.R.K.

CONTENTS

ACKNOWLEDGMENTS

We began work on this book during the fall of 1996. Since then each of us has had the assistance of a number of people who have helped make this book what it is.

John Williamson wants to thank Shari Grove, a librarian at Boston College, for her assistance in tracking down sources in the chapters he co-authored and for helping in our efforts to locate suitable selections to represent the different points of view. He wishes to thank Brenda Pepe and Eunice Doherty of the Sociology Department for the many ways in which they have helped out. He especially wants to thank David Karp and Charlie Derber for the time that they have spent reviewing drafts of the prospectus and being there to discuss the project over many months. He appreciates their suggestions and values their friendship. He also wants to thank his wife, Bette Johnson, for the various ways in which she has contributed. He appreciates her support and greatly admires the grace with which she balances the challenges of the roles of mother, daughter, wife, construction supervisor, and associate director of admissions. He has dedicated this book to two special uncles, Charles B. Butler and Blaine R. Butler, Jr. In their different ways they both have been role models for him for decades.

Diane M. Watts-Roy wishes to thank her family and friends for being a continual source of support and encouragement. She especially wants to thank her husband, Jeff, for the many ways that he contributed to this project. She has dedicated this book to the memory of her grandmother, Mary Catherine Blakeman. Her courage, wisdom, and humor remain a constant source of inspiration.

Eric Kingson wants to thank Richard Jackson, Senior Advisor to the Concord Coalition, for his helpful advice. He also wishes to acknowledge and thank his wife, Joan, and their children, Aaron and Johanna, for their support in all his efforts and, most important, for a joyful home. He has dedicated this book to his Uncle Bill, an important presence in his life. They have found much enjoyment in discussing their political differences—so much so that it is often disappointing that they agree on so much.

At Columbia University Press there are several people we want to thank: John Michel, our editor, for the role he has played at all stages; Alexander Thorp for his prompt and competent answers to the many questions that have come up along the way; and Anne McCoy for her role as managing editor. Suzanne Schafer did an excellent job as copy editor. Finally, we want to express appreciation to our anonymous reviewers for their suggestions.

CREDITS

Chapter 1 is an original contribution.

Chapter 2 originally appeared as "Testimony Submitted to the Senate Budget Committee," January 22, 1997.

Chapter 3 is copyright © 1996 by Lester C. Thurow. It originally appeared in *The Future of Capitalism*, by Lester C. Thurow. Reprinted by permission of William Morrow and Company, Inc.

Chapter 4 is in part adapted from "Generational Accounts for the United States," by Jagadeesh Gokhale, Benjamin R. Page, and John R. Sturrock," in *Generational Accounts Around the World*. Copyright © 1998 by the National Bureau of Economic Research. All rights reserved. Reprinted by permission of The University of Chicago Press.

Chapter 5 is copyright © 1989 by *The Mount Sinai Journal of Medicine*. From Richard D. Lamm, "Columbus and Copernicus: New Wine in Old Wineskins." *Mount Sinai Journal of Medicine* 56, no. 1 (1989): 1–10.

Chapter 6 is copyright © 1994 by the Gerontological Society of America. From Daniel Callahan, "Setting Limits: A Response." *The Gerontologist* 34, no. 3 (1994): 393–398.

Chapter 7 is is an original contribution.

Chapter 8 is copyright © 1996 by the Gerontological Society of America. From Jill Quadagno, "Social Security and the Myth of the Entitlement 'Crisis.'" *The Gerontologist* 36, no. 3 (1996): 391–399.

Chapter 9 appeared in *The Oldest Old,* edited by Richard M. Suzman, David P. Willis, and Kenneth G. Manton. Copyright © 1992 by Oxford University Press, Inc. Used by permission of Oxford University Press, Inc.

Chapter 10 originally appeared as "Social Security Politics and the Conflict Between Generations," by Theodore R. Marmor, Fay Cook, and Stephen Scher, in *Social Security in the 21st Century,* edited by Eric R. Kingson and James H. Schulz. Copyright © 1997 by Oxford University Press, Inc. Used by permission of Oxford University Press, Inc.

Chapter 11 is an extensively revised version of "Understanding the Coming Debate Over the Privatization of Social Security," by Eric R. Kingson and John B. Williamson. *Journal of Sociology and Social Welfare* (in press). Copyright © 1998 by Journal of Sociology and Social Welfare.

Chapter 12 is adapted from "Third Millennium Declaration." Copyright © 1993 by Third Millennium. Used by permission of Third Millennium.

Chapter 13 is adapted from *Agenda 2000,* a booklet published by the 2030 Center. Reprinted by permission of the 2030 Center.

PART I

Introduction

CHAPTER ONE

Framing the Generational Equity Debate

John B. Williamson and Diane M. Watts-Roy

John Williamson is Professor of Sociology at Boston College. He is a member of the National Academy of Social Insurance. He has written extensively on the politics of aging, public policy toward the elderly, and the privatization of Social Security. Among his books are *The Senior Rights Movement, Old-Age Security in Comparative Perspective, Aging and Public Policy,* and *The Politics of Aging.* Diane Watts-Roy is a doctoral student in the Department of Sociology at Boston College. She received her M.A. in sociology from the College of William and Mary. She is currently doing research on the way that the Social Security debate has been framed in the popular press during the past thirty years.

Williamson and Watts-Roy create a framework for a critical analysis of the articles that follow. They provide an in-depth analysis of the concept of "generational equity" that includes a discussion of the concept's historical origins. They discuss the current framing of the generational equity debate, describing how the debate is framed by both proponents and critics of the generational equity perspective. They highlight the assumptions, beliefs, and values that undergird each of these perspectives and discuss the distinctive rhetorical strategies emphasized by the proponents of each.

The issue of generational equity is central to the debate between senior advocates and their critics over what share of societal resources should be allocated to the elderly. Some proponents of generational equity are critical of the share of societal resources being consumed by the elderly today; others are concerned about the share the elderly may consume thirty years from now, when most of the baby boomers have retired.

At the core of the arguments being put forth by proponents of generational equity is the assumption that thirty years from now it will not be possible to support the retired baby boomers at the level enjoyed by those currently retired. From this perspective it is viewed as unfair that the boomers now in the labor force are being asked to pay heavy taxes to support those now retired at a level that will be unsustainable when they in turn retire. Central to the generational equity perspective is the idea that each generation should provide for itself; one generation should not be asked to support another generation, particularly if there is good reason to believe that the generation providing the support is unlikely to receive the same level of support when it retires.

The concept of generational equity is used in connection with the argument that the elderly are getting more than their fair share of societal resources, particularly federal government resources, and that unless something is done this inequity is going to get much worse in the years ahead. Although many defenders of Social Security accept the argument that it may be necessary to make cuts in projected spending on Social Security and Medicare in the years ahead, they do not accept the suggestion by proponents of generational equity that equity between generations should be emphasized to the exclusion of other forms of equity. In large measure the debate over generational equity is a debate over whether or not to focus on one specific form of equity (age related) or to try to balance needs linked to several competing forms of equity, including those linked to race, class, and gender.

GENERATIONAL EQUITY IN HISTORICAL PERSPECTIVE

EARLY ORIGINS OF THE DEBATE

The generational equity debate is the most recent incarnation of a question that has been with us since the dawn of recorded history, the question about what share of family and/or community resources should be consumed by the elderly. Historically the issue and the conflict surrounding it were typically intrafamily matters. However, it was a sufficiently prevalent issue that cultural norms evolved for handling it. In some communities those norms seemed to protect the interests of the elderly; in others they seemed to protect the rest of the community from the consumption demands of the elderly.

Conflict between young and old over the control of food, land, and other scarce resources is a common theme in historical accounts of intergenerational relations. Anthropologists have given considerable attention to the issue, particularly in their accounts of the relationship between elderly parents and their adult children. Relationships between the young and old have often reflected ambivalence, including such emotions as guilt, affection, and fear (Treas 1977). It has not been uncommon for elders to be treated with derision in some contexts while at the same time being granted a certain amount of power and respect in others (Achenbaum and Stearns 1978).

In anthropological accounts of preliterate societies, food-sharing practices are often mentioned in discussions of conflict between young and old over control of resources (Simmons 1945). These practices and the norms surrounding them were one way the elderly could protect their interests in societies that placed a high premium on youth, strength, and stamina. The elderly tended to be better treated in societies based on fishing and gathering than in nomadic societies based on herding and hunting. Among the Aleuts, a fishing-based society, the elderly tended to be well treated (Beauvoir 1972). In contrast, among the nomadic Hottentots of sub-Saharan Africa the infirm elderly were often left behind to die as the community moved on in search of better hunting grounds (Murdock 1934).

Food-sharing practices were often linked to food-related taboos. These practices were usually found in settled societies with well-developed religious beliefs that involved magic and ancestor worship. Religious beliefs reinforced superstitions about the adverse consequences of violating certain food taboos. For example, the Chukchi of Siberia believed that reindeer milk caused flabby breasts in young women and impotence in young men, but it was not viewed as harmful to the elderly. Among the Omaha, a Native American tribe, youth were told that their arrows would twist as they shot if they ate certain choice morsels thought to be harmless only to the elderly (Simmons 1945). Meats that were particularly suitable for those who had lost many of their teeth, such as soft organ meats like lungs and livers, were often involved in these food taboos. Most anthropologists do not go so far as to suggest that the elderly invented these food taboos out of self-interest, but they do seem to have manipulated them to their advantage (Webster 1932).

In feudal societies the elderly tend to be at the mercy of those who are younger and stronger. Prior to about 800 B.C. the feudal aspects of ancient

Greek society prevented elderly males from exercising real power. However, by the seventh century b.c. Greek society had evolved to a point where age had become a qualification for holding office. In many cities old men controlled the government and they enacted laws protecting their land rights. As long as Greek society was aristocratic and conservative, old men with property had power and influence. Intergenerational conflict became more open when institutions in cities like Athens became more democratic. Although an Athenian father could exercise economic power over his children by withholding inheritances, the comedies of Aristophanes illustrate that elderly parents who used their power in such ways were now subjected to derision, at least in the context of the theater. This link between democracy and the relative power of different age groups would appear two millennia later in colonial America.

In rural colonial America it was common for elderly parents to be cared for by one of their children (often the youngest), who in return was given the homestead and some land (Fischer 1978). Elderly parents who owned a substantial farm had at least some economic protection during their old age, but the landless—and particularly laborers living in towns and cities—often did not have significant assets to pass along to their children.

Colonists who lived in frontier communities had to rely upon neighborly mutual aid (Bradford 1962). This contributed to a suppression of certain aspects of Protestant individualism. It also promoted community solidarity and a willingness to provide for needy persons, including the elderly, who were members of the local community (Trattner 1974). Those living in early colonial settlements were generally willing to provide for their own elderly poor in a way that was considered adequate given the Spartan standard of living available at the time for most of the nonelderly working population. But they were generally unwilling to care for poor outsiders. Elderly strangers who were poor or at risk of becoming poor were not welcome; they would not have time to make sufficient contributions to the community to justify a claim on community resources.

In colonial America the elderly (particularly elderly men) were venerated so long as they were not poor. Yet by the late eighteenth century there were growing strains in the system of age relations. According to the social historian David Hackett Fischer (1978), the years between 1770 and 1820 saw, in addition to the American War of Independence and the French Revolution, a dramatic change in the relationship between the elderly and their adult children. That change was influenced by the ideological and psychological upheavals associated with these revolutions, and it contributed to a decline in veneration of the elderly and to the emergence of a new hierarchy of the generations—one in which the young acquired the moral advantage that the aged lost. The historian Andrew Achenbaum (1978) also notes a shift in age relations, but puts the transition a bit later, during the decades after the Civil War. He suggests that during the period after the Civil War the elderly were less likely to be praised for their moral wisdom and practical sagacity; they were now more likely to be described in terms their obsolescence and poor health.

A number of factors contributed to changes in public policy toward the elderly during the nineteenth century. During the early part of the century there was a sharp increase in the number of people on relief and a corresponding increase in the poor tax. An important source of this change was the severe depression from 1815 to 1821 linked to the end of the Napoleonic War (Coll 1969). Another source was the change in the ethnic composition of the poor in many areas. Many of the recent immigrants not only were culturally different but for a variety of reasons were failing to conform to the American norm of caring for their own dependent elderly (Kutzik 1979; Williamson 1984).

One of the most important policy changes was the shift from an emphasis on outdoor relief (relief to people living in their own homes) to indoor relief (relief in almshouses). During the colonial period almshouses were for the most part confined to the large port towns, but by the middle of the nineteenth century almost every town had one (Rothman 1971). Although a significant proportion of the poor, including the elderly poor, continued to receive outdoor relief, the tendency to emphasize the much more punitive indoor relief alternative continued for the rest of the century. This shift in policy was triggered by economic insecurity and an increase in tax rates, causes that sparked a similar reaction during the early years of the Reagan administration (Powell and Williamson 1985).

SHADES OF THE DEBATE IN THE NEW DEAL AND THE
GREAT SOCIETY

Whereas the issue of conflict between generations over the elderly's economic dependency and the control of resources has a very long history, the contemporary generational equity debate has its most direct origins in the debate over passage of the Social Security Act of 1935. One title of this legislation created a national old-age welfare program called Old Age Assistance. Another title created an old-age pension scheme called Old Age Insurance. That legislation was enacted after a long and bitter struggle between proponents and opponents of a national old-age pension scheme. At the core of the struggle was a contest between two alternative interpretive packages. Those who favored enactment of a national pension scheme attempted to frame the contest as a debate over "social security." Those who opposed it attempted to frame it as a debate that placed the "American way" in a contest with the socialistic European alternative.

Advocates for the enactment of pension legislation emphasized the issues of social security and social insecurity. The social security interpretive package eventually prevailed. One reflection of this was that the catch phrase "social security" became the informal name for the Old Age Insurance program. This conceptualizaton was used to argue that a public pension scheme was the only acceptable solution to the problem of economic insecurity among the elderly. The elderly were often depicted as poor, frail homebodies deserving of public support so they could remain at home rather than being forced into almshouses (Powell, Branco, and Williamson 1996). In one cartoon, published in 1930 in the *American Labor Legislation Review*, an elderly couple is depicted walking down a country lane. They have just come upon a fork in the road where they must choose between a road that leads to the local poorhouse and another that leads to the old-age pension office. A kindly Uncle Sam is at the side of the road urging them to take the road to the pension office (Quadagno 1988).

Critics of pension legislation were also very active, but the goal of their rhetorical efforts was to undercut support for the idea of a national public pension scheme. During the early 1930s a number of grassroots pension movements were active in California. The most influential among them was organized by Francis Townsend (Holtzman 1963; Skocpol and Amenta 1985). Within a few years the Townsend Movement became a national movement (Pratt 1976). Critics of public pensions described such groups as "radical" or "extremist" and their pension proposals as "the entering wedge of socialism." These proposals were labeled as inconsistent with the American way, that is, with such values as thrift, self-reliance, and individualism. This anti-pension interpretive package pointed to the danger of creating a new class of dependents, elderly lazy freeloaders dependent on the government. According to economist and anti-pension activist Samuel Crowther (1930:34), "there are young bums as well as old bums, and neither has any claim whatsoever upon society."

In a 1935 cartoon published in the *New York Times* we find a forerunner of the more recent "greedy geezer" image of the elderly. A fat, elderly woman with big teeth (symbolizing the tax bite that would be needed to pay for a public pension scheme) is depicted as greedily feeding on national revenue. She is at the table with a lean male dinner companion (symbolizing the taxpayers of America) who is looking on in a state of shock or bewilderment (Powell et al. 1996). This cartoon was one of many of the era depicting themes of the anti-pension framing of the debate. Others describe public pension as an unworkable bureaucratic nightmare, as hopelessly idealistic and impractical, and as a source of idle dependency.

Between 1950 and the early 1970s the original Social Security Act was frequently amended, sometimes to extend coverage to new groups and sometimes to increase the level of pension benefits. It had become a very popular program, and the large number of workers paying in relative to the number drawing benefits made voting for such legislation politically attractive for both Republicans and Democrats. However, there was considerable conflict between liberals and conservatives over the issue of health care coverage, which reached a crescendo during the mid-1960s and led to enactment of the Medicare and Medicaid programs in 1965.

Some labor groups were pushing for national medical insurance programs even before 1920. President Franklin D. Roosevelt did not make a serious attempt to include national health insurance as part of the original Social Security legislation because he knew there would be stiff opposition that could jeopardize the entire Social Security bill. But the Committee on Economic Security, the group Roosevelt selected to help shape the Social Security legislation, did insert a clause calling for a study to explore the feasibility of adding such a program. Because of very strong opposition, even this clause was removed (Feingold 1966). The issue arose again during the Truman administration. Truman endorsed several national health insurance proposals, none of which were ever enacted by Congress.

In 1961 President Kennedy asked to have a Medicare bill drafted. It differed from the proposals of the Truman era in that it covered only the elderly. It was based on a suggestion from Wilbur Cohen of the Social Security Administration to start with a program limited to the elderly that could subsequently be gradually extended to cover the entire population (Harris 1966). This incremental strategy was viewed as a possible defense against conservative efforts to label such a program as socialized medicine. Despite strong support from the president, organized labor, the American Association of Retired Persons (AARP), and many other old-age interest groups, the bill was defeated, as was a similar bill when the issue reappeared in 1964 (Berkowitz 1997). Conservatives were successful in their efforts to frame the debate as a choice between socialized medicine and the American way (Marmor 1969; Powell et al. 1996).

When Lyndon Johnson was elected in 1964 with a very large Democratic majority it became clear that Medicare legislation was going to pass. In a surprise move, Wilbur Mills added Title 19 to the Medicare bill, calling for the creation of a separate Medicaid program to cover the health care needs of the poor.

This was part of a conservative strategy to make it more politically difficult over the years to extend Medicare to cover the entire population. Those opposed to Medicare, including the American Medical Association, the American Hospital Association, the National Association of Manufacturers, and many other groups representing the interests of business and the health care industry, spent huge sums opposing the bill. Their goal again was to frame the question as a choice between socialized medicine and the American system of medicine. Their interpretive package emphasized the high taxes, loss of freedom, and bureaucratic problems that would result (Marmor 1973).

Conservatives lost in their efforts to oppose the enactment of Medicare, but they were successful in shaping the program to assure that the major actors in the health care industry would be well compensated. They also succeeded in constructing the program so that it could not easily be extended to other age groups. The creation of what has become an expensive program paid for in large part by the nonelderly has placed Medicare, along with the Social Security program, at the center of the generational equity debate.

Between the mid-1960s and the mid-1970s, much legislation responding to the needs of the elderly was enacted. In 1965 the Older Americans Act was passed. It led to the creation of a network of senior centers and to the introduction of a number of service programs designed to help the elderly with such issues as nutrition, transportation, legal counseling, and home repairs. Many advances were made during Richard Nixon's first administration (1969–1973), including (1) substantial increases in the size of Social Security benefits, (2) the introduction of indexing for Social Security benefits in order to protect them against inflation, and (3) the creation of the Supplemental Security Income (SSI) program, a guaranteed income program for the elderly poor.

THE RECENT REEMERGENCE OF THE DEBATE

During much of the period between the mid-1930s and the late 1970s, and particularly during the 1960s and 1970s, the aged benefited from what Robert Binstock (1983) has described as compassionate ageism. Advocates for the elderly were able to create a widely accepted image of the aged as discriminated against, poor, and frail. A number of interest groups advocating for the elderly promoted an interpretive package that painted a picture of the elderly as a group of people who were, with few exceptions, not only needy but also eminently deserving of public support (Kalish 1979). The promotion of these compassionate stereotypes about the elderly proved to be an effective rhetorical device, particularly between the mid-1960s and the mid-1970s.

During the 1950s, 1960s, and early 1970s these stereotypes helped sell social policies that increased the share of societal resources allocated to and consumed by the elderly. This was relatively easy to do during an era of rapid increases in both income and standard of living for the rest of the population. People were willing to increase spending on the elderly and other vulnerable groups when the size of the economic pie was rapidly expanding and most people assumed it would continue to do so indefinitely.

But changing demographics–including increased life expectancies, declining birth rates, and population aging–combined with dramatically changing economic conditions in the 1970s led to questions about whether there was too much spending on the elderly. The economic turning point came in 1973 with the first oil embargo. Inflation became a serious problem and the rate of economic growth declined. By the end of the decade there had been a second oil embargo and it was clear the nation was facing what was termed stagflation, an unusual combination of high unemployment and high inflation. Due in part to these economic problems and in part to the war in Vietnam, the Watergate scandal, the failure of various War on Poverty programs to achieve promised results, and the Iranian hostage crisis, there was a general decline in trust of government and confidence in federal programs as means to solve social problems.

During the prior couple of decades most people had been very confident about the economic future of the nation and of their families; now they became more pessimistic. That pessimism yielded greater reluctance to fund government programs for the elderly, the poor, and other needy groups. As a result of this dramatic shift in the economic environment and the level of trust in government, the nation was ripe for the ascendance of the New Right. The election of Ronald Reagan as President in 1980 reflected this shift to the right, but the increasing influence of conservative ideology on social policy was already evident by the late 1970s, exemplified by the successful "tax revolts" in several states that took the form of ballot initiatives like Proposition 13 in California and Proposition 2 in Massachusetts (Kuttner 1980). By the end of the decade the anti–welfare state backlash was under way and programs for the elderly were unusually vulnerable.

Ginsberg (1986) points out that major shifts in political thinking often emerge as the result of well-organized campaigns rather than as spontaneous events. The emergence of the New Right during the 1970s was no accident. It was in part orchestrated by a number of conservative think tanks such as the Cato Institute, the American Enterprise Institute, and the Heritage Foundation. A number of conservative foundations, such as the Olin Fund, financed the work of conservative scholars and activists. Also playing an important role were a number of public intellectuals such as William F. Buckley Jr., who edited the influential conservative *National Review* and hosted a widely syndicated television program, *Firing Line* (Powell et al. 1996).

In 1977 Social Security for the first time faced a serious short-term financing problem. Many factors contributed to the emergence of this situation, including several years of high inflation, high unemployment rates, and lower than expected wage increases (Berkowitz 1997). But there were other contributing factors as well, such as the sharp increase in the size of Social Security pension benefits resulting from the 1972 amendments and a large increase in the number of workers awarded disability benefits (Kingson 1984). And there were projections of a long-term financing shortfall, fueled by a faulty indexing system enacted at the same time and changing demographics.

In connection with the debate over the Social Security financing problem, a great deal was written in the popular press and in the publications of conservative think tanks. Claims were made that unless drastic measures were taken the Social Security system would soon go bankrupt (Kingson 1984). At the time the American public was not aware of how a pay-as-you-go social insurance program is financed. Few realized how the financing of such a public pension scheme differs from a fully funded private pension scheme such as the 401(k) and Individual Retirement Accout (IRA) plans that are so common today. Of particular note was the effort of conservatives to define the problem as a "crisis" and for liberals to define it as a "short-term funding problem."

The crisis interpretive package served a number of goals for conservatives. Conservative activists and scholars were in favor of efforts to shrink the American welfare state. It was clear to them that it would be impossible to achieve the kind of spending reduction they wanted without making cuts in the very popular Social Security program. One way to reduce the popularity of a program, and thus make it easier to reduce spending on it, is to undermine public confidence in the program. The crisis framing and the associated argument that the program might soon go bankrupt was part of the effort by conservatives to define the debate in such a way as to advance their policy objective, namely, cutting spending on social programs, including Social Security (Powell et al. 1996). Liberals wanted to defend Social Security from cuts. To this end their objective was to minimize the magnitude of the problem and at all costs avoid a "crisis" framing of the issue. Their alternative frame was that the program was facing a temporary cash-flow problem that could be easily managed with minor technical adjustments.

The 1977 Social Security legislation increased payroll tax rates and increased the upper limit with respect to how much income would be subject to payroll taxes (Meyer 1987). The cost-of-living-adjustment (COLA) formula was also changed to compensate for a fault in the formula as enacted in 1972; the earlier formula had provided benefit increases well in excess of congressional intent. Thus it reduced Social Security spending. This legislation also called for periodic increases in the upper limit with respect to how much income would be subject to the Social Security payroll tax. Within a few years it was clear that the 1977 legislation had failed to deal adequately with the program's financing problems (Berkowitz 1997). A major reason was that the economy continued to get much worse than most analysts had anticipated. In 1980 the COLA increase was 14.3 percent, but wages increased by only 9 percent because of the poor economy (Kingson 1984). As a result, retired workers were better able to maintain their standard of living than were those still in the labor force.

When it became evident that further changes in the Social Security program would be needed–changes that would be politically unpopular–the Reagan administration formed a bipartisan group called the Greenspan Commission (or the National Commission on Social Security Reform) to deal with the issue. In 1983 Congress enacted the reforms proposed by the commission with only minor changes. The changes in the Social Security program were much more substantial than those in the 1977 legislation. They included the following: (1) up to one-half of Social Security benefits would now be subject to the federal income tax (prior to this there had been no tax on Social Security benefits); (2) coverage was extended to all new federal employees; (3) the cost-of-living adjustment was delayed by six months (this amounted to a modest benefit cut); (4) the payroll tax was increased slightly; and (5) the normal age of retirement would be increased gradually from 65 to 67 between 2003 and 2027 (Berkowitz 1997). Although even these changes would not solve the financing problem indefinitely, Congress could be reasonably assured that Social Security would take in more as contributions than it paid out as benefits for the next several decades.

In connection with the debate leading up to and following the 1983 Social Security reforms there was again an effort by conservatives to frame the issue as a "crisis" and by liberals to minimize the magnitude of the required changes. By this time some of the most militant libertarians such as Stuart Butler and Peter Germanis (1983) of the Cato Institute were openly calling for "guerrilla warfare" against the Social Security program. It was common for conservative critics to describe Social Security as a pyramid scheme in which young adults end up getting little or nothing after years of supporting today's elderly at a level far in excess of what is justified based on the contributions they made prior to retirement (Longman 1982). What is the solution? In *Forbes*, Ashby Bladen (1980) argued that a major reform of Social Security was called for, and that the program should be financed the same way private pensions are financed. Today this idea is being very seriously considered by those debating whether or not we should privatize Social Security.

It was in the wake of the 1983 reforms that conservative policy analysts and the popular press began to use the term "generational equity" to describe the conflict of interest between those retired on Social Security and those still in the labor force, particularly young adults and children. In 1984 David Durenberger, a Republican senator from Minnesota, founded Americans for Generational Equity (AGE), an organization funded primarily by a number of large corporations and conservative foundations. The goal of AGE was to promote the concept of generational equity, that is, the need to reduce spending on the elderly in order to more adequately tend to the needs of other age groups, particularly young adults and children. This organization proved to be very effective throughout the 1980s (Berkowitz 1997; Quadagno 1989).

Also important in the wake of the 1983 Social Security reforms was the work of demographer Samuel Preston (1984a, 1984b), who published a couple of influential articles supporting the conclusion that in recent years the economic status of the elderly had substantially improved while at the same time the economic status of children had declined. One reason the work received so much attention was his suggestion that the improved conditions for the elderly had been achieved at least in part at the expense of children. This argument came to be cited again and again by advocates of the generational equity framing of public policy toward the elderly.

Phillip Longman (1985, 1987), then research director of AGE, wrote a very influential article on generational equity, published in the *Atlantic Monthly,* and a book entitled *Born to Pay.* Much of the conservative literature on generational equity was published in the popular press rather than in academic journals. During the late 1980s in the *New Republic,* Henry Fairlie (1988) described his own generation as "greedy geezers." In *Forbes,* an article critical of the government's policy of spending so much more on the elderly than on children was titled "Consuming Our Children" (Chakravarty and Weisman 1988). *Newsweek* columnist Robert Samuelson (1988) concluded that "The Elderly Aren't Needy." Then Governor Richard Lamm (1985) stated that "in the name of compassion for the elderly, we have handcuffed the young, mortgaged their future, and drastically limited their hopes and aspirations."

Although liberal commentators and policy analysts have been less successful than their conservative counterparts in getting headlines in the popular press, they have been responding to the arguments made by conservative proponents of the generational equity interpretive framework. In *Ties That Bind*, a report of the Gerontological Society of America that explores competing approaches to define issues associated with population aging–a book commissioned explicitly to respond to the conservative generational equity framing of public policy toward the elderly–the authors call for a "multigenerational" social policy agenda stressing the "common stake" between generations and the "interdependence" between young and old (Kingson, Hirshorn, and Cornman 1986). William Hutton (1989), executive director of the National Council of Senior Citizens, made a similar plea for intergenerational solidarity, asking Americans to respect the "compact of mutual responsibility between generations." In an article in the *New Republic*, liberal commentator Robert Kuttner (1982) rejects the claim that today's workers constitute a "gypped generation"; this claim does not, in his mind, adequately take into consideration the benefits of Social Security to the adult children of those living on Social Security. The financial independence provided by Social Security greatly reduces the potential economic burden on these adult children, preventing many more "intergenerational class wars" than it creates (Powell et al. 1996).

DEVELOPMENTS DURING THE 1990S

In books and articles dealing with generational equity issues that have appeared during the 1990s, many of the themes from the 1980s have continued; however, every few years there has been a shift in emphasis. A few years ago economist Larry Kotlikoff (1992, 1993) began calling for "generational accounting" to identify cross-generational inequities in social welfare spending. Recently such issues as the level of spending on entitlement programs, the proposal to means-test Social Security benefits, and proposals to partially privatize Social Security have also received attention.

Proponents of the generational equity interpretive package have focused attention on entitlement spending and on two related issues, the size of the federal deficit and the size of the national debt. A former secretary of commerce and cofounder of the Concord Coalition, Peter Peterson has been a particularly articulate spokesperson on the issue of entitlement spending. He and other proponents of the generational equity interpretive framework give much attention to what they describe as the entitlement "crisis" and its implications for the next generation (Peterson 1993, 1996). Although the category of entitlement spending is quite broad and includes spending on a number of programs not usually considered part of the American welfare state (such as farm subsidies), in the context of this debate the term is an abstract way of referring to spending on

Social Security, Medicare, and Medicaid. This turns out to be a useful rhetorical strategy since it is politically less risky to call for cuts in "runaway entitlement spending" than it is to call for cuts in spending on Social Security and Medicare.

Critics of the entitlement "crisis" frame take issue with the argument that spending on Social Security and Medicare are crowding out spending on other domestic programs. They do not reject the idea that discretionary domestic spending has been decreasing since the early 1980s; instead they reframe the issue by suggesting that the decline is due to the combined effects of tax cuts, the buildup in the military budget during the 1980s, and spending caps on programs funded from the discretionary domestic budget (Quadagno 1996). These critics also take issue with the argument that current spending levels cannot be sustained. With respect to Social Security their argument is that with modest technical changes such as small benefit cuts and small tax increases, it would not be difficult to keep the program in balance. In short, the interpretive frame put forth by critics is that the purported entitlement "crisis" is a myth being advanced by conservatives seeking to reduce government spending on Social Security, Medicare, and the American welfare state more generally.

At the same time the generational interdependence frame suggests that older cohorts do indeed have responsibilities toward younger ones, arising from the reciprocity across the course of life and the need (and desire) to provide a legacy. Hence, it is in the interest of older family members to invest in future generations within the family and of older cohorts to invest in the young to assure a competent voting and working citizenry in the future. And the generational interdependence frame would also imply that advocates for the old have a clear interest in advocating for the well-being of children (Kingson et al. 1986).

The debate over whether to means-test old-age security benefits predates the enactment of the original Social Security Act of 1935 (Skocpol 1990). In the past the primary goal of means-testing has been to limit social welfare benefits to the poor. The contemporary debate over the privatization of Social Security pension benefits differs in that the goal is to exclude the affluent (Howe and Longman 1992; Kaus 1994). For this reason the term "affluence testing" is often used rather than "means-testing."

Of particular note is what at first blush appears to be a reversal of roles with respect to the major actors on the opposite sides of this debate. Many conservative proponents of generational equity have advocated the means-testing of Social Security benefits, a policy that is redistributive in the sense that it would cut the benefits to high-wage earners, but not those to low-wage earners. In contrast, the critics of this proposal have often been liberals, a group generally viewed as proponents of intragenerational equity, including redistribution from rich to poor.

The means-testing of Social Security benefits is defended by proponents of generational equity on the grounds that it would help reduce the deficit and control entitlement spending, help direct Social Security benefits to those with the greatest need, and put the burden of the fiscal sacrifice on those who can most afford it, the affluent (Concord Coalition 1993; Howe and Longman 1992; Kaus 1994). This policy is rejected by critics of the generational equity perspective and by many who generally support redistributive Social Security policies. One reason is that over time the original income limit might be lowered so that more than just the affluent would be excluded, leading to the exclusion of many middle-income retired workers who need these benefits (Kingson and Schulz 1997). Another is that it would undercut the earnings-based individual equity interpretation of Social Security pension benefits. The risk is that Social Security would gradually come to be viewed as a welfare program. This would hinder its political support and, in the long run, the adequacy of the benefits provided (Ball and Aaron 1993; Meyer and Wolff 1993).

In recent years the generational equity debate has also come to include proposals to partially privatize Social Security. According to recent projections the cost of paying for Social Security pensions will begin to exceed payroll tax revenues in 2013 and the trust fund will begin to shrink as of 2019. In the unlikely event that no changes were made between now and then, the trust fund balance would, according to these projections, drop to zero in 2029 (Board of Trustees 1996). Some commentators such as Michael Tanner of the Cato Institute have suggested that as of 2029 or so Social Security will go bankrupt (U.S. Senate 1995). National polling data from 1994 suggest that only about 30 percent of the adult population feel confident that their Social Security pensions will be paid throughout retirement (Reno and Friedland 1997). Although there are not many Social Security experts who believe it is likely that Social Security will go bankrupt in 2029, there are enough people in the general public who have such concerns that privatization proposals have gained a basis of political support that extends beyond the affluent workers and those employed in the securities industry who would very likely benefit most.

The partial privatization of Social Security is being proposed as a way to deal with the anticipated burden associated with the retirement of the baby boom generation. Advocates for privatization often emphasize generational equity themes when making their case. One argument is that privatization would increase the national savings rate (Ferrara 1995). This in turn would increase the rate of investment, which in turn would increase the rate of economic growth.

With more growth the economic pie would be larger when the boomers retire, making it easier to support them in their retirement. This economic argument contains a moral element, that today's workers have an obligation to make sacrifices now (by saving more and consuming less) so as to reduce the Social Security tax burden on subsequent generations of workers. A related argument is that privatization will help protect future generations by preventing the government from spending Social Security contributions being made today to pay for current consumption; those funds should be set aside for the future to help ease the burden of paying for the retirement of the boomers.

Advocates argue that privatization would increase individual equity. That is, eventual Social Security benefits would more closely reflect differences between workers in the amount contributed over the years (Stephenson, Horlacher, and Colander 1995). A variant of this argument is that each generation has the responsibility to provide for itself, and small age cohorts should not be expected to carry larger burdens than large age cohorts. Another argument is that with privatization today's workers would get a much better return on their contributions than would be true without privatization (Steuerle and Bakija 1994). Proponents also argue that privatization would help protect future generations of workers against sharp increases in payroll taxes when the boomers retire and help protect retired boomers against sharp reductions in their Social Security benefits. They also argue that privatization would be beneficial to groups with lower rates of life expectancy.

Those critical of privatization tend to reject the generational equity framing of the debate over Social Security policy. They tend to focus on an alternative frame emphasizing intragenerational equity (which balances the imperatives of age-cohort equity with those of other dimensions of equity including race, class, and gender) (Kingson and Williamson 1996; Williamson 1997b). Some focus on the lack of precision inherent in long-term economic projections or question the economic assumptions at the core of many privatization arguments (Baker 1997; Quadagno 1996). Some point to the increase in risk for those who can least afford such risk, low-wage workers (Ball and Bethell 1997; Williamson 1997a). Some ask why we should radically alter what has proven to be one of the nation's most successful social programs when its current problems can be handled with a few modest technical fixes (Ball and Bethell 1997; Myers 1997).

Some critics of privatization point to the exaggeration, oversimplification, and distortion behind efforts to portray the Social Security system as being in a state of crisis and in need of radical change. Some are critical of privatization because it would undermine the moral basis for Social Security, reducing solidarity between generations and classes (Quadagno 1996). Others reject privatization because they believe it would reduce support for the redistributive component of Social Security and lead to an increase in the poverty rate for tomorrow's elderly (Ball and Bethell 1997; Kingson and Williamson 1996). Even some economists who do not oppose privatization agree that there is a risk that old-age poverty rates would increase (Quinn and Mitchell 1996).

FRAMING THE DEBATE

Two major groups, or "advocacy networks," to use a more precise term suggested by Gamson and Stuart (1992), have been competing to frame the debate over public policy toward the elderly. Since the mid-1980s this debate has been referred to as the "generational equity" debate, a designation that reflects both a symbolic victory and a rhetorical advantage for one of the two major advocacy networks and its interpretive package. The term "generational equity" has come to designate a number of assumptions, arguments, values, and beliefs associated with the more conservative of the two competing interpretive packages. Those making up the more liberal advocacy network are less unified behind a single catch phrase to designate their alternative interpretive package with its set of assumptions, arguments, values, and beliefs on this issue; but they often use terms such as "intragenerational equity" and "generational interdependence" (Kingson et al. 1986). In the sections that follow, we briefly summarize the major arguments that have been made by advocates of these two interpretive packages, beginning with the generational equity framing.

THE GENERATIONAL EQUITY FRAME

Advocates for the generational equity interpretive package argue that Social Security and Medicare policy makers need to give more attention than they have been giving to the issue of fairness between generations (Longman 1987; Peterson 1996). Too much public money is being spent on the retired elderly at the expense of the rest of the population, particularly children and young adults. This is doubly unfair because those paying for the very generous Social Security and Medicare benefits enjoyed by today's elderly will not receive comparable benefits when they retire.

The retirement of the baby boom generation is going to put a very heavy burden on the Social Security and Medicare programs because there will be so few workers paying into the trust funds that support these programs relative to the number of retired workers who will be drawing benefits. One consequence of this burden is that it will not be possible to support the retired baby boomers at benefit levels enjoyed by those who are currently retired.

Current recipients of Social Security are consuming more than their fair share of societal resources. As a group, in recent decades their financial situation has improved considerably while at the same time the financial situation of children has declined dramatically. Poverty rates among the elderly have decreased while at the same time poverty rates among children have increased sharply. Over the years federal spending on the elderly has increased considerably; today such spending makes up more than 25 percent of the federal budget. Were we not spending so much on the elderly it would be possible to spend more on children and young adults, a policy that would help alleviate the unacceptably high poverty rates for children.

Relative to what they actually paid into Social Security and Medicare as contributions over their working years, those who are currently retired have generally done very well. During much of their working lives payroll taxes were low by contemporary standards. As a result, within a few years most retired workers have collected pension benefits that correspond to the value of contributions made. This is true even if we take into consideration the interest that would have been earned had these contributions been invested in long-term Treasury bills. Most of those currently retired will live to receive from Social Security and Medicare benefits far in excess of what they would have been due, in a strict actuarial sense, based on their actual contributions over the years. This will not be true for the baby boomers. Many boomers will receive less by way of Social Security and Medicare benefits than they will have contributed over the years, particularly if we take into consideration interest income and adjust for changes in the cost of living.

Advocates for the generational equity interpretive package are committed to the idea that each generation should be expected to provide for itself. It is not fair for one generation to be expected to provide for another generation at a level that the generation providing the support is itself unlikely to realize. The structure of a pay-as-you-go, social insurance–based Social Security scheme assumes that each generation will provide support to those currently retired and will in turn be supported by a younger generation when it moves into retirement. A privatized Social Security scheme, in contrast, is more consistent with the idea that each generation should be responsible for itself.

Generational equity advocates often point out that the elderly constitute a very strong voting bloc. They, and interest groups such as the AARP that represent them, have a great deal of influence on public policy. The elderly and their interest groups often use their political clout in selfish ways to support programs that benefit themselves to the exclusion of others. One example that is sometimes mentioned is voting down school bond issues in some communities. More common is their lack of support for politicians who suggest serious cuts in Social Security or Medicare as a way to balance the federal budget.

If we are going to be able to provide for baby boomers when they retire without putting a very heavy burden on those in the labor force at the time, we need to do all we can between now and then to grow the economy. The more economic growth we have between now and then, the larger the economic pie will be and the easier it will be to support a large retired population. To do this we need to increase the savings rate, which will increase the investment rate, which in turn will increase the rate of economic growth. To increase the savings rate we need cuts in current consumption, including a variety of government social programs. We also need new policy initiatives such as a shift to a partially privatized Social Security scheme.

In recent decades there have been dramatic increases in spending on entitlements. An important part of this increase has been the increase in spending on Social Security, but an even more important component has been the increase in spending on health care, particularly Medicare and Medicaid. The rate of increase in government spending on health care has been higher than the overall rate of inflation; for much of the past three decades it has been far in excess of the general inflation rate. It is impossible for this trend to continue indefinitely, and something must be done. Serious thought needs to be given, as Callahan (1987), Lamm (1989), and Longman (1996) suggest, to finding ways to more openly and effectively ration health care. In this era of tight budgets it does not make sense to spend huge sums on expensive procedures for very elderly patients when the prospects of significantly adding to life expectancy, particularly healthy life expectancy, are negligible.

As a society we need less emphasis on an entitlement ethic and more emphasis on a work ethic. We need to emphasize such values as thrift, self-reliance, independence, personal freedom, and limited government. In short, advocates for the generational equity interpretive package make it a point to link their arguments to the widely and deeply held values in American society that define individualism.

THE GENERATIONAL INTERDEPENDENCE FRAME

Advocates for the generational interdependence interpretive package argue that Social Security and Medicare policy makers need to take into consideration the interdependence of generations when making and changing policy. They reject the idea that each generation can or should be expected to provide for itself. In part because of demographic fluctuation and in part because of unique historical events such as the Great Depression or the Second World War, it is not possible for each generation to be assured a standard of living during retirement at least equal to that of its parents' generation. When there are demographic, economic, or other factors that make it difficult to provide for the retirement of a particular generation, the burden should be shared by both generations, those who are retired and those still in the labor force. It is unreasonable to expect either generation bear the entire burden in such situations.

Advocates of this perspective point out that sharp cuts in benefits for the retired or the soon to be retired will also have an adverse impact on their adult children. Due to interdependence between generations at the family level, such cuts would produce pressure on their adult children to take in older family members or to supplement their Social Security and Medicare benefits. Whereas the generational equity perspective emphasizes the need for each generation to be responsible for itself, the proponents of the generational interdependence perspective argue that the generations are and should continue to be highly interdependent. This is true at both the family and the societal level. Advocates of generational interdependence accept the idea that we should be making an effort to plan for the retirement of the boomers, but they emphasize the need to balance considerations of generational equity and of generational interdependence.

A distinctive aspect of the generational interdependence perspective is its emphasis on what different generations have to offer one another as opposed to what one is or will be consuming at the expense of the other. More explicitly, it tends to emphasize the many transfers taking place among the generations, within the family and society. At the level of individual families this includes transfers of income, child care support, psychological support, and advice. In 1994, 3.7 million grandchildren were being raised in households headed by grandparents (Saluter 1996); many of the elderly also provide countless hours assisting functionally disabled family members. In addition the elderly are making major artistic, intellectual, and leadership contributions to society more generally.

Closely linked to the generational interdependence framing of these issues is the intragenerational equity framing. Advocates of this perspective point out that when deciding on Social Security and Medicare policy changes, generational equity is only one form of equity that needs to be taken into consideration. It is not a good idea to focus on generational equity to the exclusion of other forms of equity such as those based on race, class, and gender.

With respect to Social Security we are facing a long-term financing problem, but not the crisis described by many proponents of generational equity. Policy changes are needed to deal with these long-term financing problems, but such changes can be made without radically altering Social Security, the most successful social program the nation has ever created. Why replace a popular and very successful program with an unproved alternative that might not work nearly as well?

There is a great deal of diversity in economic circumstances among the elderly. When we base policy decisions on what is best for average-wage workers or for the affluent, we do so at the risk of potential harm to some vulnerable groups such as low-wage workers, minority workers, and the very old, particularly very old women. The mean and median income for the elderly have increased in recent decades, but there are still millions of elderly people living in or very near to poverty. When the elderly are treated as a homogeneous aggregate for policy purposes, as is often the case in policy analysis from the generational equity perspective, the special needs of these vulnerable groups tend to be neglected (Binstock 1992).

There has been an increase in poverty among children in recent decades— the same decades that have seen a decrease in poverty rates among the elderly. Proponents of the intragenerational equity perspective do not view these two events as causally linked. Many factors have contributed to the increases in poverty rates among children, including changes in the American economy, the increase in single-parent families, and changes in public willingness to support public spending on the poor. If the current level of spending on Social Security and Medicare is a contributing factor, a claim that has not been demonstrated, it most likely is a very minor factor.

Steps are needed to deal with the rapid increase in spending on Medicare and on health care in general. Evidence from other countries shows that there are ways to organize the delivery of health care services so that the entire population is adequately covered using a much smaller share of the GDP than we spend in the United States. A way to control spending must be found, but it must not produce a sharp reduction in the quality of health care available for the less affluent.

The issue of the means-testing of Social Security benefits poses special problems for proponents of the generational interdependence perspective. The issue tends to come up in the context of "affluence testing," a form of means-testing in which only the affluent would be excluded from benefits. One might expect advocates of intragenerational equity to support such a policy due to its redistributive implications. Some do support the means-testing of Social Security benefits on those grounds, but most proponents of the generational interdependence perspective oppose it. One reason is that affluence testing might end up stigmatizing those who continue to be recipients. However, a much more important reason is that it might reduce the level of political support for Social Security. The affluent are a powerful political constituency; the loss of their support could have serious adverse long-term consequences for the program. The risk is that over time the income limit at which means-testing would kick in would be lowered, and Social Security would eventually evolve into an underfunded program for the poor.

Proponents of generational interdependence and intragenerational equity argue that we need to take a close look at the values that inform our policy decisions. In contrast to the individualistic values emphasized by proponents of generational equity, proponents of generational interdependence emphasize solidaristic values such as community obligation to provide for those in need and the right of all citizens to adequate health care, food, and shelter; and goals such as reduction of poverty and inequity, and income redistribution to compensate for our economy's tendency to increase income inequality.

VALUES, BELIEFS, AND RHETORICAL STRATEGIES

Each of the competing advocacy networks we have described must make strategic choices about the symbolism it will use to promote its preferred interpretive package. Central to advocacy strategies are attempts to use symbols that resonate with larger cultural themes, thereby increasing the appeal of certain packages and making them appear natural and familiar (Gamson 1992). Those who respond to the larger cultural theme will find it easier to respond to a package with similar themes. Some frames "resonate with cultural narrations, that is, with the stories, myths, and folktales that are part and parcel of one's cultural heritage and that thus function to inform events and experiences in the immediate present." (Snow and Benford 1988:210).

For example, in recent years those working within the generational equity interpretive framework have often made a case for privatizing Social Security and have linked that idea to such broad cultural themes as self-reliance and personal freedom (Borden 1995; Ferrara 1995; Porter 1995). In contrast, those advancing the generational interdependence perspective generally oppose privatization, support the redistributive social goals of Social Security, and include in their arguments such themes as the obligation to protect low-wage workers and other vulnerable groups (Baker 1997; Ball and Bethell 1997; Quadagno 1996). Because the value of individualism emphasized by generational equity advocates is more widely and deeply held in American society, it can be described as a dominant value or theme. In contrast, the less widely and deeply held value of community obligation to provide for the needy can be described as a countertheme or countervalue. Counterthemes often share a number of the same assumptions, but they generally challenge some aspect of a corresponding dominant or mainstream theme; they tend to be adversarial or oppositional (Gamson 1992).

Symbolic contests are waged with metaphors, catch phrases, and other symbolic devices that mutually support an interpretive package used to make sense of an ongoing stream of events as they relate to a particular issue. The catch phrase "generational equity," for example, economically conveys a set of related ideas and assumptions about Social Security and Medicare that most readers could readily articulate with little or no prompting.

The generational equity debate has largely taken place in the mass media, primarily via newspaper editorials and editorial cartoons. The mass media play a central role in the construction of political meaning. According to Gurevitch and Levy (1985:19) they become "a site on which various social groups, institutions, and ideologies struggle over the definition and construction of social reality." The media, in this view, provide a series of arenas in which symbolic contests are carried out among competing advocacy networks.

The dominant values and beliefs embodied in the generational equity framing of the debate over the future of Social Security and Medicare center around the theme of individualism. Central to individualism are such values as autonomy, personal freedom, and personal responsibility. Individualism is one of the strongest themes in American culture. As Robert Bellah and his colleagues point out (1985:142), "We [Americans] believe in the dignity, indeed the sacredness, of the individual. Anything that would violate our right to think for ourselves, judge for ourselves, make our own decisions, live our lives as we see fit, is not only morally wrong, it is sacrilegious." Individualism is strongly supported by the media. This is revealed in the media's use of news stories that focus on individuals acting on their own (Gamson 1992). News stories involve narratives that focus on individual actors rather than on social structure because people identify better with narratives that place human agents at the center of moral dilemmas.

Those who support the generational equity perspective generally oppose redistributive social policies. But redistribution within one's family is a special case and often is supported in discussions of public policy by those who subscribe to individualistic values. More generally, advocates of individualism are often not opposed to intrafamily redistribution or voluntary redistribution by churches, charities, and civic organizations; rather they are opposed to redistributive government programs, particularly tax-supported federal government programs.

The generational interdependence perspective emphasizes a set of alternative values and beliefs contrary to the individualistic values linked to the generational equity perspective. Advocates of this interpretive package also make an effort to link their arguments to widely held values, but they are at a disadvantage because the values they typically tap into are less widely and deeply held. Under some special circumstances such as the Great Depression or the Second World War, solidaristic and communitarian values come to the fore, but throughout most of American history values linked to individualism have been dominant; as a result, values such as redistribution and providing for the needy have been relegated to the status of countervalues.

Rhetorical strategy is central to the generational equity debate. Those who support the generational equity framing tend to focus on the mass media as the arena in which to present their message. That arena is supportive of flamboyance, simplification, polarization, and the related styles that emphasize the crisis nature of social problems and issues. Much of the response from the generational interdependence perspective is presented in professional journals and academic books. This literature tends to present arguments in more qualified and nuanced terms. The rhetorical strategy here includes efforts to appear value-free, objective, and scientific. This strategy tends to attract less media attention, and the message is more difficult for a general audience to understand. Those advocating the generational interdependence interpretive package are more likely to refer to a financing "problem" to describe what those advocating the generational equity interpretive package would describe as a financing "crisis."

Why frame the issue as a crisis? If you want a major policy change, one way to accomplish it is to convince the general public that we face a crisis that cannot be solved in any other way than with the proposed structural change. Such a profound shift as the change from Social Security with its present structure to a partially privatized alternative will not be possible without very strong popular support. Therefore, advocates of privatization use generational equity themes and dramatic expressions such as "demographic earthquake" and "colossal debt" to help frame the issue as a crisis in the hope of engaging a wide audience.

One rhetorical strategy used by proponents of the more liberal generational interdependence perspective is to generate suspicion and undercut the credibility of supporters of the generational equity interpretive package by linking them to well-known ideological organizations that oppose spending on Social Security and on social welfare programs that benefit children and young adults. By the same token they present evidence that at least some conservative critics of Social Security seek to undermine public confidence in the program as part of a more general strategy to roll back the nation's welfare state commitments. Liberals portray the apparent efforts of conservatives to undermine confidence in Social Security as part of a rhetorical as well as a political strategy. What do they gain by such portrayals? Perhaps the goal is to generate suspicion, fear, and anger among the "have-nots" and guilt on the part of the "haves" in society.

Both advocates of generational equity and advocates of generational interdependence tend to suggest that they are being more objective about the issues than are those who disagree with them. Neither side pays much attention to the possibility that what people see as the objective truth with respect to these issues is shaped by differing, and deeply held, sets of beliefs and values.

Proponents of generational equity sometimes play upon people's emotions; so too do those who prefer to frame Social Security and Medicare policy in terms of generational interdependence; but the emphasis is different. Proponents of the generational equity framing often adopt a moralistic tone that condemns people for "credit-card spending" and the "me generation" ethos they claim is rampant in American society. Those who emphasize the generational interdependence framing also tap into people's emotions, primarily with arguments designed to foster feelings of guilt and concern about selfishness. An example of this is the argument that the partial privatization of Social Security probably would benefit the affluent, but at the same time it would quite likely harm the low-income population.

CRITICALLY EVALUATING THE ALTERNATIVE INTERPRETIVE FRAMEWORKS

Despite the claims of some policy analysts, it is certainly difficult, and perhaps impossible, to analyze the issues encompassed by the generational equity debate in an entirely value-neutral, objective way. A number of the arguments made on both sides of the debate turn out to be linked to fundamental but opposing values. Empirical facts are part of the story, but only part. Much of the analysis hinges on the interpretation of factual evidence and on an assessment of long-term projections. Some of these projections, such as the number of people over age 65 who will be alive in the year 2030, may be quite accurate. But in general we need to be more aware of the uncertainty that necessarily surrounds long-term economic projections, projections that all too many commentators treat as if they involved no margin of error. Most long-term projections call for what statisticians refer to as wide confidence limits because there is a great deal of room for error. Arguments based on such projections are particularly susceptible to the influence of fundamental values. Depending in part upon one's values, different assumptions will be made, and those assumptions will have considerable impact on long-term projections.

Those who write about the generational equity debate are in large measure engaged in a social construction of reality—a construction based on the values and beliefs they choose to embrace in an effort to reach their desired outcomes, whether that outcome is fundamental change, such as the privatization of Social Security, minimal change, for example, maintaining Social Security more or less as it is, or something in between, such as the introduction of means-testing or a modest step in the direction of partial privatization. The values and beliefs that inform the "reality" each analyst proposes do not exist as independent and external truths; rather, they are shaped by his or her socialization, life experiences, religious and ethnic background, and social network.

Our values and beliefs are the lenses that shape and color the way in which we view the world. They influence what we consider to be "objective truths." If we conclude that objectivity and value neutrality in the traditional sense are impossible, does this mean we must accept absolute relativism (anything goes)? Many scholars have argued that there is a middle ground (Griswold 1987; Natter, Schatzki, and Jones 1995). Finding the middle ground requires that both authors and readers become more aware of their own values and beliefs and the extent to which those factors influence the way in which they interpret evidence and evaluate arguments linked to controversial social policy issues.

There are a variety of ways to evaluate the interpretive package being used in a particular article. From the major arguments made it should be clear whether the author is drawing more on the generational equity or on the generational interdependence perspective. However, in some cases the author attempts to maintain an impartial stance by drawing more or less equally on both. The interpretive package the author emphasized should suggest a related set of assumptions, beliefs, and values that are likely to be present. Some may be expressed explicitly, others implicitly. Our prior discussion of these alternative interpretive frameworks is a useful as a starting point for such analysis; however, some authors may rely on other assumptions, beliefs, and values that we have not mentioned.

The analysis of an article may also benefit from a critical assessment of the rhetorical strategies used by the author. Is the author using emotional language designed to appeal to the reader's basic values with little or no attention to potentially relevant empirical evidence? Is the author attempting to discredit critics by linking them to ideological organizations without giving adequate attention to the potential validity of their arguments? It is possible that an author with strong links to a highly ideological organization will offer some valid arguments that should be taken seriously even by those who do not share the values embraced by that organization?

It may be relevant to ask who is likely to benefit or who risks being harmed by the use of a particular framework for analyzing an issue such as Social Security or Medicare policy. This question can be asked when comparing interpretive packages as a whole, and it can also be asked when analyzing a specific frame that is part of one or another of these interpretive packages. For example, in response to the proposed crisis framing of the future of Social Security, which some would view as a rhetorical strategy that is part of the generational equity interpretive package, it is reasonable to ask who stands to benefit and who is most likely to be hurt by the policies proposed to address the purported crisis.

It is sometimes useful to assess an author's ideas about fairness with respect to the distribution of societal resources. Those working within the generational equity frame tend to emphasize fairness between generations and policies that make an effort to assure that one generation is not favored over another. Some within this same advocacy network favor fairness in the form of individual equity, for example, Social Security pension benefits that are linked as closely as possible to actual payroll tax contributions over the years with very little in the way of redistribution.

In contrast, those working within the generational interdependence frame generally support a different conception of fairness—one that sees a need for redistribution to those who reach old age with very low incomes. This group of analysts and commentators urge us to make an effort to even out some of the inequality our market economy tends to produce among those reaching old age, particularly inequality linked to race, class, and gender. They are also likely to emphasize the need under some circumstances, such as the retirement of the baby boom generation, for two generations to attempt to share the dependency burden.

Having carried out a preliminary analysis, readers should be in a better position to assess the overall credibility of the arguments made. Having read articles by authors on both sides of the debate, readers will be aware of relevant empirical evidence that has been neglected by a given author and that may undercut his or her argument. Such reading should also make readers aware of alternative assumptions about values, which lead to very different arguments and to varying interpretations of the empirical evidence. Comparing articles written from opposing perspectives will help sensitize readers to differences in rhetorical style and to the biases associated with the various styles. It will often be useful to ask why a particular rhetorical strategy is being used, and why some rhetorical strategies are more successful than others.

As readers analyze the interpretive package associated with a particular article, it may be of interest to ask whether an argument seems to hold under all circumstances or only under some. If the argument is based in large part on future projections about economic or demographic conditions, it may make sense to ask questions about how reliable such projections are likely to be. Has the author adequately taken into consideration possible errors in those projections? All projections about future conditions will involve some error, and the margin of error can become substantial when when the projections reach several decades into the future.

A comparison of the factual information given by authors on different sides of the issue may reveal some inconsistencies. When this happens it might be useful to go to other sources to check the facts. Who has done the best job of getting the facts straight? Does an author present facts that are correct in a narrow technical sense, but present them in a way that might be misleading? Is the author highly selective with respect to the evidence, presenting only evidence that supports his or her conclusions?

A goal of this anthology is to encourage our readers to become more informed critics as they attempt to evaluate arguments made on both sides of the generational equity debate. We do not expect to change our readers' basic values, but we do feel that it is worthwhile to help our readers see clearly the alternative sets of values, beliefs, and assumptions that are linked to the different interpretive packages involved in the generational equity debate.

OVERVIEW OF THE ARTICLES

One of our goals is to present all sides of the generational equity debate. From the articles written by the editors that have been included in this volume, it will be clear where we stand on these issues. Although this debate has focused on policy issues concerning Social Security and Medicare, it is actually a somewhat broader debate that encompasses many other aspects of public policy toward the elderly (e.g., organ transplant policy, housing policy, and tax policy). However, in our selection of readings we focus on the core of the debate, Social Security and health care for the elderly.

Chapters 2 through 6 make extensive use of the generational equity interpretive framework. Some of the authors are considered conservatives; others
are considered liberals. What they share is support for the generational equity
frame. Peter Peterson (chapter 2) calls for across-the-board sacrifice, but with a
progressive emphasis. Lester Thurow (chapter 3) is alarmed at the trend in this
country with respect to the amount the government is spending on the elderly
relative to other age groups, but he points out that the pattern is similar and the
situation more severe in a number of other industrial nations. Jagadeesh
Gokhale and Laurence Kotlikoff (chapter 4) write about what they call "generational accounting," which they view as a way to assess the extent to which our
efforts to help one generation (such as spending on Social Security and
Medicare) potentially end up doing harm to another.

Richard Lamm (chapter 5) is concerned that we are spending far too large a
share of our societal resources on health care, particularly treating the chronic
diseases of old age. Daniel Callahan (chapter 6) proposes that we use the concept of a "natural life span" as a way of deciding when to limit expensive medical procedures on the elderly. He suggests that we provide health care to the
poor, but with restrictions on high-cost medical procedures and with the
assumption that the affluent who can pay on their own will have access to additional health benefits.

Chapters 7 through 11 focus on arguments that are critical of the generational equity framing of these issues. In these articles we find such concepts as
generational interdependence, intragenerational equity, and generational and
class solidarity presented in a favorable light. Suggesting that the nation can
afford a growing population without placing an extraordinary burden on
future workers, Alicia Munnell (chapter 7) suggests that exaggerated claims
about generational conflict and economic catastrophe potentially undermine
efforts to develop policy responses based on sound economics. Jill Quadagno
(chapter 8) is critical of the distortion, oversimplification, and exaggeration
associated with the expression "entitlement crisis" frequently used by advocates
of the generational equity perspective. Robert Binstock (chapter 9) is skeptical
of the call for a greater commitment to the rationing of health care resources,
particularly with respect to the needs of the oldest old, and rejects the idea that
huge sums are being expended on wasteful high-technology medicine from
which the elderly are unlikely to benefit. Theodore Marmor, Fay Lomax Cook,
and Stephen Scher (chapter 10) view the efforts of those who attempt to frame
the debate over the future of Social Security in terms of generational equity as
part of a more general drive to divide the young and the old. Describing Social
Security as an outstanding example of public policy reflecting the notion of

generational interdependence, Eric Kingson and John Williamson (chapter 11) suggest that privatization proposals reflect the highly individualistic notions of the generational equity advocates and that, if adopted, they would undermine the well-being of many Americans.

The final two chapters present excerpts from position papers representing two very different Generation X organizations. In chapter 12 the Third Millennium warns that generational war is a real possibility if efforts are not taken to restrain spending on Social Security, a program it views as fiscally unsound and generationally unfair. In contrast, the 2030 Center (chapter 13) has a positive view of Social Security. It urges us to modernize Social Security in such a way as to preserve the program's current community-enhancing and poverty-reducing goals.

REFERENCES

Achenbaum, W. Andrew. 1978. *Old Age in the New Land: The American Experience Since 1790*. Baltimore: Johns Hopkins University Press.

Achenbaum, W. Andrew, and Peter N. Stearns. 1978. "Old Age and Modernization." *The Gerontologist* 18:307–312.

Baker, Dean. 1997. "The Privateers' Free Lunch." *American Prospect* (May–June): 81–84.

Ball, Robert M., and Henry J. Aaron. 1993. "The Myth of Means-Testing." *Washington Post*, (November 14): C4.

Ball, Robert M., and Thomas N. Bethell. 1997. "Bridging the Centuries: The Case for Traditional Social Security." Pp. 259–294 in *Social Security in the 21st Century*, edited by Eric R. Kingson and James H. Schulz. New York: Oxford University Press.

Beauvoir, Simone de. 1972. *The Coming of Age*. Translated by Patrick O'Brian. New York: G. P. Putnam's Sons.

Bellah, Robert N., Richard Madsen, William M. Sullivan, Ann Swidler, and Steven M. Tipton. 1985. *Habits of the Heart: Individualism and Commitment in American Life*. Berkeley, Calif.: University of California Press.

Berkowitz, Edward D. 1997. "The Historical Development of Social Security in the United States." Pp. 22–38 in *Social Security in the 21st Century*, edited by Eric R. Kingson and James H. Schulz. New York: Oxford University Press.

Binstock, Robert H. 1983. "The Aged as Scapegoat." *The Gerontologist* 23:136–143.

Binstock, Robert H. 1992. "The Oldest Old and Intergenerational Equity." Pp. 394–417 in *The Oldest Old*, edited by Richard M. Suzman, David P. Willis, and Kenneth Manton. New York: Oxford University Press.

Bladen, Ashby. 1980. "The Shocking Shape of Things to Come." *Forbes* (May 26): 39–40.

Board of Trustees, Federal Old Age and Survivors Insurance and Disability Insurance Trust Funds. 1996. *1996 Annual Report of the Board of Trustees, Federal Old Age and Survivors Insurance and Disability Insurance Trust Funds.* Washington, D.C.: U.S. Government Printing Office.

Borden, Karl. 1995. "Dismantling the Pyramid: The Why and the How of Privatizing Social Security." The Cato Project on Social Security Privatization, SSP. No. 1. Washington, D.C.: Cato Institute.

Bradford, William. 1962. *Of Plymouth Plantation.* New York: Capricorn Books.

Butler, Stuart, and Peter Germanis. 1983. "Achieving Social Security Reform: A Leninist Strategy. *The Cato Journal* 3:547–556.

Callahan, Daniel. 1987. *Setting Limits: Medical Goals in an Aging Society.* New York: Simon and Schuster.

Chakravarty, Subrata N., and Katherine Weisman. 1988. "Consuming Our Children." *Forbes* (November 14): 222–232.

Coll, Blanche D. 1969. *Perspectives in Public Welfare.* Washington, D.C.: U.S. Department of Health, Education, and Welfare.

Concord Coalition. 1993. *The Zero Deficit Plan.* Washington, D.C.: Concord Coalition.

Crowther, Samuel. 1930. "The Need for Old-Age Pensions." *Forbes* 25 (8): 15–34.

Fairlie, Henry. 1988. "Talkin' 'bout My Generation." *New Republic* (March 28): 19–22.

Feingold, Eugene. 1966. *Medicare: Policy and Politics: A Case Study and Policy Analysis.* San Francisco: Chandler and Sharp.

Ferrara, Peter J. 1995. "A Private Option for Social Security." Pp. 205–213 in *Social Security: Time for a Change,* edited by Kevin Stephenson. Greenwich, Conn.: JAI Press.

Fischer, David Hackett. 1978. *Growing Old in America,* expanded edition. New York: Oxford University Press.

Gamson, William A. 1992. *Talking Politics.* New York: Cambridge University Press.

Gamson, William A., and David Stuart. 1992. "Media Discourse as a Symbolic Contest: The Bomb in Political Cartoons." *Sociological Forum* 7:55–86.

Ginsberg, Benjamin. 1986. *The Captive Public: How Mass Opinion Promotes State Power.* New York: Basic Books.

Griswold, Wendy. 1987. "A Methodological Framework for the Sociology of Culture. *Sociological Methodology* 15:1–35.

Gurevitch, Michael, and Mark R. Levy, eds. 1985. *Mass Communication Review Yearbook.* Vol. 5. Beverly Hills, Calif.: Sage.

Harris. Richard. 1966. *A Sacred Trust.* New York: New American Library.

Holtzman, Abraham. 1963. *The Townsend Movement*. New York: Bookman Associates.

Howe, Neil, and Phillip Longman. 1992. "The Next New Deal." *Atlantic Monthly* (April): 88–99.

Hutton, William R. 1989. "The Young and the Old Are Not Enemies." *USA Today Magazine*, (March): 63–65.

Kalish, Richard. A. 1979. "The New Ageism and the Failure Models: A Polemic." *The Gerontologist* 19:398–407.

Kaus, Mickey. 1994. "The Case for Means-Testing Social Security." Pp. 117–124 in *Social Welfare Policy at the Crossroads: Rethinking the Roles of Social Insurance, Tax Expenditures, Mandates, and Means-Testing*, edited by Robert B. Friedland, Lynn M. Etheredge, and Bruce C. Vladeck. Washington, D.C.: National Academy of Social Insurance.

Kingson, Eric R. 1984. "Financing Social Security: Agenda-Setting and the Enactment of the 1983 Amendments to the Social Security Act." *Policy Studies Journal* 14:131–155.

Kingson, Eric R., Barbara A. Hirshorn, and John M. Cornman. 1986. *Ties That Bind*. Washington, D.C.: Seven Locks Press.

Kingson, Eric R., and James H. Schulz. 1997. "Should Social Security Be Means-Tested?" Pp. 41–61 in *Social Security in the 21st Century*, edited by Eric R. Kingson and James H. Schulz. New York: Oxford University Press.

Kingson, Eric R., and John B. Williamson. 1996. "Undermining Social Security's Basic Objectives." *Challenge* 39 (November-December): 28–30.

Kotlikoff, Laurence J. 1992. *Generational Accounting*. New York: The Free Press.

Kotlikoff, Laurence J. 1993. "Justice and Generational Accounting. Pp. 77–93 in *Justice Across Generations: What Does It Mean?* Washington, D.C.: American Association of Retired Persons.

Kuttner, Robert. 1980. *The Revolt of the Haves: Tax Rebellions and Hard Times*. New York: Simon and Schuster.

Kuttner, Robert. 1982. "The Social Security Hysteria." *New Republic* (December 27): 17–21.

Kutzik, Alfred J. 1979. "American Social Provision for the Aged: An Historical Perspective." Pp. 32–65 in *Ethnicity and Aging*, edited by Donald E. Gelfand and Alfred J. Kutzik. New York: Springer Publishing Company.

Lamm, Richard D. 1985. *Mega-traumas: America at the Year 2000*. Denver: Center for Public Policy and Contemporary Issues.

Lamm, Richard D. 1989. "Columbus and Copernicus: New Wine in Old Wineskins." *Mount Sinai Journal of Medicine* 56 (1): 1–10.

Longman, Phillip. 1982. "Taking America to the Cleaners." *Washington Monthly*

(November): 25–30.

Longman, Phillip. 1985. "Justice Between Generations." *Atlantic Monthly* (June): 73–81.

Longman, Phillip. 1987. *Born to Pay: The New Politics of Aging in America*. Boston: Houghton Mifflin.

Longman, Phillip. 1996. *The Return of Thrift*. New York: Free Press.

Marmor, Theodore R. 1969. "The Congress: Medicare Politics and Policy." Pp. 3–66 in *American Political Institutions and Public Policy*, edited by Allan Sindler. Boston: Little, Brown.

Marmor, Theodore R. 1973. *The Politics of Medicare*. Chicago: Aldine.

Marmor, Theodore R. 1981. "Enacting Medicare." Pp. 105–134 in *The Aging in Politics: Process and Policy*, edited by Robert B. Hudson. Springfield, Ill.: Charles C. Thomas.

Meyer, Charles W. 1987. "Social Security: Past, Present, and Future." Pp. 1–34 in *Social Security*, edited by Charles W. Meyer. Lexington, Mass.: Lexington Books.

Meyer, Charles W., and Nancy L. Wolff. 1993. *Social Security and Individual Equity*. Westport, Conn.: Greenwood Press.

Murdock, George P. 1934. *Our Primitive Contemporaries*. New York: Macmillan.

Myers, Robert J. 1997. "Will Social Security Be There for Me?" Pp. 208–216 in *Social Security in the 21st Century*, edited by Eric R. Kingson and James H. Schulz. New York: Oxford University Press.

Natter, Wolfgang, Theodore R. Schatzki, and John Paul Jones III. 1995. "Contexts of Objectivity." Pp. 1–15 in *Objectivity and its Other*, edited by Wolfgang Natter, Theodore R. Schatzki, and John Paul Jones III. New York: Guilford Press.

Peterson, Peter G. 1993. *Facing Up: How to Rescue the Economy from Crushing Debt and Restore the American Dream*. New York: Simon and Schuster.

Peterson, Peter G. 1996. *Will America Grow Up Before It Grows Old?* New York: Random House.

Porter, John E. 1995. "Individual Social Security Retirement Accounts." Pp. 197–203 in *Social Security: Time for a Change*, edited by Kevin Stephenson. Greenwich, Conn.: JAI Press.

Powell, Lawrence Alfred, Kenneth J. Branco, and John B. Williamson. 1996. *The Senior Rights Movement: Framing the Policy Debate in America*. New York: Twayne.

Powell, Lawrence Alfred, and John B. Williamson. 1985. "The Reagan-Era Shift Toward Restrictiveness in Old-Age Policy in Historical Perspective." *International Journal of Aging and Human Development* 21:81–86.

Pratt, Henry J. 1976. *The Gray Lobby*. Chicago: University of Chicago Press.

Preston, Samuel H. 1984a. "Children and the Elderly: Divergent Paths for America's Dependents." *Demography* 21:435–457.

Preston, Samuel H. 1984b. "Children and the Elderly in the United States." *Scientific American* 251 (6): 44–49.

Quadagno, Jill S. 1988. *The Transformation of Old-Age Security: Class and Politics in the American Welfare State*. Chicago: University of Chicago Press.

Quadagno, Jill S. 1989. "Generational Equity and the Politics of the Welfare State." *Politics and Society* 17:353–376.

Quadagno, Jill. 1996. "Social Security and the Myth of the Entitlement 'Crisis.'" *The Gerontologist* 36:391–399.

Quinn, Joseph F., and Olivia S. Mitchell. 1996. "Social Security on the Table." *American Prospect* (May–June): 76–81.

Reno, Virginia P., and Robert B. Friedland. 1997. "Strong Support but Low Confidence: What Explains the Contradiction?" Pp. 178–194 in *Social Security in the 21st Century*, edited by Eric R. Kingson and James H. Schulz. New York: Oxford University Press.

Rothman, David J. 1971. *The Discovery of the Asylum*. Boston: Little, Brown.

Saluter, Arlene F. 1996. "Marital Status and Living Arrangements: March 1994." *Current Population Reports*, Series P–20, No. 484. Washington, D.C.: U.S. Department of Commerce, Bureau of the Census.

Samuelson, Robert J. 1988. "The Elderly Aren't Needy. *Newsweek* (March 21): 68.

Simmons, L. W. 1945. *The Role of the Aged in Primitive Society*. New Haven: Yale University Press.

Skocpol, Theda. 1990. *Protecting Soldiers and Mothers: The Political Origins of Social Policy in the United States*. Cambridge, Mass.: Harvard University Press.

Skocpol, Theda, and Edwin Amenta. 1985. "Did Capitalists Shape Social Security?" *American Sociological Review* 50:572–575.

Snow, David A., and Robert D. Benford. 1988. "Ideology, Frame Resonance, and Participant Mobilization." Pp. 197–217 in *From Structure to Action: Comparing Social Movement Research Across Cultures*, edited by Bert Klandermans, Hanspeter Kriesi, and Sidney Tarrow. Greenwich, Conn.: JAI Press.

Stephenson, Kevin, David Horlacher, and David Colander. 1995. "An Overview of the U.S. Social Security System: Problems and Options." Pp. 3–23 in *Social Security: Time for a Change*, edited by Kevin Stephenson. Greenwich, Conn.: JAI Press.

Steuerle, C. Eugene, and Jon M. Bakija. 1994. *Retooling Social Security for the Twenty-first Century: Right and Wrong Approaches to Reform*. Washington, D.C.: The Urban Institute Press.

Trattner, Walter I. 1974. *From Poor Law to Welfare State*. New York: Free Press.

Treas, Judith. 1977. "Family Support Systems for the Aged: Some Social and Demographic Considerations." *Gerontologist* 17:486–491.

U.S. Senate. 1995. *Privatization of the Social Security Old Age and Survivors Insurance Program*. Hearing before the Subcommittee on Social Security and Family Protection of the Committee on Finance, 104th Congress, 1st session, on S. 824, August 2. Washington D.C.: U.S. Government Printing Office.

Webster, H. 1932. *Primitive Secret Societies: A Study in Early Politics and Religion*. New York: Macmillan.

Williamson, John B. 1984. "Old-Age Relief Policy Prior to 1900: The Trend Toward Restrictiveness." *American Journal of Economics and Sociology* 43:369–384.

Williamson, John B. 1997a. "A Critique of the Case for Privatizing Social Security." *The Gerontologist* 37:561–571.

Williamson, John B. 1997b. "Should Women Support the Privatization of Social Security?" *Challenge* 40 (July–August): 97–108.

Williamson, John B., Linda Evans, and Lawrence A. Powell. 1982. *The Politics of Aging: Power and Policy*. Springfield, Ill.: Charles C. Thomas.

PART II

The Generational Equity Frame

CHAPTER TWO

How Will America Pay for the Retirement of the Baby Boom Generation?

Peter G. Peterson

Peter G. Peterson is president of the Concord Coalition. He is also chairman of the Blackstone Group, a private investment bank. He served as secretary of commerce under President Nixon, and more recently as a member of the Bipartisan Commission on Entitlement and Tax Reform (1994–95). He has written a number of books, including *Facing Up* and *Will America Grow Up Before It Grows Old?*

Peterson is a passionate advocate for cuts in projected increases in entitlement spending in the years ahead. He argues that unless major changes are made and made soon, it will not be possible to pay for the retirement of the baby boom generation. This article focuses on nine criteria that should be taken into consideration as we undertake reform of Social Security, Medicare, and Medicaid policy in the years ahead. The article concludes with the author's own proposed reform package as described in his recent book, *Will America Grow Up Before It Grows Old?* Among the changes he calls for is a program to supplement and eventually replace Social Security as we know it with an alternative that will emphasize personally owned mandatory retirement savings accounts.

A momentous question now looms over America's economic future. The way we face this question will likely have vast bottom-line consequences for the institution of retirement. It may also determine whether our children participate in the American Dream of rising affluence or whether our nation's wealth-producing engines will fail within their lifetime.

The question is this: How will America prepare and pay for the growing retirement and health-care costs of our rapidly aging population? Graying means paying—paying more for public and private pensions, more for hospitals and doctors, more for nursing homes and other social services. Under our present system, we, as a nation, cannot begin to meet these costs when the huge Baby Boom generation begins turning sixty-five a mere fifteen years from now.

America is just now beginning to understand our need to act. Over the last couple of years, a growing number of voices—in Congress, in academia and think tanks, and on official federal commissions—have begun to advocate thorough reform of our senior entitlement programs. As for the public, over 90 percent now believe that Social Security will eventually require "major change." Sixty-five percent agree that the program "is in need of major reform now." This latter figure includes 37 percent of Americans age 65 and over—and an amazing 80 percent of Boomer-age Americans between 30 and 49. . . .

The only real choice we face is whether that reform will come sooner, with benign consequences and with more time for Americans to prepare for their future, for our national future, or later—after the long-term social and economic harm has already been done and when public retirement promises must be broken violently and without warning. . . .

I've been studying and speaking out on these issues for many years. One lesson I've learned is to refrain from jumping too quickly into this plan or that, a tactic that invariably creates instant allies and enemies. I've learned that the more effective way to approach reform is to start by identifying and explaining the criteria that must underlie any successful package. . . .

Allow me to . . . explain those criteria.

NINE CRITERIA UNDERLYING ANY SUCCESSFUL REFORM PACKAGE

1. Any reform package must confront the total federal cost of the coming age wave.

Too often policymakers approach various senior benefit programs—Social Security Old Age and Survivors Insurance, Medicare Hospital Insurance, Medicare Supplementary Medical Insurance, Medicaid long-term care, and so on down the list—as though they constituted separate and self-contained problems. Not only does this lead to a lack of coordination in policies affecting the same people, it fosters the illusion that the rising cost of any individual program is bearable because it alone won't bankrupt tomorrow's workers. It's as if no single pebble matters in the landslide that buries us.

The projected federal cost of the senior boom, in its totality, is truly staggering. From now to 2030, federal spending on Social Security, Medicare, and Medicaid will, according to the Congressional Budget Office (CBO), rise by 10 percent of GDP. Already by 2020—assuming we don't raise taxes—we could zero out all other federal spending except interest on the debt and still not balance the budget. To pay promised Social Security and Medicare benefits without adding to the debt, taxes would have to rise to 35 percent of workers' payroll by 2040. Add in Medicaid for seniors, and the total tax burden rises to over 40 percent of payroll—enough to erase all growth in real after-tax worker earnings over the next forty-five years.

It is true that much of this cost growth is due to the rapid projected rise in health benefit outlays—and that controlling spending on Medicare poses a more daunting challenge than controlling spending on non-health-care programs. But this fact does not take the heat off cash benefits like Social Security. In fact, just the opposite is true. Since spending on Medicare is likely to keep growing faster than the economy even if we enact draconian cost controls, it is all the more urgent to reform Social Security and free up fiscal resources. This is especially true since the two programs pay benefits to the same people (mostly retirees) and derive revenues from the same people (mostly workers).

Defenders of the entitlement status quo apparently assume that future Americans won't mind paying a stupefying total tax burden so long as many different government agencies are collecting and spending the money. This assumption will be proven wrong. It is the total cost of the age wave that threatens to overwhelm the federal budget and flatten future living standards—and it is the total cost of the age wave that any reform package must strive to contain.

There's an irony in the status quoists' refusal to confront economic and budget reality. After all, many of the same people who tirelessly defend our current entitlement system are also outspoken advocates of a greater public investment role for government. Let me remind them of the sobering conclusion of the Bipartisan ("Kerrey-Danforth") Commission on Entitlement and Tax Reform on which I served. On our current course, entitlements will consume the entire federal budget by 2030, leaving nothing to pay for interest on the debt, much less any progressive social or economic agenda, new or old.

2. Any reform package must be based on prudent projection assumptions.

It has become standard practice to base long-term budget projections on the "intermediate" Social Security and Medicare financing scenario prepared each year by the actuaries at the Social Security and Health Care Financing Administrations. Rarely, however, do policymakers ask whether this scenario is plausible (in the sense that it is at all likely to happen)—much less whether it provides a prudent basis for policymaking.

Many experts believe that the intermediate scenario is actually a "best case" scenario, since its key assumptions about demographic and economic trends are fiscally optimistic relative to recent historical experience. Consider the three most important:

Elderly longevity. Despite the prospects for medical advances on so many fronts, the intermediate scenario assumes that the future rate of improvement in life expectancy at age sixty-five will slow to just half its historical rate over the past two decades. While this slowdown might seem pessimistic to most of us, it brightens the annual reports of the Social Security and Medicare Trustees.

Productivity growth. The intermediate scenario assumes that future productivity (which determines real wage growth and hence the payroll tax base) will accelerate at a rate one-third faster than America's historical record to date since 1973.

Health care costs. Over the past quarter century, real Medicare spending per beneficiary has risen at the blistering rate of 5 percent a year, several times faster than real per capita income growth. Over no five-year period since 1970 has the growth in real per-beneficiary costs been less than 3 percent. Yet the intermediate scenario assumes that this growth will slow to about 1 percent per year by 2020.

As it turns out, the actuaries calculate another scenario whose key demographic and economic assumptions more closely reflect recent historical experience. According to this so-called high-cost scenario, the cost of Social Security and Medicare as a share of workers' taxable payroll is due to rise to 55 percent (not 35 percent) by 2040. Paying for the panoply of current-law senior benefits would not merely flatten after-tax worker earnings over the next forty-five years, it would cause a catastrophic decline of 59 percent.

In the interest of prudence, any reform package should take into account the risk that things will turn out worse than the official projections suggest. . . .

3. Any reform package must raise national savings.

How can an aging America help a relatively smaller number of workers support the exploding cost of a much larger number of retired dependents? By 2040, there will be no more than 2 workers to support each Social Security beneficiary and perhaps as few as 1.6—down from 3.2 today and 16.5 in 1950. Our best hope is to raise the real growth rate of our economy, and to do that we have to raise the growth rate of labor productivity. As the economist Paul Krugman has observed, "Productivity isn't everything, but in the long run it is almost everything. A country's ability to improve its living standard over time depends almost entirely on its ability to raise its output per worker."

Admittedly, economists are divided about the relative importance of the many factors affecting productivity growth. But they all agree that investment (which must ultimately be financed by savings) plays a major role—and, moreover, is the one factor over which public policy can exercise direct control. Capital formation is the inescapable bottom line insisted on by economists from Adam Smith to Alfred Marshall to John Maynard Keynes to Paul Samuelson. It is the economic dynamic by which the choice to consume less today generates the ability to consume more tomorrow.

Yet if we regard savings as a long-term leading indicator, the recent trend is a cause for concern. From an average of 8.1 percent of GDP in the 1960s, the U.S. net national savings rate plunged to 3.9 percent of GDP in the 1980s and to 2.3 percent of GDP thus far in the 1990s. Not only is today's savings rate far beneath our own historical average, it is far beneath the rates in most other industrial countries.

Given this trend, America probably needs to raise its savings rate simply to achieve the rate of productivity growth already assumed in the intermediate scenario underlying the official Social Security and Medicare projections. Unfortunately, on our current fiscal course we will get less savings, not more. If we simply leave the federal budget on autopilot, the CBO projects that the federal deficit—public dissavings, really—will climb to 5 percent of GDP by 2010. By the mid-2020s, the deficit would shoot past 20 percent of GDP—enough to devour all the net private savings of the domestic economy several times over. Deficit projections of approximately the same magnitude have been calculated by the General Accounting Office (GAO) and the Bipartisan Entitlement Commission on which I served.

It is impossible to exaggerate the importance of productivity growth. Everything consumed tomorrow must be produced tomorrow. The only sure way we have of easing the dependency burden projected for the next century is to increase the stock of physical and human capital at the disposal of tomorrow's workers. To do this, we must, at the very least, prevent the currently projected decline in the U.S. net national savings rate. Better, we should plan to raise our savings rate substantially above today's anemic level.

4. Any reform package must help reduce federal borrowing from the public.
There are two important components of national savings: government and private. Government savings is dominated by the annual unified federal budget balance—that is, by net Treasury borrowing from the public. Federal Reserve Chairman Alan Greenspan has stressed this point repeatedly: The annual unified federal budget balance provides the only bottom-line measure of how overall fiscal policy helps or hurts our economy's rate of capital formation.

In assessing the future impact of senior benefit programs on the economy, therefore, it is essential that we look at their effect on precisely this unified budget measure in each and every future year. For so-called self-financing programs, we measure this effect by looking at the extent to which their outlays exceed their earmarked tax revenues in each and every future year. Current projections show that the aggregate impact on savings of all senior benefit programs will be hugely negative. They are in fact the primary cause of the spiraling future deficits calculated by so many policy experts. (The secondary cause is the cumulative interest charges attributable to these senior programs.)

Consider the numbers for the two major self-financing senior benefit programs: Social Security now has a small operating surplus, but, under the intermediate scenario, will begin running a widening operating deficit beginning in 2012. By 2020, that deficit will rise to $216 billion per year; by 2030, it will rise to $703 billion per year (or to 2 percent and then to 4 percent of taxable payroll). Medicare Hospital Insurance is already running an operating deficit that will, by 2020, rise to $455 billion per year; by 2030, it will rise to $1.1 trillion per year (or to 3 percent and then to 5 percent of taxable payroll).

Many official agencies highlight another measure of the financial health and sustainability of some of the largest senior benefit programs. This is called *actuarial balance*, and it measures the extent to which trust-fund assets will be able to provide sufficient budget authority to cover future outlays. In 1996, the Trustees determined that the actuarial balance of Social Security is now minus 2.2 percent of taxable payroll. In theory, this is the total amount by which we would have to raise taxes or cut benefits, starting today, to keep the Social Security trust funds solvent over the next seventy-five years. Without this savings, Social Security would be solvent until 2029—meaning that, until then, its trust funds are projected to possess sufficient assets to cover current-law benefit promises.

This measure, however, is highly misleading. Actuarial balance assumes that interest-earning trust-fund surpluses accumulated in prior years constitute genuine economic savings that can later be drawn down to cover trust-fund deficits incurred in future years. They don't. Since the surpluses are immediately spent by Congress on non–Social Security outlays, trust-fund assets consist of nothing but a special series of intragovernmental Treasury IOUs. When the time comes to redeem them, Congress will have to increase taxes, cut other spending, or borrow from the public to raise the cash.

Status quoists will counter that trust-fund assets do indeed constitute genuine savings because, if Social Security had not run surpluses, the federal government would have run larger deficits. This is an interesting argument—but there's little evidence to support it.

Behaviorally, the argument implies that our political system tracks and targets some desired balance in the rest of government, rather than in the unified budget. This isn't so. Over the past dozen years (the era in which we built up today's trust-fund assets), there have been many plans and processes aimed at balancing the unified budget, but none aimed at balancing the budget excluding Social Security. Remarking on Washington's failure even to attempt this, Senator Moynihan notes that Social Security's surpluses have simply allowed Congress to tax less and spend more than it otherwise would, and so denounces them as a "fraud." As for the future, no one, least of all the status quoists, is insisting that we run a $96 billion unified budget surplus in 2002–which is what will then be required to balance the budget excluding Social Security.

To repeat, what matters is Social Security's operating balance—the simple annual difference between its outlays and its earmarked tax revenues. Under current law, this balance is due to turn negative in 2012 and widen to an annual deficit of $650 billion by 2029, the last year the trust funds are technically solvent. Even if the "2.2 percent solution" were enacted, Social Security would still face large and steadily growing operating deficits starting in 2021. Thereafter, the trust funds would only remain solvent by cashing in a mountain of paper Treasury IOUs for the next fifty straight years.

The supposed 2.2 percent solution is misleading for other reasons as well. It assumes that the reform would be effective as of last year, in 1996. This is impossible, of course, yet every year we wait the requisite cost will grow. [For instance, by] the year 2002, it will become the "2.6 percent solution." . . .

The bottom line is that accounting techniques will not do our savings for us. To say that the Social Security trust funds are a bit richer and Treasury is a bit poorer makes no difference for national savings or the economy—either now or in the future.

The truth is, the Trust Fund is a Distrust Fund. Rather than pretend that the fiscal oxymoron has any real economic meaning, I would suggest to this committee that you invite some of America's premier bond traders and equity traders to review the government's treatment of trust funds. Ask these experts to assume the Social Security Trustees attempt to redeem their Treasury IOUs. Then ask them to discuss the possible effects on interest rates and capital markets generally. I believe you would find such an exercise as informative as it would be sobering.

5. Any reform package must encourage—perhaps even require—households to save more.

Now let's turn to the private component of national savings. Just as government savings is dominated by the behavior of the federal government, private savings is dominated by the behavior of households. Increasing household savings would increase economic growth, which would take pressure off public budgets while also making seniors less dependent on government to begin with. In other words, it would make it easier for us to pay for future benefits while also making it easier to reduce future benefits if necessary.

The instance of higher household savings can hardly be overstated. Over the post-war era, net household saving has averaged roughly twice the size of net corporate saving—a ratio that has been rising slightly over time. Moreover, because the national savings rate has fallen to such lows (thus far in the 1990s, we're lingering well below 3 percent of GDP), even a small rise in the household rate would have a hugely positive impact.

The fact that most working-age households today are doing very little to prepare for their own retirement is also a key consideration here. Less than half of all private-sector workers have an employer pension, and the coverage rate is declining among younger workers. In 1992, according to Federal Reserve Board data, 43 percent of U.S. families spent more than their income while only 30 percent accumulated assets for long-term savings. In 1993, according to Census Bureau data, half of all households had less than $1,000 in net financial assets. Among adults in their late fifties, the age at which workers are staring directly at retirement, median net financial assets are still about $10,000. According to Stanford economist Douglas Bernheim, even if current-law senior benefits are paid in full (which is unlikely), the typical Boomer household would have to triple its current savings rate to enjoy an undiminished standard of living in retirement.

Even the optimists admit that a bleak future awaits the estimated one-third of all Boomers who are expected neither to accumulate financial assets nor to receive a private pension. Among these will be many of today's burgeoning number of divorced and single mothers, who have well below average incomes and few opportunities to save—and who, of course, are less likely than married couples to belong to a household with at least one pension.

How to get households to save more? Many strategies have been suggested—some using incentives, others compulsion. Whichever we adopt (and I believe that a mandatory approach is necessary), we should keep in mind the positive feedback between benefit reductions and household savings. Most economists assume and most surveys confirm that household savings rises or falls when people expect less or more generous public benefits upon retirement. Thus, if benefits must be reduced for some households in the future, we should by all means let those households know now so that they can plan in advance. That planning will almost certainly include more savings, which will help the economy onto the trajectory we should hope for.

6. Any reform package must fully pay for its transition costs.
In many reform plans, raising household savings is part of a larger strategy to escape the pay-as-you-go chain letter and to transform Social Security into a funded system of personally owned accounts.

There are two enormous benefits to funding Social Security: Not just higher returns on contributions, and hence higher benefits for retirees, but more national savings, and hence higher wages for workers in the years before retirement. The rate of return in a pay-as-you-go system is limited by the rate of growth of national product or income. The rate of return in a funded system is limited by the rate of return to capital. Almost all economists agree that the latter greatly exceeds the former. This difference, even after adjusting for risk, could be as great as 2 to 4 percent per year—enough to double the real return on contributions over time. A personally owned system would have another great benefit: security. Social Security was originally set up because people trusted government more than markets. Today, most Americans under fifty feel just the opposite. They know that Congress must ultimately renege on its pay-as-you-go promises—but that no politician can take away personal assets invested in the real economy.

Yet any effort to move in the direction of full funding and personal ownership must acknowledge the huge transition cost. It must recognize that the only way we can arrive at a positive-sum result in the long term is to raise aggregate savings—that is, to lower aggregate consumption—in the near term. One generation will have to pay for two retirements: its own, which now must be prefunded, and that of its parents, who will naturally continue to rely on pay-as-you-go benefits. This means that workers will have to save more. In fairness, retirees (those retirees who can afford it) would also have to give up some fraction of the benefits they are now receiving.

Some plans (and here all too many liberals and conservatives find common ground) pretend that this sacrifice is not necessary. Simply allow government or workers to invest a portion of current FICA revenues in the stock market, they say, and everyone will be better off. But this will compel government to borrow an equal amount from the public, offsetting the private savings boost. What we get is a budgetary three-card monte. Future generations will be saddled with a permanent debt service charge that will take away with one hand what we are promising to give them with the other.

These "reformers" sometimes concede that their plans may not raise national savings—but claim that this doesn't matter. According to this logic, the mere fact that workers' contributions are invested in private capital markets will ipso facto make everybody better off in the long run. Apparently they believe that Treasury—or each worker's personal retirement account—can indefinitely earn greater returns (with no greater risks) on the new equity assets than would be lost on the new debt liabilities.

The truth is that any plan that simply relies on the spread between stocks and bonds is a dicey and perhaps even dangerous proposition. Take proposals to have government invest the Social Security surpluses in private capital markets. Since no new savings—the indispensable element—are involved that would raise the aggregate returns to the economy as a whole, won't this massive shifting of funds affect the relative returns of government bonds (raise them) and on equities (lower them)? Thus, if the government starts buying stocks and selling bonds on a large scale, the yield on bonds will rise and the yield on stocks will fall—narrowing the favorable spread on which the proposal depends. Moreover, the very fact that government is betting on the stock market to defray the cost of future benefits will increase the riskiness (and hence the interest cost) of government debt. This narrows the spread even more—perhaps to the vanishing point.

No major government engages in this sort of high-risk gamble, and for good reason. But if it did make sense for the government to go into the arbitrage business, one wonders why it should stop with Social Security. Why doesn't it always make sense for Treasury to borrow trillions from the public, invest the funds in the stock market, then refund the profits to taxpayers? To ask the question is to answer it. This is the stuff of pipe dreams.

Let's not waste our time on zero-sum games. Only if reform raises national savings will we all be better off.

7. Any reform package must preserve and strengthen the safety net.

Some reformers have advocated a system of personally owned Social Security accounts under the rubric of "privatization." I believe this is a serious mistake, for privatization would violate at least two basic commitments America made over a half century ago: first, that public authority can be used to require people to set aside some minimal share of income to prepare for their own old age, and second, that no old person in America should live in poverty. These are settled issues.

So let me clarify: A system of personally owned accounts is not necessarily a privatized system. It could be mandatory so that workers cannot overconsume—and regulated so that workers cannot invest recklessly. Nor need it put lower-income workers at greater risk of poverty in old age. In my own proposal, I advocate that government provide a dollar-for-dollar match to all personal contributions by lower-income workers and back that up with a means-tested guarantee against poverty for all seniors.

The purpose of reform is not to dismantle our system of old age benefits, but to fashion a new system that is at once economically sustainable and generationally equitable. Along the way, I am convinced that some of the fiscal resources we free up should be used to create a more generous floor of protection against poverty in old age than the remarkably meager provision we can currently afford.

8. Any reform package must recognize that the age wave is a global challenge.
It is tempting to take some comfort in the fact that other industrial countries are aging more rapidly and face even larger old-age benefit costs. Presumably, we might think, this will put us at a competitive advantage. But think again. As rates of consumption rise in other industrial countries, we will not be able to rely on foreign capital (as we have in recent years) to finance our budget deficits. And if the global savings shortage is serious enough, it could plunge the industrial world into an economic and social crisis that might take America with it.

I've looked carefully at the data from the Organization for Economic Cooperation and Development, and the public-pension projections for the G-7 nations are sobering. Between 1995 and 2020, the combined deficit swing of these programs will be equivalent (as a share of G 7 GDP) to 23 percent of today's G-7 savings rate. By 2035, that figure will rise to 53.5 percent and remain well over 50 percent in the decades that follow. The entire world, in short, is en route to cannibalizing its global savings in order to fund its pensions.

As a share of GDP, Japan tops the list of nations with large deficit swings. (Germany is not far behind.) And small wonder when we consider that its age wave is already hitting with tsunami-like force. By 2010, when the ratio of workers to retirees in the United states will still be about 3 to 1, plunging birth rates and record longevity gains may have pushed the ratio down to 1 to 1 in Japan—a level we are not likely to reach even at the peak of the Baby Boom's retirement.

That year, Japan's public pension deficit is projected to hit 3 percent of GDP; by 2040, it is projected to hit 8 percent of GDP.

But as a share of national savings, the United States tops the list—because our savings rate is so low to begin with. By the year 2035, in fact, the operating deficit in Social Security alone will be enough to absorb 92 percent of U.S. national savings, by far the highest figure for any nation. To finance our pension deficits and still continue to make any net domestic investment at all, we would have to rely on imported capital. But, again, the savings dearth abroad could mean that we will be unable to do so except at prohibitive real interest rates.

Let me emphasize that these numbers reflect the trends in cash pensions only. They don't reflect the far more catastrophic growth trends in health-care benefits. If projections of total senior benefits for the G-7 were available, I'm certain that they would show critical savings shortages occurring much earlier.

In theory, the industrial world could avoid this future by changing policy course—that is, by raising taxes or cutting benefits. Will this be politically possible any time soon? On the one hand, I was chagrined to learn at a recent conference in Europe that, however daunting a political obstacle to reform the 34-million-member AARP may be, other countries (as the situation in France underscores) could face still more intense opposition from their powerful labor unions. On the other hand, I recently heard the prime minister of Japan, Mr. Hashimoto, say that his country's "aging society" was his "priority imperative." If President Clinton could join him in a similarly honest declaration, this issue could move to the G-7 summit level, where it deserves to be. . . .

9. Any reform package must begin now.
Many people have come to me and said, "Pete, I think you're absolutely right. We've got to act. But why now—when the public is still uncertain, when the leaders are still divided, when the country as a whole is still so politically unfocused? Can't we wait a while?" My answer is: Yes, we can wait—but not without closing a unique window of opportunity. If we wait until it closes entirely, I believe, the only choices left will be far more painful and dangerous and uncertain than those we face now.

This window of opportunity has three dimensions.

First, America is currently passing through an extremely favorable *demographic* era (that began around 1990 and will end around 2010) in which a large (Baby Boom) generation is still in the labor force and approaching the peak of its earnings and a small (Depression) generation is retiring. That translates into a relatively swift growth in the tax base and a relatively slow growth in senior benefits. Some economists are calling this America's demographic "Indian

Summer." But soon, of course, the season will change and the age profile will reverse. That huge generation of Boomers will turn from workers into retirees, and the tax burden will fall upon the next generation of workers (the so-called Busters)—who are neither numerous nor affluent. At this point, say the projections, the relative cost growth of every senior program will accelerate. . . .

Second, America is currently passing through a *global era* of unprecedented peace. The lack of clear threats abroad has allowed us to reduce our defense budget to the lowest level as a share of GDP since before Pearl Harbor. We cannot be certain this era will last indefinitely. Does it not, then, make sense to take some of this peace dividend and to steer it in a direction—personal retirement accounts, for example—that will help solve another national problem we know is just over the horizon? Would we rather wait until some future year when, perhaps, we face both foreign crises and fiscal crises piggybacked on top of one another? Finally, America is currently passing through an *economic era* of sustained recovery and of booming equity markets. There are, I suppose, times when people can say: No, we can't risk fiscal drag now—because the economy's in recession, or because the recovery's still too weak, or because the recovery's already exhausted. But right now, no one has that excuse. From a macro standpoint, this is clearly an ideal moment to launch a reform package. . . .

Elected officials often complain that the short-term worries don't allow the long-term solutions. But right now . . . our short-term and our long-term needs point in the same direction. All we need to do is take advantage of the opportunity while it lasts. History may never offer us a better one.

MY OWN PROPOSED REFORM PACKAGE

Having laid out my views on the purpose of reform, allow me to go ahead and summarize my own concrete reform proposals—which, I believe, together reflect and meet the criteria just outlined. I describe these proposals in more detail in my recent book, *Will America Grow Up Before It Grows Old?*

REFORM CASH BENEFIT PROGRAMS

Reduce COLAs. We should at a minimum legislate a 0.5 percentage-point reduction in the annual COLA adjustment. There's no justification for overindexing benefit payments—and most experts agree that the CPI overindexes inflation by at least this amount.

Affluence test. We must begin to adjust benefits according to need. The senior lobby still talks as if "old" is just another way of saying "poor." The reality is that over one-third of Social Security and Medicare now goes to Americans with incomes above the national median. We need an "affluence test" (which I would apply to all federal benefits programs) to progressively reduce the entitlement benefits of higher-income households.

Raise the retirement age. We must raise the Social Security's "normal" retirement age to 70. Since the New Deal, life spans have risen dramatically. An aging America can no longer afford to encourage it citizens to spend the last third of their adult lives in subsidized leisure.

REFORM HEALTH BENEFIT PROGRAMS

As it now stands, Congress and the executive branch do not really control most health benefit spending. They merely observe and monitor it—and sometimes change regulations in the hope of moderating its growth. I suggest that we regain control by putting all federal health spending into a fixed annual budget. We would then enforce that budget by capitating everyone's benefit. This might mean giving Medicare beneficiaries fixed-dollar vouchers to buy insurance (a voucher that might vary depending on the person's income). Or it might mean—for those who insist on fee-for-service medicine—premiums, copayments, and deductibles that change yearly to ensure that the federal cost per capita stays within budget. Republicans and Democrats alike pretend that there exists some painless way to control this most explosive dimension of senior dependency. The truth is that there's no solution that doesn't require someone to give something up.

SHIFT THE TAX BASE TO CONSUMPTION

We must ensure that households begin to save more on their own—not just to raise the economy's overall savings rate, but to avoid stranding millions of tomorrow's Boomer elders in what might be called a "Demographic Depression." One way to encourage savings is to replace the current income tax with a progressive consumption tax. An aging society should tax people on what they take out of the economy, not what they put into it—i.e., it should tax what they consume, not what they save.

INSTITUTE MANDATORY PERSONAL RETIREMENT ACCOUNTS

We should also supplement (and ultimately replace) today's pay-as-you-go Social Security system with a mandatory system of funded and personally owned retirement accounts. I have already explained the huge economic advantages of funding—and the huge credibility advantages of personal ownership. If we want to get from here to there without burdening posterity, however, we will have to face up to the "transition cost." Today's workers will have to set aside more of their current income, today's retirees will have to give up a portion of their benefits, or some combination of the two. Again, I warn against "privatization" schemes that claim no sacrifice is needed: All they do is shift assets around in a sort of budgetary three-card monte. Remember: If there's no net new savings, there will be no gain in future living standards and no real solution to the age wave challenge.

LAUNCH A NATIONAL SAVINGS CRUSADE

For decades, Americans have been indoctrinated to believe that consumption, not savings, is the key to prosperity. This campaign has worked all too well. Now it's time for a different kind of campaign—one in which our political and business leaders explain that a graying America must become a saving America. Pessimists will say that America will never agree to a reform program that requires them to make near-term sacrifices. But I'm an optimist. I believe that Americans are not spoiled children, that they are capable of making choices between today's consumption and tomorrow's higher living standard, and that when the real options are put to them honestly, they will face up.

There are moments in the history of great nations when a single choice can mean the difference between alternative futures—one bright, the other dark.

Imagine what America might be like if we could simply reattain the rates of national savings and productivity growth that we achieved throughout most of the last century. Once again, grown children could look back on their parents as relative paupers; once again, voters would find plenty of extra fiscal resources with which to build a better community; and once again, parents could take pride in the opportunities they would be passing on to their children. Such a difference is the stuff the American Dream is made of.

I believe the president must play a crucial role in leading us to such a future—and that his success or failure will define his legacy in American history.

If I were to write a letter to the president about this challenge, it would go something like this:

Dear Mr. President:

You, the president who campaigned this last year on your success in reducing the deficit over four straight years, know that our entitlement programs will blow not a hole, but a giant crater in the long-term deficit and in our national economy if we don't start the process of reform soon. You, the president who campaigned on the need for middle-class tax relief, know we cannot possibly allow the cost of Social Security and Medicare to rise to between one-third and one-half of payroll, as it is now projected to do, without destroying the very middle class you champion. You, the president who has focused so much on the problems of our youth and the need to invest in our collective future, know that benefits to senior citizens are already crowding investment in the young out of the federal budget and will eventually consume *all* government revenues, leaving *nothing* for worthy causes you have advanced, from the environment to Head Start.

Presidents are remembered best for stepping boldly out of character: Eisenhower, the war hero who warned against the military-industrial complex; LBJ, the Southern senator who championed the Civil Rights Act; Richard Nixon, the anti-Communist who went to "Red" China.

Mr. President, you are, to most Americans, the quintessential Boomer. Your fiftieth birthday recently was treated by the media as a watershed in the life cycle of an indulged generation that has made a virtue of youthfulness and has yet to acknowledge the inevitability of its old age. You, like so many Boomers, came of age in a time of great expectations for the permanence of economic plenty and the munificence of government—expectations that were created by the sweat, teamwork, and good fortune of your "Great Society" parents.

Mr. President, you could play against type by facing the crisis ahead and by understanding that your generation's reputation for vision and values will be utterly squandered if it is not soon matched by some modest capacity for realistic self-sacrifice. As a Democratic president and a Boomer yourself, you could be the leader who finally urges his party to redefine seniorhood as a type of "productive aging" and ongoing contribution, rather than subsidized dependency. You could lead the crusade for the personal savings and fiscal balance so desperately needed by your generation as preparation for its own old age. You could urge your contemporaries to moderate the me-first consumption that has always marked your generation and to instead relinquish some measure of material reward in return for the knowledge that they are contributing to the security and prosperity of the America they leave to their children and grandchildren.

I would also urge you to think about history's judgment if you don't find it politically feasible to take the lead on this issue. You, like other Boomers, are likely to live into your eighties. That means you will be very much alive when the Social Security system's operating deficit exceeds *one trillion dollars annually*. What will you, a former president still known for his grasp of policy detail and economic fact, say then? That you didn't know? That you were unaware that your daughter's generation was going to be denied the American Dream?

As you approach this challenge, you will want to bear in mind that this is not just an American problem but a global problem. Indeed, other industrial nations are aging more rapidly, and many face even larger retirement liabilities. Avoiding a global financial and economic crisis early in the next century when these liabilities come due demands a kind of leadership that I believe an American president can best provide.

Respectfully yours,

Well, that's what I would say to the president. But what if he doesn't get the message? And what if, despite the good work of this committee, your Senate and House colleagues don't get the message?

Then we would be in for another future—a dark future in which we close our eyes to the inevitable and condemn our own posterity. This is the future in which an aging society, flattered by cheap talk about inevitable prosperity and the inviolability of entitlement programs, does nothing—and by doing nothing, grows old gracelessly and destructively.

If we want the best of all worlds for our children—and even for ourselves— we must do more than hope. We must plan now to redirect ourselves toward the goal we all desire: a future worth preparing for. None of the choices are pleasant. Yet the longer we wait, the less pleasant they'll become.

CHAPTER THREE

Generational Equity and the Birth of a Revolutionary Class

Lester C. Thurow

Lester Thurow is professor of economics and management and a former dean of the MIT Sloan School of Management. He has served as vice president of the American Economics Association and is the author of a number of books, including *The Future of Capitalism, Head to Head: The Coming Economic Battle Among Japan, Europe, and America,* and *The Zero-Sum Society.*

In this selection taken from his recent book, *The Future of Capitalism,* Thurow argues that a demographic crisis is looming. He asserts that intergenerational competition is posing major problems because the elderly have become self-interested voters. He warns that politicians are intimidated by the voting power of the elderly and that the growing needs of the aged are leading the social welfare state to financial destitution.

GROWING OLDER

. . . The aging of the population [represents an explosive demographic shift]. A new class of people is being created. For the first time in human history, our societies will have a very large group of economically inactive elderly, affluent voters who require expensive social services such as health care and who depend upon government for much of their income. They are bringing down the social welfare state, destroying government finances, and threatening the investments that all societies need to make to have a successful future.

Back in 1900, 4 percent of America's population was over 65 years of age. Those over 65 now account for 13 percent of the population.[1] After 2013 the number of elderly will grow very fast in America, since the baby boom generation, the first of whom were born in 1947, will reach 65 and start to retire. Where there are now 4.5 workers working to pay for every pension, in 2030 there will be only 1.7 workers available to be taxed to pay for every pension.[2]

In many rich and poor countries the percentage of the population over the age of 65 will double by 2025.[3] In Japan in 2025 the elderly are expected to account for 26 percent of the population. In the United States, projection of the proportion of the population that will be elderly depends heavily on what is assumed about immigration—a source of young people—but the elderly will be at least 20 percent of the population.[4]

The United States faces what might be called the "double forty whammy." On average, those over 65 receive slightly more than 40 percent (41 percent to be precise) of their income from government.[5] And slightly less than 40 percent (38 percent to be precise) of the elderly receive 80 percent or more of their income from government. (Sixty-two percent get 50 percent or more.) In contrast, only 35 percent receive money from private pensions.[6]

This enormous transfer of resources has made the elderly into one-issue voters (whether government increases or decreases their monthly pension payments or health care benefits). In democracies, one-issue voters have a disproportionate impact on the political process, since they don't split their votes because of conflicting interests in other issues.

Already the needs and demands of the elderly have shaken the social welfare state to its foundations, causing it for all practical purposes to go broke. If one adds payments to the elderly to interest on the national debt, remembering that today's budget deficits are being produced by our unwillingness to pay for today's expenditures on the elderly, interest plus entitlements are swallowing government budgets. Project the numbers forward and government simply goes broke. It will have promised its elderly more than it can collect in taxes from those who are working.

Today the welfare state plus interest payments (most accumulated in recent years to make payments to the elderly) take 60 percent of total tax revenue. . . . By 2003 they will take 75 percent and by 2013 they will take 100 percent if current laws remain unchanged.[7] In Western Europe today's programs for the elderly will take 50 percent of the GDP by 2030. . . .

Everything else is being cut in government budgets to make room for the elderly. Leaving the elderly aside, domestic spending has fallen from 10 to 7 percent of the GDP in the last twenty years in the United States.[8] In the Organization for Economic Cooperation and Development (OECD), the association of developed nations as a whole, five times as much money is spent on social expenditures on those over 65 per capita as on those from 15 to 64 years of age.[9] Most important, expenditures on the elderly are squeezing government investments in infrastructure, education, and research and development out of the budget—down from 24 to 15 percent of the federal budget in twenty years.[10]

Spending on the elderly is not an issue of equity or deprivation. In 1970 the percentage of the elderly in poverty was higher than for any other part of the population. Now there are fewer poor people among the elderly than any other group in the population. For many in the United States, real standards of living actually rise with retirement. . . .

Adjusting for household size, capital gains, taxes (state and federal), noncash benefits such as health insurance and school lunches, and imputed returns on equity in owner-occupied housing, the elderly have a per capita income a whopping 67 percent above that of the population as a whole.[11] . . .

The elderly are also much wealthier than those who are not elderly.[12] Those 65 to 74 years of age have $222,000 in net worth vis-à-vis $66,000 for those aged 35 to 44.[13]

The elderly obviously don't want their benefits cut. The alternative is raising taxes, but that is also a very unattractive option. Today's 15 percent Social Security tax rate would have to be boosted to 40 percent by 2029 to provide the benefits that have been promised.[14] Moving out farther and assuming no changes in current laws, future payroll tax rates can rise as high as 94 percent if one is pessimistic about controlling health care spending on the elderly.[15] What is called generational accounting leads to some very disturbing future tax rates. The tax system implodes.

Over the past twenty-five years many of our entitlement programs have implicitly been paid for by cutting defense spending from peak Vietnam War levels. But even with the end of the cold war and a willingness to cut military

budgets (and the new Republican majority say they are not willing to have further defense cutbacks), there is not much room left for such shifts. Defense
spending is now down to less than 4 percent of GDP, and even if America were
willing to take defense spending down to zero, the day of reckoning for the
social welfare state would only be postponed by a few years.

Pensions are a matter of benefits and numbers. Health care for the elderly is
also a matter of technology. New, more costly technologies constantly escalate
per capita costs. While per capita costs differ greatly across countries, in the last
decade health spending as a fraction of the GDP has escalated right across the
OECD with only Sweden and Ireland bucking the trends.[16]

Expenditures on the elderly have fundamentally altered our fiscal systems. In
the 1960s government generated what was then called the fiscal dividend.
However large its current deficit, if government simply did nothing—passed no
new laws—within a few years it would be producing a budget surplus. With
economic growth, tax revenue grew faster than government expenditures.
Today the exact opposite is true. Even with rapid economic growth and no new
programs, government spending rises faster than tax revenues because of entitlements for the growing population of the elderly. If government does nothing,
deficits expand rapidly.

All of President Clinton's budget cutting and tax increases in his first two
years in office only brought a small amount of breathing space. By 1996 the
deficit will again be rapidly rising even if no new spending programs are passed.
What is faced by President Clinton is faced by every government. Even Sweden,
which is in many ways the inventor of the social welfare state, and is still the place
where it enjoys some of its greatest political support, is having to cut back.[17]

Instead of a fiscal dividend, governments all around the world now confront
structural fiscal deficits that cannot be cured by economic growth. . . .

Across the OECD between 1974 and 1994, government debt has risen from 35
to 71 percent of GDP, and that does not count the unfunded pension and health
care liabilities that lie ahead.[18] In 1995 only one of the OECD countries, oil-rich
Norway, was expected to run a budget surplus.[19]

Technically, in the United States the elderly can argue that the pension part
of their benefit package does not contribute to government debts, since the
pension part of social security, but not the health care part, is running a surplus—tax revenues from earmarked taxes exceeds expenditures. But that is an
illusion. To evaluate the impact of government budgets, it is necessary to look
at total revenue and total expenditures as a whole. If governments are running
a deficit in their overall budgets, the fact that one part of the budget has a surplus because there is an accounting convention that earmarks more taxes than

this sector of the budget needs is irrelevant. Whatever the earmarking, governments are net dissavers and that is what affects the economy. What matters is what is driving the expenditure side of the budget. The driver is the elderly.

The problem of running up debts to pay for the elderly is straightforward. Just to take the arithmetic, simply suppose that taxes collect 30 percent of GDP and suppose that market interest rates are 10 percent. When government debt reaches 300 percent of GDP, all of government revenue has to be used to make interest payments on outstanding debt and nothing is left for anything else. Belgium, Italy, and Canada already can see this limit ahead of them. . . .

While all of our economic resources are not going to be given to the elderly (there are other things such as police and fire departments that simply have to be financed), no one knows how the growth of entitlements for the elderly can be held in check in democratic societies. Even when they are only 13 percent of the population, they are so powerful that no political party wants to tangle with them.

House Majority Leader Newt Gingrich's Contract with America does more than explicitly exclude the elderly from its cutbacks. It promises to spend more on the elderly by raising the amount of income that can be earned before social security benefits are cut and to reduce the taxes paid on social security benefits by high-income individuals.[20]

A conservative French finance minister, Alain Madelin, was forced to resign just for suggesting that public employees be forced to contribute more to their own retirement.[21]

Long before they are a technical majority of the population, the elderly will be unstoppable politically, since those under age 18 legally cannot vote and those between eighteen and thirty tend not to vote. Democracy is going to meet its ultimate test when it has to confront the economic demands of the elderly. Can democratic governments cut benefits for a group of voters that will be close to being a majority?

Today it cannot. President Clinton appointed a panel to recommend changes in the system, but it could only report back that it could "not agree on any specific proposals to slow the growth of Social Security, Medicare, or other government benefit programs," even though it could agree that the current programs would raise the government deficit eightfold by 2030 if nothing was done.[22]

Democracy is not yet a survival-of-the-fittest species. In terms of letting everyone vote, it is less than one hundred years old. It is going to meet the ultimate test in the elderly. Can it cut the benefits that go to a majority of its voters? If the answer is no, democracy has no long-run future. Other investments have to be made that will not and cannot be made unless those benefits are under control.

The political problems are not created entirely by the political power of the ever more numerous elderly. Means-tested benefits (benefits that decrease as income and wealth increase) would result in dramatic cost savings, but it is not just the elderly with above-average incomes and wealth who are opposed to it. All of us will eventually become old and all of us, especially the near elderly, would rather use our own money for the luxuries of life and let the government pay for our necessities when we are old. Less generous programs are ultimately less generous programs for *us* and not just for *them*.

Even for the young not yet worried about retirement, the shift toward making the elderly pay more of their own bills is not without a downside. The shift means that the young may have to pay, or feel the guilt associated with not paying, for some of the costs of taking care of their parents if their parents don't budget their income appropriately. More dire, for those with parents who have assets, making the elderly pay means smaller inheritances.[23] One will not inherit the house or the stock portfolio that one expected to inherit if it was sold to pay medical bills or provide the equivalent of a monthly pension. The young would rather not lose their inheritances.

The political message is simple. Targeting benefits to low-income elderly families reduces costs and improves economic efficiency (gets the money to those who need it most), but it quickly loses political support.

A balanced budget amendment is often offered as a solution. But it isn't. A balanced budget amendment can be passed, but it has no meaning unless politicians are willing and able to cut back on the entitlements for the elderly. If those who make the laws don't want to obey the spirit of a law, they can always avoid doing so. They can simply spend more than incoming revenues and justify it with some of the fine print that has to accompany any balanced budget amendment.

Any balanced budget amendment has to have some exceptions and some implementation provisions. How are revenues and expenditures to be forecast? What happens if an unexpected recession occurs? What happens if a major war breaks out? How are expenditures to be counted—do the expenditures of government corporations such as the postal service count? Do asset sales count as revenues? Do major infrastructure investments count as current expenditures? How are loan guarantees to be counted? All of these "details" make it possible for any government that does not want to obey a balanced budget amendment to avoid obeying it. If spending is to be cut, in the end those who have been elected have to cut it.

The problem of the elderly is not just a government problem. Private firms face the same dilemma in private pension and health programs for the elderly.[24] In the private sector, health care programs are universally underfunded and pension programs are often less than fully funded. In the United States there is a 20 percent shortfall in private pension plans, yet 75 percent of the companies with underfunded programs are financially healthy companies. Older companies such as the auto companies with a lot of retirees and generous pension and health plans for those retirees would have little or no corporate equity if these obligations were fully reflected on their books.

The elderly are not the big dissavers that they are sometimes portrayed to be (spending all of their accumulated wealth so that they die on the day when their assets run out), but they quite understandably are not big savers for the future. The results can be seen in savings rates. In OECD countries gross savings rates have fallen from 24 percent to 19 percent of GDP between 1977 and 1992.[25]

Much of the decline in personal savings rates in the United States, from about 9 percent in the decades after World War II to 3 percent in the 1990s, can be attributed to the elderly or those about to be elderly.[26] The near elderly, being more confident about public and private employers providing pensions, are saving less than they used to right before retirement, and the elderly who know that they have monthly pension checks and health coverage are spending more during retirement. Savings rates fall just when . . . man-made brainpower industries will require a significant increase in savings.

If one is looking for a group in need, it is not the elderly. The group with the highest proportion now in poverty is children under the age of 18. Yet government spends nine times as much per person on the elderly (those who do vote) as it does on the young (those who don't vote).[27] Precisely the group that most needs investments if there is to be a successful American economy in the future is the group that is getting the least. How are they to pay taxes to support the elderly if they don't have the skills to earn their own incomes?

In the years ahead, class warfare is apt to be redefined to mean not the poor against the rich but the young against the old. As a young Frenchwoman said during a strike to protest government laws that would have lowered the wages of the young, "We have no future! That's why we're out here."[28] In America this conflict is already clear. The elderly systematically vote against education levies when they have a chance.[29] The elderly establish segregated, restricted retirement communities for themselves where the young are not allowed to live so that they do not have to pay for schools.

The most dramatic recent example of impending social conflict occurred in Kalkaska, Michigan, a retirement haven, where elderly voters essentially robbed the school budget to pay for other things such as snow plowing and then refused to vote the funds to allow the schools to finish the school year. Schools closed months early and some of Michigan's schoolchildren missed much of a year's schooling.[30] While the elderly are probably still interested in their own grand-children, they no longer live in the same communities with their grandchildren. Each of those elderly Kalkaska voters could vote against educating someone else's grandchildren yet convince themselves that somehow voters elsewhere in America would treat their grandchildren differently.

The implicit post—World War II social contract has been that parents will take care of children but that society, the taxpayer, will take care of parents. Both parts of that bargain are collapsing. More and more parents are not taking care of children, and the taxpayer is going to have to retreat from his promise to take care of the elderly.

REFORMING THE SOCIAL WELFARE SYSTEM

What has to be done is as economically clear as how to do it is politically opaque. Single-issue politics where large voting groups fight over income redis-tribution is what democracies do worst.[31] By always being willing to exempt the elderly from budget cuts, those who know politics best, our elected politicians, have already decided that the problem is politically impossible to solve. But the problem has to be solved, since 100 percent of any society's tax revenue cannot be given to the elderly.

No society, no matter how it pays for it, can afford to let ever larger fractions of its population live in idleness for ever longer periods of time. Societies can guarantee a fixed number of years in retirement (ten years, fifteen years, twenty years), but no one can any longer guarantee retirement at some fixed age such as 65 as life expectancy lengthens. There is also no reason why any social welfare system should transfer so many resources to a group that it ends up with above-average incomes. That leads to the social absurdity of the poorer members of society paying taxes to subsidize the richer.

The answer to what must be done has to begin with some explicit goals. How much of a person's preretirement income should be replaced with a system of compulsory government pensions? The mirror image of that question is, how much should someone be expected to save if they wish to have a retirement standard of living equal to their preretirement standard of living? Just to moti-vate the thought processes, let me suggest a possible set of goals.

The maximum benefit should be a public pension that would guarantee a retired couple no more than two-thirds of the median earnings of the average workingman and average workingwoman (jointly $23,876 in 1992) since the average couple supports a family of three.[32] The minimum benefit should be a pension that ensures that all elderly families have an income at least equal to the poverty line.

Whatever a family's preretirement earnings, it would be guaranteed a poverty-line pension. Above this level, families should get a pension equal to half of their preretirement earnings in the ten years before retirement. When a family's preretirement earnings reached twice the national average, they would be guaranteed a pension equal to two-thirds the earnings of the average working man and woman. Earnings more than this would not yield higher pensions. With the exception of the working poor, everyone would be expected to save if they wish to have an income equal to that of their preretirement earnings.

The age of retirement is easy to calculate. How much taxes are people willing to pay? What essential services have to be provided and what essential investments have to be made? Subtracting the latter two numbers from the first yields the funds available to support the social welfare system. Make another subtraction for everything else other than spending on the elderly that has to be done in the social welfare system. Take the resulting funds, the annual income needed in retirement to have a per capita income equal to that of the nonelderly, and the number of elderly, and it is easy to calculate the maximum number of years that the average elderly person can be supported in retirement. Subtract this number from average life expectancy at age 65 (now seventeen years) and one has the retirement age society can afford.

The age of retirement has to be raised and early retirement eliminated. When Bismarck set the retirement age at 65 in the German pension system in 1891, the average German lived to be less than 45.[33] Today that would be roughly equivalent to saying that there is a government pension for all those over the age of 95. If this were the actual rule, there wouldn't be any problem.

Raising the retirement age will not be popular. While 65 used to be the age at which the largest number of people retired, it is now 62 and falling.[34] Already by age 61 labor force participation rates are about 10 percentage points lower than they were at age 55. Yet no one can finance a system where life expectancy rises and the age of retirement falls.

Pundits can talk about letting people voluntarily take care of themselves when they are elderly, but there is a simple reality—too many won't. At retirement, 16 million Americans have no voluntary savings and nothing but their pensions to sustain them.[35] The average American family has only $1,000 in accumulated net financial assets, and to finance a future pension income equal to what today's retirees receive they would be required to save a sum equal to eleven times their own current income.[36] Those with thirty years of their working life left would be required to save one-third of their pretax incomes each and every year for the next thirty years to reach this goal.

Those 54 to 65 years of age and just about to retire have less than $7,000 in net financial assets and are in even worse shape.[37] Many of course have some equity in their homes, but with home equity loans, housing equity is not building up nearly as fast as it did in the past. Including home equity, the fiftieth-percentile households of those 51 to 61 years of age have only $99,350 in accumulated assets.[38] . . .

When Americans get a chance to rob their pension plans, they do so. Thirty-eight percent of workers who change jobs and have a chance to take money out of their pension plans take the money and run.[39] Workers in general and lower-paid workers in particular don't take advantage of tax-free opportunities to save. The baby boom generation systematically uses home equity loans. . . . to raise their current consumption.[40] Today's baby boomers are saving only one-third of what they need to in order to have the standard of living in retirement that their parents currently enjoy.[41] . . .

There is a fundamental reality that Americans don't save unless they are forced to save.

Employers are getting out of the pension business. They have cut their pension contributions in half (from $1,039 to $506 per worker) between 1980 and 1991, and this trend will only accelerate.[42] Jurisdictions requiring employer-financed pension plans will only find employers relocating elsewhere.

History will record that Lee Kuan Yew got it right in Singapore with his Provident Fund (self-financed social welfare benefits), while Bismarck got it wrong in Germany with his social welfare system of intergenerational transfers. In Singapore every person must contribute 20 percent of their wages to a personal savings account where it is matched by 20 percent from employers. The account's investments are half managed by the individual and half managed by the government and can only be used for health care, education, housing, and one's old age. Taxes are not levied on the young to pay for the old. The old live on what they have been forced to save and the additional saving that they have voluntarily done.

But once a system of intergenerational transfers exists, it is only possible to move to self-financing very slowly. The problem is simple. The big winner in a system of intergenerational transfers is the first generation. They receive benefits when they are old without having had to pay anything into the system when they were young. The system did not exist when they were young. They get but did not pay. The big loser is the last generation. They pay into the fund for their entire lifetimes but there are no young people behind them to pay benefits to them. They pay but do not get.

Today's retirees are essentially the first generation and they are the big winners in social security. While no one will be the last generation in terms of humankind, if the generations are very different in size or benefit levels have expanded dramatically, the smaller and later generations (today's baby-dearth generation born after 1963) will to some extent be the last generation having to pay for the much larger generation (the baby boom generation born between 1947 and 1963) ahead of them.

While those born in 1900 received a real, inflation-adjusted, 12 percent rate of return on their social security contributions (far more than they would have gotten in private capital markets), those born in 1975 will earn less than a 2 percent real rate of return.[43] ... That is simply unfair, yet most of the elderly have convinced themselves that they have "paid for" their current benefits and are not on welfare. They have "earned" what they get.

Nothing could be further from the truth. The average elderly male now is repaid all of his social security tax payments plus interest in less than four years.[44] After that he is on welfare in exactly the same sense that a welfare mother is on welfare.

While more saving for retirement should be encouraged, such actions cannot solve the current problem. They in fact compound it. If today's workers are essentially forced ("encouraged") to save for their own old age, but if nothing is done to cut the costs of the current system for those who are already elderly, today's workers must simultaneously finance both today's elderly and their own old age. They have their economic burdens essentially doubled. As a result, the shift from a system of intergenerational transfers to self-financing can occur only very slowly—one would have to think about a fifty- to seventy-five-year period of time. The shift to more self-financing should be slowly made in the long run, but doing so will not change what needs to be done in the medium term.

Whatever is done has to be announced far in advance, so that families can plan for their retirement. No one can change their retirement plans quickly. Retirement benefits and ages have to be known fifteen to twenty years in advance. New laws have to be written not so much to cut current benefits but to cut the increases in the benefit stream that are programmed into current laws. Only very gradually will the elderly have to pay more out of their own savings. But benefits do need to be selectively cut to bring the per capita income of the elderly back into balance with that of the nonelderly. There is simply no justification for a social welfare system that taxes those with lower incomes (the young) to give it to people with higher incomes (the elderly). There is no need to return to the "bad old days" when the elderly had much less than the nonelderly. . . .

While the direct means testing of benefits may be impossible since it undercuts the political viability of the system, the elderly have to pay income taxes that are consistent with their incomes. In the United States a couple with one child earning $30,000 pays $2,449 in federal income taxes. An elderly couple needing to support only two with an equally large income of $30,000 (40 percent of it coming from social security) pays only $791 in taxes.[45] Equally wealthy elderly should pay equal taxes.

Since pensions and health care benefits are consumption activities, the right way to pay for pensions and health care benefits for the elderly is not a payroll tax on work but a consumption tax—a value-added tax—on other forms of consumption. If pensions are not to squeeze out investment, they must be set up in such a way that they squeeze out other forms of consumption. A progressive consumption tax also means that the elderly continue to help pay for their pensions after they cease working unless they are willing to contribute to society by savings.

Using the payroll tax to finance benefits for the elderly creates what economists know as the tax wedge. When employers look at workers, they see expensive workers—labor compensation, which includes wages, private fringe benefits, and public payroll taxes, is high. When workers look at those same jobs, they see low-wage jobs, because the only part of that compensation package that is relevant to them is take-home wages. The rest of it either goes to others (the elderly) or yields benefits in a distant future that are completely discounted.

Both sides essentially bail out of the tax-paying economic system. The employer moves his operations to some other part of the world where private fringe benefits and public social benefits don't exist. From offshore production bases the employer continues to sell his products in the old home market, but he no longer makes his products or pays his taxes in his home market. By doing this, he lowers costs and raises profits. The employee seeks to do the same. He seeks to get whatever social welfare benefits are available (unemployment insurance, disability payments) and moves into the illegal black economy where taxes are not paid and where cash wages are often higher than after-tax wages in the legal white economy, because the employers do not have to pay for public or private fringe benefits.

Because both sides have quit paying the taxes that are necessary to finance the social welfare system, the costs of the welfare system rise for those who are left in it, and their incentives to bail out increase. In the long run, a payroll-tax-financed system of social welfare spending is simply not viable.

Whatever is done, the sooner it is done the easier it is to do. Bringing the system into balance now leads to fewer debts tomorrow. Lower interest payments mean that fewer taxes need to be collected to finance the system. Politically, the same interest in speed exists. The electoral power of the elderly can only grow as they become more numerous. The longer the elderly are addicted to government pensions, the harder it is going to be to stop that addiction. What humans have always had quickly seems a right and not a privilege. Such a shift in attitudes is already clearly visible.

But the elderly are not the entire social welfare problem. In Sweden two-thirds of the population gets some kind of a regular check from the government.[46] In northern Europe it is clear that there is something that might be called a "second generation" problem. When welfare systems were first established, the existing ethos limited usage so that people didn't use the system unless they badly needed to. Such attitudes still exist . . . but to a much lesser extent. But over time such inhibitions died away and what was initially regarded as a system only to be used in case of dire need became an entitlement to be used whenever it was convenient to do so.

These same inhibitions, however, allowed the politicians of a few decades ago to think that the long-run costs of the systems they were designing were much lower than they actually were. Since few people used the system in the first generation, costs were low, and the system could be made more generous because benefit hikes could be easily afforded. Over time the systems were expanded to the point that benefits often yielded wage-replacement rates of more than 90 percent (107 percent for pensioners in Greece, 100 percent for being an invalid in Germany, 124 percent for maternity benefits in Portugal, 97 percent for disability benefits in Belgium), so that when work expenses were subtracted, large numbers of people were actually better off not working.[47] But what was cheap in the first generation became expensive in the second generation as more and more people got used to using the system.[48] . . .

With all of the talk about paying less taxes, one would think that Americans wanted fewer social benefits. It is important to remember that nothing could be further from the truth. The elderly want their benefits. They are not alone. Rather than paying privately for health, flood, hurricane, or earthquake insurance, middle-class voters want government to provide the necessary insurance. But when government does pay, those who bought private flood or earthquake insurance become suckers—paying privately for their own coverage and publicly through taxes for someone else's coverage. Every flood or earthquake for which the government offers disaster relief reduces the number of those who in the future will buy the private coverage that makes them ineligible for public benefits. They are not stupid. In the flood-prone zones of the Midwest, only 7 percent now carry flood insurance.[49] The same attitudes can be seen in health insurance. More than 50 percent of those who were covered under Medicaid cut back on their private insurance as a result.[50]

Rather than being interested in insurance policies that only pay for catastrophic unusual occurrences—the unexpected huge costs that few can afford and no one expects—the public wants first-dollar coverage. It wants government or corporations to pay for the unusual risks, but also to pay for the everyday expected expenses that most should, and could, easily pay for themselves.

The increasing unwillingness to live with risk in our modern societies probably comes from the shift out of agriculture. In an agricultural world, annual incomes rise and fall dramatically depending upon the weather. People have no choice but to live in a world with a lot of uncertainty about their annual incomes. Having to live with big risks that cannot be eliminated makes living with the little risks of life seem natural. But in an industrial world everything seems more controllable. There may be uncertainties but they are uncertainties created by other humans and at least in principle are avoidable. Not having to live with unavoidable big risks to their incomes makes humans less willing to live with the little unavoidable risks of life.

Fatalism and "caveat emptor" are gone and have been replaced by the social insurance state.[51] The result is an enormous mismatch between redistribution wants and the willingness to pay taxes to pay for those wants.

. . . A big increase in the number of elderly people has to profoundly change the nature of [a capitalistic] system. Not expecting to live too much longer and no longer working, they simply are not, and should not be, interested in investments in the future. But investments have to be made if the young are to be economically viable and generate the income necessary to finance the pensions and health care of the elderly. One cannot tax what does not exist. Nothing should be more important to the old than the economic success of the young.

We have met the financial "enemy" and he is the elderly "us" in both the public and the private sector.

NOTES

1. Arsen J. Darney, ed., *Statistical Record of Older Americans* (Detroit: Gale Research, 1994), pp. 47, 48, 49, 64.

2. "Aging Population Puts the Strain on Pensions," *European*, October 28, 1994, p. 20.

3. Aline Sullivan, Retiring Baby Boomers Dread the End of the Boom Times," *International Herald Tribune*, March 11, 1995, p. 16.

4. U.S. Bureau of the Census, *Statistical Abstract 1994* (Washington, D.C.: U.S. Government Printing Office), p. 16; Keizi Koho Center, *Japan 1995: An International Comparison*, p. 9.

5. Advisory Council on Social Security, *Future Financial Resources of the Elderly: A View of Pensions, Savings, Social Security, and Earnings in the Twenty-first Century*, December 1991, pp. 12, 13.

6. Ibid., p. 39.

7. *Financial Times*, Editorial, December 19, 1994, p. 13.

8. "A Powerful Political Lobby," *Financial Times*, March 28, 1995, p. viii.

9. Barry Bosworth, *Prospects for Savings and Investment in Industrial Countries*, Brookings Discussion Paper No. 113, May 1995, pp. 12, 14.

10. Office of Management and Budget, *Budget of the United States Government, Fiscal Year 1996*, Historical Tables (Washington, D.C.: U.S. Government Printing Office, 1995), p. 122.

11. U.S. Bureau of the Census, *Income, Poverty, and Valuation of Noncash Benefits: 1993, Current Population Reports, Consumer Income*, Series P60-188 (Washington, D.C.: U. S. Government Printing Office), pp. 41, 45.

12. Daniel B. Radner, *The Wealth of the Aged and the Nonaged 1984, Social Security Administration*, ORS Working Paper No. 36, 1988.

13. Edward N. Wolff, "Changing Inequality of Wealth," *American Economics Review*, May 1992, p. 554.

14. Anne Reilly Dowd, "Needed: A New War on the Deficit," *Fortune*, November 14, 1994, p. 191.

15. "The Budget Pain Will Come and the Young Will Suffer," *International Herald Tribune*, February 18, 1995, p. 6.

16. "Health Spending," *The Economist*, June 24, 1995, p. 98.

17. Richard W. Stevenson, "A Deficit Reigns in Sweden's Welfare State," *New York Times*, February 2, 1995, p. 1.

18. "House of Debt," *The Economist*, April 1, 1995, p. 14.

19. "Public Sector Finances," *The Economist*, July 8, 1995, p. 115.

20. Newt Gingrich, *Contract with America* (New York: Times Books, 1994), p. 115.

21. "French Finance Minister Resigns," *Boston Globe*, August 26, 1995, p. 2.

22. Robert Pear, "Panel on a U.S. Benefits Overhaul Fails to Agree on Proposals," *New York Times*, December 15, p. A24.

23. "Taking Care of Granny," *The Economist*, June 3, 1995, p. 25.

24. Health and Wealth, special issue of *Daedalus*, Journal of the American Academy of Arts and Sciences, Fall 1994.

25. John Pender, "Not Such a Safe Haven," *Financial Times*, December 23, 1994, p. 15.

26. Sylvia Nasar, "Older Americans Cited in Studies of National Savings Rate Slump," *New York Times*, February 21, 1995, p. 1.

27. Wallace C. Peterson, *Silent Depression* (New York: W. W. Norton, 1994), p. 149; David Popenoe, "The Family Condition of America," in *Values and Public Policy*, ed. Henry J. Aaron, Thomas E. Mann, and Timothy Taylor (Washington, D.C.: Brookings Institution, 1994), p. 104.

28. Quote in Alan Riding, "Passions Ignited, French Students Protest Wage Policy Again," *New York Times*, March 26, 1994, p. 3.

29. Dennis Kelly, "Seniors Much Less Likely to Back Local Education Bonds," *USA Today*, June 30, 1993, p. 1.

30. William Celis, "Schools Reopen in Town That Made Them Close," *New York Times*, September 2, 1993, p. A14; Isabel Wilkerson, "Tiring of Cuts, District Plans to Close Schools," *New York Times*, March 21, 1993, p. 20.

31. Mancur Olson, *The Rise and Decline of Nations* (New Haven: Yale University Press, 1982), p. 8; Stephen P. Magee, William A. Brock, and Leslie Young, *Black Hole Tariffs and Endogenous Policy Theory* (New York: Cambridge University Press, 1989), p. xv.

32. U.S. Bureau of the Census, *Money Income of Households, Families, and Persons in the United States, 1992, Current Population Reports*, Series P60-184, pp. 148, 150.

33. John Eatwell, Murray Milgate, and Peter Newman, eds., *The New Palgrave: Social Economics* (New York: W. W. Norton, 1987), p. 10; "Statistisches Budesamt," *Statistisches Jahrbuch* 1994, Federal Republic of Germany, p. 82.

34. Michael V. Leonesio, *The Economics of Retirement: A Nontechnical Guide*, ORS Working Paper No. 66, Social Security Administration, April 1995, pp. 65, 66.

35. Leslie Wayne, "Pension Changes Raising Concerns," *New York Times*, August 29, 1994, p. 1.

36. "Skimpy Savings," *Fortune*, February 20, 1995, p. 38.

37. Ibid.

38. "Why Baby-Boomers Won't Be Able to Retire," *Fortune*, September 4, 1995, p. 48.

39. Ibid.

40. Ibid.

41. "The Economics of Aging," *Business Week*, September 12, 1994, p. 60.

42. Scott Lehigh, "Social Security," *Boston Globe*, August 20, 1995, pp. 81, 82.

43. Dean R. Leimer, *A Guide to Social Security Money's Worth Issues*, ORS Working Paper No. 67, Social Security Administration, April, 1995, p. 28.

44. Ibid, p. 26.

45. Dowd, "Needed: A New War on the Deficit," p. 191; Internal Revenue Service, "Form 1040A, 1994" (Washington, D.C.; U.S. Government Printing Office, 1993).

46. "Sweden: Judgement Day," *The Economist*, February 18, 1995, p. 37.

47. "The Enlightened Welfare Seeker's Guide to Europe," *The Economist*, March 12, 1994, p. 57.

48. Assar Lindbeck, *Overshooting, Reform, and Retreat of the Welfare State*, Institute for International Economic Studies at University of Stockholm, No. 499, 1994.

49. Damon Darlin, "A New Flavor of Pork," *Forbes*, June 5, 1995, p. 146.

50. "Expanded Medicaid Crowded Out Private Insurance," *The NBER Digest*, 1994, p. 1.

51. Yair Aharone, *The No Risk Society* (New Jersey: Chatham House, 1981), pp. 48, 62.

CHAPTER FOUR

Generational Justice and Generational Accounting

Jagadeesh Gokhale and Laurence J. Kotlikoff

Jagadeesh Gokhale is an economist at the Federal Reserve Bank of Cleveland who has published extensively on such topics as generational accounting, intergenerational equity, and the sustainability of fiscal policies. He has also written about the desirability and feasibility of privatizing the Social Security system. Laurence J. Kotlikoff is professor of economics at Boston University and a research associate of the National Bureau of Economic Research. He has served as a senior economist on the staff of the President's Council of Economic Advisors. He has published a number of books, including *Generational Accounting, Dynamic Fiscal Policy*, and *Pensions in the American Economy*.

Gokhale and Kotlikoff suggest that unless dramatic fiscal changes are made, future generations will experience enormous tax burdens relative to the burden on those currently in the labor force. They propose and describe a system of generational accounting to help estimate and track the amount each generation pays over the life span. The goal of generational accounting is to make the system more accountable and reduce the extent to which one generation takes out more than it pays in. The authors apply this method of long-term fiscal analysis to assess alternative fiscal policies.

Governments spend money in order to purchase goods and services for the citizenry.[1] These purchases are financed by levying taxes on the citizens. A part of total revenue is immediately handed back to the public as public pensions (Social Security), health care benefits (Medicare and Medicaid), and welfare and other transfers. Hence, it is *net taxes* (taxes minus transfers) that finance government purchases. This chapter focuses on the issue of generational justice in fiscal policy—that is, on whether the *net tax burden* of paying for government purchases is spread equitably across living and future generations.[2] Although important in and of itself, this issue has considerable bearing on those of fiscal sustainability and economic efficiency.

Present and future purchases plus the government's existing liabilities must be paid for out of net taxes levied today and in the future—that is, the government's long-term budget must be balanced. This requires that the discounted value of all future net taxes be equal to the government's outstanding debt plus the discounted value of all scheduled purchases. However, net taxes in any particular period need not equal purchases plus debt service in that period. The time profile of net tax receipts can be altered—for example, by lowering taxes this year and increasing them in the future in a manner that preserves their present value and hence maintains the balance between the discounted values of net taxes and purchases plus debt.

A present-value-neutral change in the time pattern of net taxes will, in general, produce a different generational distribution of net tax burdens. For example, reducing income taxes today and increasing them several years later such that the present value of income taxes remains unchanged will reduce the net taxes of some living generations (for example, old, some of whom may die in the intervening period) but impose larger net taxes on younger (possibly future) generations.

The foregoing may suggest that comparing different streams of net taxes and purchases (in effect, monitoring budget deficits) is sufficient to reveal the generational stance of fiscal policy. It can be shown, however, that the net tax burdens facing different generations can also be altered *without* changing the time profile of aggregate net taxes and purchases. For example, increasing both payroll taxes and Social Security transfers by the same amount in each future year leaves the time path of total net taxes unchanged. However, current retired generations gain (via larger Social Security benefits) and young and future generations lose (because their larger taxes exceed their larger transfer receipts in present value). The same holds true for "revenue neutral" changes in the structure of taxes (for example, substituting income for sales taxes) or transfers (for example, cutting welfare benefits and increasing health care benefits).

Evaluating a given fiscal policy for generational justice therefore involves looking beyond budget deficits. Indeed, one must look at precisely which generations pay and receive the various taxes and transfers under that policy. Generational accounting is a method of long-term fiscal analysis designed for doing just that.[3] This method uses demographic projections, cross-sectional profiles of taxes and transfers by age and sex, and official budget projections to calculate the prospective net tax burdens facing living generations under the prevailing set of fiscal policies. It combines future projections with past data on generation-specific tax and transfer payments to compute lifetime net tax rates. Combined with the government's long-term budget constraint, the lifetime net tax rates enable a comparison of the fiscal treatment of different generations (including future ones) on a lifetime basis. In addition, generational accounting can also evaluate the impact of policy changes on different generations and inform us about the sizes of alternative policy changes that are necessary to establish a generationally balanced fiscal policy. The remainder of this chapter describes how generational accounting evaluates generational equity and fiscal sustainability and reports conclusions from its application to United States fiscal policy.

EVALUATING GENERATIONAL EQUITY AND FISCAL SUSTAINABILITY

Under "reference" projections, we calculate that the present value of the government's bills amounts to $31.5 trillion ($29.4 trillion in purchases plus $2.1 trillion in outstanding debt).[4] Of this, living generations (those born in 1995 or earlier) are scheduled to pay $22.1 trillion in net taxes over their remaining lifetimes. The requirement of long-term budget balance therefore implies that future generations (those born after 1995) must pay net taxes amounting to $9.4 trillion.[5] It is this latter figure rather than the outstanding government debt that more meaningfully reflects the fiscal burden imposed on future generations as a whole.

To evaluate the net tax treatment of different generations, we calculate generation-specific lifetime net tax rates.[6] For a given generation, this rate is its lifetime net tax burden—the discounted value as of its year of birth of net taxes during the entire lifetime—viewed as a percentage of its discounted lifetime labor earnings. For a newborn generation, the lifetime net tax rate is calculated by dividing the present value of its prospective lifetime net tax payments under reference projections by the present value of its projected lifetime labor earnings. The lifetime net tax rate for an older living generation is calculated in the same manner except that its past net tax payments must be included.

If fiscal policy was maintained indefinitely, the lifetime net tax rate of each new generation would equal that of the current 1995 newborn generations.[7] Doing so, however, will not necessarily generate the $9.4 trillion in present value from future generations as required to satisfy the long-term budget constraint. We calculate the *average* lifetime net tax rate that all future generations would have to pay in order to balance the long-term budget if current newborn and older generations paid no more in net taxes than scheduled under reference projections and if government purchases remained as projected. To find the required rate on future generations, we distribute the residual aggregate burden (the $9.4 trillion) equally among all future generations (except for an adjustment for labor productivity growth). This yields their generation-specific per capita lifetime net tax burdens. Dividing these burdens by the present values (at birth) of their per capita projected labor earnings yields the uniform lifetime net tax rate that future generations will have to bear to achieve long-term budget balance.[8]

One can assess the sustainability of current policy (the projected purchases and scheduled net taxes for all living generations) by comparing the lifetime net tax rate that future generations must pay to achieve long-term budget balance with that facing current newborns under reference policy. That policy is deemed unsustainable if the rate facing future generations is different than that facing current newborns. If future generations' rate is larger, taxing successive new generations at the same rate as current newborns won't suffice to pay for the government's bills. If the opposite is true, then maintaining the same rate for future generations as that for current newborns will ultimately result in the government owning the entire wealth of the nation. In essence, a policy that is not generationally balanced is also unsustainable.

U.S. GENERATIONAL ACCOUNTS

Figure 4.1 presents lifetime net tax rates of generations born in this century as well as future generations under "reference" projections.[9] Generations born at the turn of this century paid just under 23.9 percent of their lifetime labor income in net taxes. Under reference policy, the rate is higher for later birth cohorts; at 33.4 percent, it is highest for those born in 1950 but declines for generations born later. Those born in 1995, for example, face a lifetime net tax rate of 28.6 percent under reference policy. The rapid expansion of Social Security and health care programs after the 1960s explains the lower lifetime net tax rates faced by most generations born during the postwar period. Despite the higher rates facing generations born during the latter half of the twentieth century, future generations (those born in 1996 and later) face a dramatically higher average lifetime net tax rate—one equal to 49.2 percent![10]

The wide divergence between the rate facing 1995 newborns under reference policy and the average rate facing future generations indicates generational inequity and imbalance in reference policy. It implies that living generations are not picking up their fair share of the tab for the government's projected purchases or that, given the amounts living generations are contributing in net taxes, current purchase policy is extravagant and will impose inequitable net tax burdens on future generations. It also indicates that fiscal policy is unsustainable and will have to be changed. Either taxes must be increased, transfers reduced, or government purchases cut in order to restore solvency to the government's intertemporal budget.

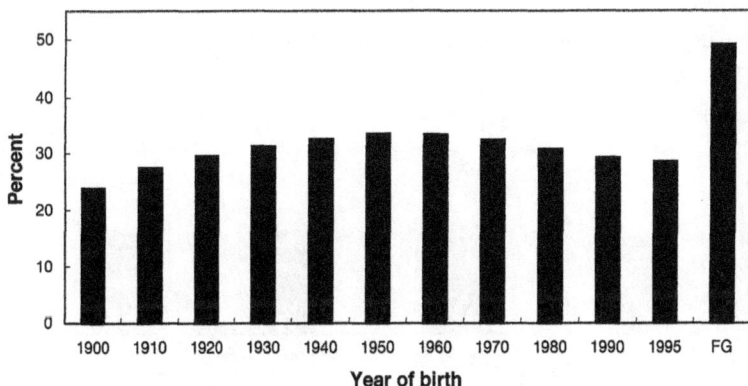

FIGURE 4.1
Lifetime Net Tax Rates for Selected Generations Under Reference Fiscal Policy, 1900–1995
Note: FG stands for "future generations."
Source: Gokhale, Page, and Sturrock 1998, table 3.

ALTERNATIVE PROJECTIONS

Although it represents the best guess of future outcomes, the reference policy is just one particular projection of future taxes, transfers, and government purchases, all of which are uncertain. To study the implications of alternative projections, we estimate lifetime net tax rates for newborn and future generations under the assumption that government purchases will stay constant in real terms after the year 2000 (see figure 4.2).[11] Under this alternative, the rate on current newborns is the same as under reference policy because their projected taxes and transfers are unchanged. However, because projected purchases are reduced, future generations face a lower fiscal burden—44.6 percent instead of 49.2 percent under reference projections.

Next, we recalculate lifetime net tax rates under the assumption that health care outlays (Medicare plus Medicaid) will grow only 2 percent faster than GDP through 2003, and that per capita health care outlays will grow at the same rate as labor productivity thereafter.[12] Figure 4.2 shows that the net tax rate of 1995 newborn generations is higher (30.9 percent) under these projections because of lower future transfers from Medicare and Medicaid.[13] The higher net tax payments by living generations lowers the net tax rate facing future generations from 49.2 percent under reference projections to 38.1 percent.

Finally, figure 4.2 shows that assuming both constant real purchases after the

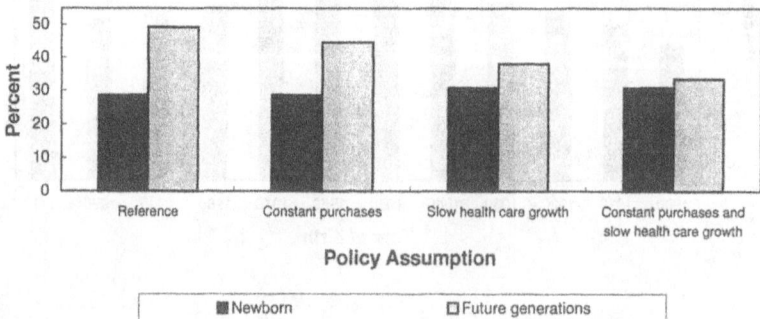

Policy Assumption

FIGURE 4.2

Lifetime Net Tax Rates Under Alternative Assumptions: Newborn Versus Future Generations

Source: Gokhale, Page, and Sturrock 1998, table 7.

year 2000 and slower health care outlay growth does not reduce the rate on future generations (33.5 percent) below that of 1995 newborns (30.9 percent). Hence, the conclusion that fiscal policy is inequitable and unsustainable is maintained despite incorporating very optimistic projections of future budgetary outcomes.

EVALUATING POLICY CHANGES FOR GENERATIONAL EQUITY

Besides comparing the lifetime net tax rates facing future generations with that of current newborns, generational accounting also calculates the present value changes in net taxes of generations, both living and future, resulting from changes in fiscal policies. Suppose Social Security benefits are permanently increased by 20 percent and payroll taxes are hiked as required to finance the higher benefits (also known as pay-as-you-go financing). Figure 4.3 shows the extent to which this policy helps current older, and harms current younger and future generations.[14] Because living generations as a whole bear a smaller net tax burden as a result of this policy, future generations' net tax burden is larger: The net tax burdens of future generations increase by $4,300 per capita for males and $1,600 per capita for females.[15]

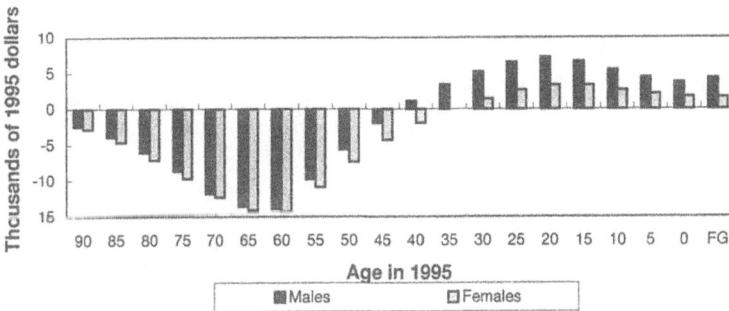

FIGURE 4.3
Changes in Generational Accounts: A 20 Percent Pay-as-You-Go Increase in Social Security Benefits

Note: FG stands for "future generations."
Source: Authors' calculations.

ACHIEVING GENERATIONAL BALANCE IN THE UNITED STATES

This section addresses the question: What additional measures are required to achieve generational balance? Figure 4.4 provides some answers. It shows alternative policies beginning either in 1998 or 2003 which would equalize the lifetime net tax rates facing newborns and future generations.

Each of the alternatives considered involves a permanent percentage change in the respective instrument: a tax hike, a transfer cut, or a purchases reduction. For example, figure 4.4 shows that beginning in 1998, income taxes would have to be increased permanently by 20.4 percent to achieve generational balance. If payroll taxes were to be used, the required increase would be 31.0 percent. The higher rate reflects the fact that the payroll tax base is smaller than the income tax base. Raising other taxes (excise, sales, and property taxes) would involve a 39.7 percent tax hike. Alternatively, all taxes together would have to be increased immediately and permanently by 8.9 percent.

Achieving a generationally balanced policy via transfer cuts would require permanently cutting either Social Security benefits by 47.5 percent or health care (Medicare and Medicaid) benefits by 36.8 percent beginning in 1998. The lower required percentage cut for health care spending compared to Social Security benefits reflects the fact that the former is projected to grow more rapidly because of rapid growth in the cost of medical care per capita. As a

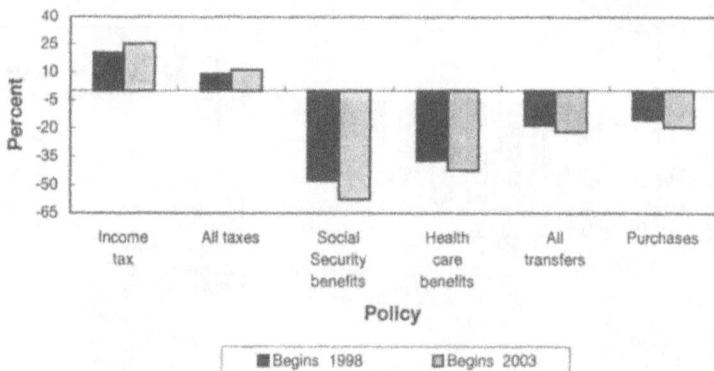

FIGURE 4.4
Policies for Achieving Generational Balance
Source: Gokhale, Page, and Sturrock 1998, table 11.

result, living generations receive more, in present value, from health care transfers than from Social Security benefits and a given percentage reduction
increases the net taxes of all living generations much more than in the case of
health care compared to Social Security. In general, cutting transfers involves
larger percentage cuts than does increasing taxes.

Balance could also be achieved by cutting government purchases by 15.4 percent every year beginning in 1998. All of these policies are sustainable, that is,
once undertaken, no additional adjustments are needed to satisfy the government's intertemporal budget constraint.[16] Figure 4.4 also shows that waiting
for a few years before implementing policies for achieving generational balance
will be costly. It shows that the required tax hikes, transfer cuts, or purchase
reduction would have to be larger if we wait for five years before implementing
them.[17]

SHORTCOMINGS OF GENERATIONAL ACCOUNTING

Generational accounting does not take into account the feedback effects of policy changes that emerge as people adjust their behavior in response. Instead, it
combines the government's forecasts of receipts and payments with other
information in a simple and straightforward way. This simplicity is both a
strength and a weakness. We would prefer policymakers to consider methods
that incorporate these effects more fully when formulating policy. But, as a
practical matter, generational accounting may be the best long-term fiscal planning tool that policymakers would actually use.

Because generational accounting does not consider feedbacks, it only provides an approximation of the true generational welfare effects (incidence) of
changes in fiscal policy.[18] The quality of this approximation depends on the
extent to which the actual incidence of fiscal changes is distributed across generations in accordance with generational accounting procedures for allocating
aggregate changes in taxes and transfers to specific generations. However, a
recent study suggests that the quality of these approximations is likely to be
quite good in the case of a large economy like the United States.

Perhaps the most important concern about generational accounting is the
choice of the proper discount rate to use in an uncertain world featuring multiple assets and incomplete markets. The key question is how to properly discount future tax payments and transfer receipts in light of the riskiness of these
payments and receipts. This is an important area for future research on generational accounting.

Notwithstanding all the attention they receive, fiscal deficits are largely irrelevant when it comes to evaluating fiscal policy for generational equity and sustainability or estimating the fiscal burdens being foisted on young and future generations. In contrast to deficit accounting, generational accounting is a direct method for assessing the sustainability of fiscal policy and for determining which generations will pay more and which less for the government's bills. The application of generational accounting to the United States indicates that U.S. fiscal policy is inequitable and unsustainable and that recent budget initiatives fall far short of what is needed to prevent placing enormous fiscal burdens on today's and tomorrow's children.

NOTES

1. In this chapter the word "government" encompasses federal, state, and local governments. "Purchases" refers to spending on national defense, legislative, judicial, and administrative services, infrastructure for transportation and trade, public parks, education, etc. The public provision of these goods is justified on grounds that private firms would fail to provide them in sufficient quantity. This is likely to occur when the provision entails significant "externalities." Firms, then, are unable to charge a price [for a good] to all who benefit from it. For example, the existence of public parks improves the environment and benefits even those who never visit them.

2. We recognize that government purchases also confer benefits on current and future generations. However, it is difficult if not impossible to allocate these by age and sex because of their "public" nature (see endnote 1). We make the operational assumption that these benefits are equally distributed across living and future generations.

3. See Auerbach, Gokhale, and Kotlikoff (1991), and Kotlikoff (1992). Generational accounts have also been constructed for 24 countries including the United States, Germany, Italy, Norway, Sweden, Canada, New Zealand, Australia, Japan, Portugal, Argentina, and Thailand.

4. All dollar numbers reported in this paper are in constant 1995 dollars. Strictly speaking, the budget projections evaluated here do not incorporate the policy changes enacted in the Balanced Budget and Taxpayer Relief Acts of 1997 because the long-term budget projections under the new policies were not available at the time of making the calculations. The "reference" projections used here are generic in the sense that they cut base spending, health care, and other (non–Social Security) programs in about the same proportions as under those acts. Hence, the

results reported here should roughly correspond to those under the reconciliation package. The long-range projections are provided by the Congressional Budget Office. See Gokhale, Page, and Sturrock (1998) for more details.

5. At the time of making the calculations, 1995 was the latest year for which a full set of actual budgetary and other data necessary was available. Hence, we use 1995 as the base year: Living generations are defined as those born in 1995 or earlier.

6. A generation includes all individuals of a given age and sex.

7. This assumes that all fiscal programs and labor income grow at the same rate as labor productivity.

8. The equal-except-for-growth-adjustment distribution of the aggregate residual burden implies that lifetime net tax burdens grow at the same rate as the present values of lifetime labor incomes.

9. See endnote 7. The lifetime net tax rates reported are population-weighted averages across male and female generations.

10. Again, this figure is high, in part, because it is based on a counterfactual experiment in which currently living generations are assumed to pay, over the remainder of their lives, only the net taxes implied by reference policy. Please note that this is a net, not a gross tax rate. Since future generations would receive positive transfer payments, their gross tax rate would exceed 49.2 percent.

11. Under reference projections discretionary spending *declines* through 2007 and grows thereafter at the same rate as population plus labor productivity growth. The Balanced Budget Act of 1997 limits discretionary spending only through 2002. However, these limits may be extended in the future.

12. This represents slower growth than under reference projections. Under those projections Medicare outlays grow 2.4 percentage points faster, on average, than labor productivity through the year 2020. Thereafter they are assumed to grow at the same rate as labor productivity.

13. Indeed, the lifetime net tax rates of all living generations are higher.

14. This statement assumes that the return to capital exceeds the growth rate of the economy.

15. We assume that future males and females pay net taxes in the same proportion as newborn males and females.

16. These policy experiments are based on reference projections and a 6 percent real discount rate. All of the policies equalize the lifetime net tax rates of newborn and future generations, but the equalized rate is different for different policies. For example the policy of raising income taxes yields an equalized lifetime net tax rate of 31.9 percent; that of raising payroll taxes yields a rate of 32.4 percent; hiking other taxes produces 33.3 percent; and increasing all taxes equalizes the rates at 32.3 percent. Cutting Social Security benefits yields an equalized rate of 30.1 percent whereas

reducing health care benefits produces an equalized rate of 31.3 percent. Cutting purchases by 15.4 percent does not affect the rate on newborns; it reduces future generations' rate down to 29.6 percent, to equal that on newborns.

17. Waiting until 2003 before implementing the policies equalizes the lifetime net tax rates of newborn and future generations at higher rates than those achieved by beginning in 1998. For example, raising income taxes permanently by 25.3 in 2003 produces an equalized lifetime net tax rate of 32.6 percent.

18. For a critique of generational accounting and a reply, see Haveman (1994), and Auerbach, Gokhale, and Kotlikoff (1994).

REFERENCES

Auerbach, Alan J., Jagadeesh Gokhale, and Laurence J. Kotlikoff. 1991. "Generational Accounts: A Meaningful Alternative to Deficit Accounting," Pp. 55–110 in *Tax Policy and the Economy*, edited by David F. Bradford. Cambridge, Mass.: MIT Press.

Auerbach, Alan J., Jagadeesh Gokhale, and Laurence J. Kotlikoff. 1994. "Generational Accounting: A Meaningful Way to Evaluate Fiscal Policy." *Journal of Economic Perspectives* 8 (1): 73–94.

Gokhale, Jagadeesh, Benjamin R. Page, and John R. Sturrock. 1998. "Generational Accounts for the United States: An Update." In *Generational Accounting Around the World*. National Bureau of Economic Research, forthcoming.

Haveman, Robert. 1994. "Should Generational Accounts Replace Public Budgets and Deficits?" *Journal of Economic Perspectives* 8 (1): 95–111.

Kotlikoff, Laurence J. 1992. *Generational Accounting*. New York: The Free Press.

CHAPTER FIVE

Care for the Elderly: What About Our Children?

Richard D. Lamm

Richard Lamm is director at the Center for Public Policy and Contemporary Issues at the University of Denver. He is a former three-term governor of Colorado. Among his books are *Megatraumas: America in the Year 2000, The Brave New World of Health Care,* and *The Uncompetitive Society.*

Lamm points to the rapid pace at which the nation is aging. He argues that the miracles of modern medicine are outpacing our ability to pay for them. When these trends are combined with evidence of a long-term trend toward slower economic growth, the result is a nation that is consuming more than it is producing. His concern is that the spending frenzy Americans are engaged in will leave future generations with an unacceptably heavy burden. Much of the article outlines his proposals for dealing with these problems, solutions that call for health care rationing and other strategies to increase the efficiency of health care spending. He suggests that the greatest causes and cures for premature mortality lie not within the institution of health care, but within the individual. For this reason he emphasizes the importance of greater self-reliance and self-control at both the individual and the institutional level.

Let me start off with a parable: An admiral in the U.S. Navy was on the high seas and all of a sudden a little blip shows up on the radar screen. The admiral tells the ensign, "Tell that ship to change its course 15 degrees." The word came back on the radio, "You change *your* course 15 degrees." The admiral said, "Tell that ship that we're the U.S. Navy and to change its course 15 degrees." The word came back on the radio, "You change *your* course 15 degrees." The admiral himself got on the radio and said, "I am an admiral in the U.S. Navy—change your course 15 degrees." The word came back, "You change *your* course 15 degrees— I am a lighthouse."

I call this a parable because it reflects my views that we are sailing into a whole new and much more volatile world of public policy. Specifically I believe we are heading for shoals. I believe we can navigate around them; I believe we can change course—but unless we do so in some important areas we shall crash into the future.

Let me describe for you the new world of public policy into which I believe we are sailing. There have been four major revolutions in the last twenty years which will permanently change public policy in the United States.

1. We have gone from a continental economy to an international economy. New York used to compete with New Jersey, Pennsylvania, and Illinois. Today it is competing with Japan, Korea, Singapore, and West Germany. We have not fully explored or fully understood the implications of living in an international economy.

2. Public policy makers no longer have a rapidly growing pie to solve all our problems. . . . We no longer have the wherewithal to be indiscriminately generous. We must understand, as one economist once told me, that "capital is the stored flexibility we have to build our children a better future." How we spend that limited capital will dictate what kind of lives we will leave our children.

3. America is aging—fast. . . . Between 1986 and 2040 the population aged 65 to 74 will grow by about 85 percent, the population aged 80 and over will grow by about 300 to 400 percent, and the population aged 90 and over will grow by an astounding 500 to 700 percent. We must better assess and more candidly discuss the implications of this demographic earthquake.

4. There is a revolution of medical technology. We now have people working on transplants or artificial organs (or both) for all the organs of your body. There has been an explosion of new treatments, techniques, and procedures we can give to people. We can now keep a corpse alive. The miracles

of modern medicine are clearly outpacing the public ability to pay for them. Infinite medical needs, especially for the elderly, have run into finite resources.

All of these together create a new world of public policy. America is consuming more than it is producing, and spending far more than we earn. Our politicians spend far more than the income generated by taxes, and we as a society want more than we can afford. In all areas of American activity, but especially in the health care field, infinite demands have run smack into finite resources.

Thus we must adjust ourselves to this new world of public policy. This requires a change in our thinking and our public policy. . . .

The public policy kaleidoscope is forever turning, presenting us with a new pattern. We must be sensitive to those changed circumstances. If I could leave anything carved over the capitol in Denver, it would be "Beware of solutions which were appropriate to the past but are disastrous to the future." There is an old hymn out of my youth which goes:

New occasions, teach new duties
Time makes ancient good, uncouth

We must adjust our public policy to meet the new realities we are faced with. We must do this for our children's sake. Dietrich Bonhoeffer said during his fight with Hitler: "The ultimate test for a moral person is how the coming generation will live." I would like to use that ethical theme, expand upon it, and give you a list of new public policy considerations I think are important to the new world of public policy into which I see us sailing.

This brings us to Copernicus. Copernicus made his contribution to history by asking the right question. He asked, "Perhaps, instead of the sun going around the earth, does the earth go around the sun?" In that spirit I ask:

1. *Instead of society adjusting itself to rising health care costs, doesn't health care have to adjust itself to society's limited resources?* Just as man can't live by bread alone, a society can't live by health care alone. But that's exactly where we almost seem to be going in the United States. We have other desperately important functions in which we have to invest to leave the kind of world we want to leave for our children and grandchildren. We must invest in education, infrastructure, and retooling America. Where are we going to get the jobs for our kids? Yet our whole system is tilting toward health care and toward the military.

When I entered high school in 1950, health care was 45.9 percent of what our society spent on education. This last year it was over 100 percent. In 1950, we spent $1 billion a month on health care—in 1986, it's well over $1 billion a day. We have many important things to do with our limited societal resources. Health care is one of them, no question. But it isn't the only one. Yet it is the one that we seem to give such precedence to, so much so that it almost dominates all of the others. One of the governors calls health care the "Pac-Man of his budget." If you want to build up a great university, you want to build up your infrastructure; you want to help retool your industries—here comes Pac-Man, coming through your budget, eating up your flexibility. . . .

We spend more than a billion dollars a day for health care, but our bridges are falling down, our teachers are underpaid, our industrial plants are rusty. This simply can't continue. . . . We have money to give smokers heart transplants, but no money to retool our steel mills. . . . We are great at treating sick people, but we are not very great at treating a sick economy. We are not succeeding in international trade. . . . Where are the industries the United States is succeeding in? They are very few and far between.

I believe one of the challenges of America's future is, How do we wisely invest our scarce resources? To do this, we must be realistic, we must ask heretical questions, we must question sacred cows. We can't simply stand back and let one segment of our economy, no matter which one it is, dominate all the others. . . .

Dr. Phil Caper, who with Dr. Jack Wennberg is doing some very creative thinking in the health care area, puts it this way: "Despite the doubling of resources devoted to medical care over the past two decades, we are hardpressed to point to specific improvements in the health status of Americans sufficient to justify such a massive transfer of wealth from other sectors of the economy."

I couldn't agree more. . . . Our health care system has become part solution, part problem. We wouldn't want to be without it, but it has become a heavy burden. It is definitely interfering with the public's ability to invest in our public goods, and with private industry's ability to retool itself. Health care insurance now costs U.S. corporations approximately $125 billion per year, which is 50 percent of their pretax profits. That's money that is desperately needed elsewhere. The 10 percent of the price of an American automobile that represents health care (and that is rising at two and a half times the rate of inflation) is rapidly making our goods more uncompetitive on the international marketplace.

In short, if we want an efficient and successful society, we must examine closely every institution in America, but especially health care. It's the Willie Sutton theory of bank robbery. When asked why he robbed banks, Willie replied: "That's where the money is." That's true today about health care.

2. *Who buys more health for society: doctors, or sewage disposal plant workers, or public health workers?* . . . There is little correlation between how much money is spent on doctors and hospitals and how healthy the society is.

We are too easily seduced into thinking that health care means doctors and hospitals, when actually the great advances in health care have been made in sanitation, pasteurization, chlorination, antibiotics, and refrigeration. Screened windows to keep out mosquitos were an incredible forward advance of health. Public health officials have saved more lives than hospitals have.

If we look at how we can improve the health of the average American, we find a similar figure. The greatest causes of premature mortality, not of total mortality, are very simple: smoking, drinking too much, eating the wrong things, and not wearing your seat belt. If you really want to know how you get America healthy, you start attacking those things. . . .

It becomes clear that there are many paths to health, and certainly doctors and hospitals are one of them. I would rather have a dollar-a-pack tax on cigarettes than I would another $100 billion put into the health care area. Smoking kills the equivalent number of people as a 747 crash every day in America. Three hundred sixty thousand people a year die from cigarettes. So when you look at the kind of alternatives available—you give me some of those empty hospital beds to lock up drunk drivers and I'll save more lives than the hospitals would. A mandatory seat belt law would probably save more lives than all the CAT scans in America.

America has to look at what we are getting for our money. The United States spends $2,000 per capita on health care, Great Britain spends $500 per capita on health care, Singapore spends $200 per capita on health care, and yet we all have the same mortality and morbidity rates. How can anyone justify this discrepancy? You have asked for cost-conscious politicians. Well, how can the political system allow the recent dramatic increases in health costs, when other nations provide full medical care to all their people and at a fraction of the per capita cost as we do in the United States, and they still have comparable health statistics? You're going to say that doesn't include cataract operations and hip replacements, and you're right. But I'll tell you again, mortality and morbidity rates are an immensely important yardstick—at least one of the yardsticks—I think it's very important. There is an inverse correlation in our industrialized world between how many doctors you have and how healthy your society is. West Germany has the largest number of doctors per capita; they've got the worst health statistics. Japan has the least number of doctors per capita; they're the healthiest. . . .

We are not as healthy as some countries that spend only one-eighth what we spend. Health care is a black hole of public policy into which you can pour infinite assets and often get only marginal returns. We have given health providers the highest social status in our society, we have made medicine the highest-paid profession in America, we have made running a hospital one of the most profitable sectors of the economy, we have given that system 11 cents out of every dollar spent in America; and yet if you're an American male you're only fifteenth in world life expectancy and if you're a female you're eighth in world life expectancy.

I am reminded of Jack Kent Cook, owner of the Washington Redskins. When asked why he fired his football coach George Allen [he said]: "I gave him an unlimited budget and he exceeded it." That's how I feel about health care.

3. *Don't we inevitably have to ration medicine?* We are not wealthy enough to base our health care system on the assumptions that we can give everything our genius has invented to all of the people out there. I believe clearly that the United States must ration medicine. It is clear to me that we already ration medicine. We deny it, and, as Linus in Peanuts says, "There's no issue too big you can't run away from it," but clearly we already live in a society that rations medicine. . . .

No society, anywhere in the world, has figured out how not to ration health care. We must be open about the values and stakes involved. . . . Rudolf Klein, a very thoughtful observer from England, says, "Rationing is inherent under any health care system." A portion of the Oregon Health Decisions says:

> We cannot live under the idea that we can give everybody all the health care that they need. Rationing of health care is inevitable because society cannot or will not pay for all of the services modern medicine can provide. People in this state must search their hearts and their pocketbooks and decide what level of health care can be guaranteed to the poor, the unemployed, the elderly, and others who depend on publicly funded health services.

They point out that we already ration medicine—chronologically, economically, geographically, politically, scientifically, by disease, etc. Thirty-three million Americans lacked hospital insurance in 1982, and perhaps another 16 million had inadequate coverage.

In short, rationing is not a future possibility—it is a present reality. . . . If we ask ourselves, How do we avoid rationing, I believe that we do our society an injustice. If we ask, How do we allocate finite resources to meet infinite demand, and do it compassionately and justly, then I believe that we can increase rather than decrease medical care in our most basic areas. Rationing can be described in the same words that Mark Twain said about Wagner's music . . . : "It's not as bad as it sounds."

4. How do we take limited dollars and buy the most health? Humana's budget for the artificial heart is roughly equivalent to what society spent on eradicating smallpox. Consider the difference between those two. The fact is we have a system that seems to give dramatic high-technology medicine the health care dollar, when a third of the kids in America have never seen a dentist, and 20 percent of the kids in America don't have their polio shots. . . .

We must thoughtfully weigh the way we spend our health care dollars. We must develop a "sense of limits" in spending health care dollars, an objective sense that we are making an intelligent allocation of limited dollars.

Lester Thurow talks about an exercise for doctors in which every time they order an expensive procedure, they would have to pick an American worker to be sentenced to a period of slavery long enough to pay the medical bill for that procedure. . . . Celebrity doctors performing dramatic, highly publicized procedures may gain national recognition but they do not add to the total national well-being. It may make a doctor or a hospital famous but it is not a cost-effective expenditure of public funds. The "opportunity costs" of these resources are obviously much, much higher elsewhere. . . . For every person it saves, it condemns two or three more who today die because we are not allocating our dollars where they will buy the most health for America. We are, unfortunately, faced with a series of Hobson's choices. Harvey Cox, the theologian, says, "Not to decide is to decide." So in fact by avoiding these issues, we are deciding. Deciding often in favor of the most inefficient and wasteful ways to spend our dollars. By not challenging our sacred cows, we are creating a tougher and more chaotic world for our children.

5. Is it an economic asset to have two-thirds of the world's lawyers and the highest ratio of doctors and hospitals in America? It is not an economic asset for America to have two-thirds of all the lawyers practicing in America; it is an economic cancer. Forty percent of the Rhodes scholars in this country go to law school. Japan trains a thousand engineers for every hundred lawyers. We train a thousand lawyers for every hundred engineers. Now which society in a technologically based, information-based society is going to win? The one that trains lawyers? The same thing applies in the physician field. It is estimated that there may be as many as 145,000 more physicians than needed by the year 2000. Duke points out that every excess doctor, or every doctor in practice, increases the nation's health care costs by $300,000 annually. Thus, in an average career spanning forty years, a single physician would create health care costs of some $12 million. You've got to limit the number of people going into those two fields. . . .

There are two hundred thousand excess hospital beds in the United States. That's equivalent to at least, let's say, a thousand hospitals out there that we don't need, that we've overbuilt. Then, a recent study found that 25 percent of all hospital days are inappropriate because the services rendered do not require hospitalization—services like oral medication. A hospital should be an institution of last resort. . . .

I really believe there's no way we are going to come to grips with this problem until we also look at some of these areas that aren't going to go away. One of the toughest of those is what Victor Fuchs calls "flat-of-the-curve medicine"—those medical procedures that are the highest cost and achieve little or no improvement in health status. He says they must be reduced or eliminated. We must demand of professional societies and licensing authorities that they establish some norms and standards for diagnostic and therapeutic practice that encompass both costs and medicine. We're going to have to come up with some sort of concept of cost-effective medicine.

It seems to me the empirical evidence is overwhelming that there are massive inefficiencies in our health care system.

- Medical expenditures for the elderly in Miami, Florida, are twice as high as for the elderly in Rochester, New York.
- There is strong evidence that one-third or more of coronary bypass operations are medically unnecessary.
- Hospital use is 60 percent higher in the Midwest than in the West.
- CAT scans are utilized seven times more often in certain parts of the country than in others.
- In Detroit in 1981, 10 percent of women delivered by caesarean section; in Washington, D.C., in the same year it was 24 percent.
- Rates of knee replacements among the elderly, when age adjusted, vary sixfold in different parts of the country.

Some experts postulate that anywhere from 30 to 50 percent of the nation's health bill consists of expenditures that produce little or no demonstrable health benefit. In a country that is losing the economic race to the Pacific Rim, that is both a tragedy and a disgrace.

6. Is death the enemy of the health care system, or is pain, suffering, degradation? In the words of William Shakespeare, do we not all "owe God a death"? There are certain new realities which we have not fully incorporated into either our public policy response or our thinking.

First is the explosion of the elderly. We all intellectually know the numbers but we haven't begun to absorb this new public policy reality. The total U.S. population tripled between 1900 and 1980—but the aged population grew eight times. The population over 85 grew twenty-one times. This is not change, it is a demographic revolution.

Second, approximately 2 million people die each year in the United States, and with today's medical miracles, rapid fatal disease is shrinking as a cause of death. Heart disease takes 34 percent of us, malignancies take 22 percent, whereas sudden deaths (accidents, homicides, suicides) take only 13 percent. Thus, chronic conditions cause 87 percent of all deaths. Treating these chronic diseases causes the overwhelming majority of health care costs in the United States. In my opinion this treatment is taking massive amounts of resources desperately needed elsewhere, and they should be spent on the living, not on the dead.

Third is the reality of our technologies. We can now keep a corpse alive. The new standard of care includes a whole range of Faustian technologies: resuscitation, intravenous feeding, stimulants, oxygen tanks, respirators, heart pumps, drainage tubes, etc. These technologies have made us scientific giants but, alas, we are still moral pygmies. We are technically smart enough to obscure the line between life and death, but not morally intelligent enough to draw the line. We have a hard time even deciding "What is death?" and "When does it occur?" It is a daily practice in hospitals to bring terminally ill patients back to life—just so they can die a second time—at great cost to the taxpayer. . . .

Tragically, many people who experience death in a family come out of the experience thinking medical treatment is the enemy. . . .

I think it is desperately important to discuss much more candidly and openly death and dying. We treat death as if it were optional. People talk about the right to die, as if we have the right to refuse to die. Once we stop treating death as an enemy and recognizing an inevitability, we can save massive resources. . . .

We cannot afford a system in which, on our way out the door, we take $100,000 to $200,000 of our children's limited resources to give us a couple of extra days of pain-wracked existence. Such a practice is more than bad policy, it is intergenerational larceny. It is wasting resources our children desperately need elsewhere to compensate for the kind of world we leave for them.

If you can make people better, terrific. But in American medicine, it often seems to be against the law to die in peace. Most elderly don't fear death as much as they do the pain and suffering and degradation and loss of autonomy that our Faustian technologies have brought to them. Alas, truth be told, all our biological clocks must strike midnight. We must learn again what the early churchmen called "the grace of dying well."

7. *Why should we give taxpayer money to people merely for reaching the age of 65?* Is it good public policy to have the highest life expectancy at age 80 in the whole world, while we are twentieth in infant mortality? This is another sensitive subject, and that's the way this whole system is slanted toward our benefit. When my wife and I bought our first house, our house payments were $49 PITI. A recent congressional study said less than 50 percent of the kids under 30 are going to be able to buy their own homes. One of the great issues of the future, I believe, is going to be intergenerational equity. Our kids will wake up and find out how badly we've cheated them.

I argue that America doesn't need any more age-based programs. Our programs should be based on need rather than age. Which leads me into the thought of Medicare, the ultimate sacred cow. But when Medicare was passed in 1965, the elderly were disproportionately poor. There was every good reason in Congress to vote for Medicare then. But the elderly are no longer disproportionately poor. In 1970, 23 percent of the elderly were poor and 12 percent of the kids were poor. Today, 12 percent of the elderly are poor and 23 percent of the kids are poor. You no longer have those same reasons. And yet we give 254,000 millionaires Medicare and we are closing well-baby clinics. We have socialized the cost of health care and given it to all the elderly while ignoring needy kids.

But income-adjusting Medicare will not be enough. There must be even tougher choices, and one of those I suggest is that we must make age a consideration in choices on the delivery of health care. . . .

The delivery of expansive medical miracles to the explosive growing number of elderly is creating an unsustainable economic and social burden. We are allocating our governmental benefits to those who lobby us the hardest and comprise the biggest voting bloc, but we are not making rational allocations. Our present policies, in the face of those realities, will prevent adequate health care for other generations, especially younger generations. It is already having a distorting effect and is bound to have an increasing distorting effect. . . .

I believe that we shall inevitably have to recognize age as a valid ethical consideration in the delivery of medical care. Is it not only fair, but desirable, to have a different level of care for a ten-year-old than for someone who is a hundred? Should not public policy recognize that some people have far more statistical years ahead of them than others?

The aged are not a static group. It is a status that we all pass through. We are all locked in as males or females, all locked in as black and white. Once a white male, always a white male. But we all age daily. In a marvelously egalitarian way, time takes its toll on all of us. The elderly are the same people—at a different stage of their lives—whom we worry about when we deny prenatal care to pregnant women.

I turn 65 in the fast-approaching year of 2000. I am not shooting a bullet in an intergenerational war, I'm not trying to take something from another generation, I realize that I'm arguing for new rules that I know I will have to live and die by. . . .

I care a great deal about myself, but I care also for my children. To repeat Bonhoeffer's observation: The ultimate question for a responsible person is, How will the coming generation live? Economists tell us that "capital is stored flexibility" that we have to build better lives for our children. I feel it is morally repugnant if I use $100,000 or $200,000 of our kids' limited resources as I'm on my way out the door unless it gives me substantially more of a quality life. I want to be valued as a senior citizen but I don't want to unnecessarily impose on my children and spend massive resources for a few more months of pain-wracked existence.

All cultures distinguish between death after a normal life span and a death which is premature. Death due to age is universally accepted and understood. Death before the end of a normal life span is universally distinguished and is usually invested with elements of tragedy, as it is in our society.

We shrug and call pneumonia an "old man's friend" and yet rage with Lear at the death of the young. We understand with an atavistic wisdom that we cannot live forever and that death in old age is natural and inevitable. At some point, to fight against death is not only useless, but unseemly.

I find it morally offensive even at the age of 51 to demand the same level of medical treatment as someone who has their whole life ahead of them.

Yet there is reason to pause. The ghost of the English system hovers over this debate, a system that seems cruel to our eyes because it rations certain scarce resources on the basis of age. I do not argue for such a system.

We have other ethical options between massive oppressive technology imposing a slow painful death on us, and arbitrary rationing using age as the criteria. I do not argue that age should be the only criteria, but that it should be one of the criteria.

I find it hard to believe that the health care system should consider a person's blood pressure, whether or not they smoke, how much alcohol they drink, what their cholesterol count is, but not consider their age. I believe age should not be *the* consideration, but one consideration along with many others in the allocation of medical resources. It should not dictate, but it should be considered. That doesn't give anyone a license to abandon me, or treat me as superfluous. Far from it. But I should not and will not object if age is laid on the scale in deciding medical treatment.

I consider it relevant in how I treat me—why shouldn't the health care system? I no longer climb trees or play rugby. I don't lower myself in my own self-esteem that I realize I have an older body. I treat it with more care. I recognize that my time is limited. I spend more time smelling the flowers.

If I consider it relevant, why shouldn't my doctor? . . .

In rationing scarce resources, age is an ethical and valid consideration.

8. Has not our health care system taken on a Stalinist view of public policy? We have in this country a media-driven humanitarianism. Whoever we can get on TV we try to save; we forget the rest. We treat individuals we can see, but we forget the statistics (who are no less individuals) we can't see.

I believe we must weigh the marvels of our health care technologies with other less visible but more cost-effective strategies. You see the Barney Clarks of the world, you see the Baby Fayes; everybody is pulling for them; it's marvelous technology. But we don't see the third of women in America who don't get prenatal care in their first trimester. Stalin said, in a horrible way, but he was right, "One man's death—that's a tragedy. A million men's death—that's a statistic." It really is true. We look at the individuals and we don't look at the statistics. The money we spent on the heart transplant for Mr. Schroeder could have been far more productively spent on the replacement of heart valves for two hundred patients or 40–50 percent of the poor, pregnant American women who receive no prenatal care in their first trimester. The quality of our mercy should rain on both identified and unidentified lives. We need non-emotional but compassionate yardsticks to measure how we spend limited resources, and we must be concerned with the total population—not merely those we see on TV.

9. Are we not worshiping graven images of high technology? In fact, in the area of artificial organs I would announce right now that until other needs are met, no taxpayer's money will be spent on artificial organs. Are we going to wait until a politically active group of chronic heart patients—many of them smokers— wheel a bunch of artificial heart recipients before a congressional committee . . . and plea for the taxpayers to save their lives. . . . Is that how we want to set our health care priorities?

I am not a medical Luddite. I admire the miracles of medicine. But I contrast cornea transplants, cataract operations, and hip replacements, which add tremendously to the quality of life for many elderly, to artificial hearts. That doesn't mean we shouldn't experiment with artificial hearts; we shouldn't eliminate any place where medical science wants to go. Medical science has made its greatest discoveries from the unexpected. But it is only when all of a sudden the taxpayers say, "OK, we're going to start to pay for this." In California they did something like this last year, they decided they were going to pay for transplants and then they knocked 200,000 low-income people off Medicare. That's not a good trade.

I believe if we zero-base budgeted the money we now spend in many areas, it clearly would not meet the test of effective medicine. If we zero-base budgeted the $2 billion we spend on end-stage renal disease, the $3 billion we spend on coronary artery bypasses, the $5 billion we spend on intensive care units, the $500 million a year it costs us for CAT scans, we would probably dramatically reduce the amount of money we spend in all these areas and transfer that money to other, more cost-effective areas. . . .

My criticism is not of high technology. There are certain high technologies that deserve to be worshiped, certainly deserve to be respected. A kidney stone crusher can eliminate the need for 80,000 surgical procedures. My criticism is the mindless way in which we invent certain high technologies and then are forced to use them, at the same time forgoing many more high-benefit procedures and technologies that could save so many more lives.

An artificial heart is a high-technology, low-benefit invention because its cost is very high and it only benefits a few people.

The ultimate goal to which this society should apply its high technology is the understanding of the mechanisms that are the underlying causes of disease. . . .

Just as we would never have cured polio by putting all our money in artificial lungs, so also we will not understand and cure heart disease if we put our money into artificial hearts. In a world of limited resources such choices become clear.

Shouldn't we all be raising some of the heretical questions? I am not going to give you any more heretical questions, but there are obviously many others. We should all think of some. Perhaps the question of fee-for-service medicine? Too many doctors believe fee-for-service medicine is a theology. It is not. We obviously can and are organizing medical care delivery through a wide variety of imaginative alternatives. HMO, PPO, and alternative delivery systems of all kinds must be encouraged if we are not to bankrupt America. . . .

Another notable absence on the tablets was any absolute stricture against two levels of health care. I believe the principal task of the health care system today is to provide health care to those who do not have access to it. But I believe it is counterproductive to paralyze ourselves over this issue when we already have a number of levels of health care in the United States. Does anyone think that those with resources don't get a better level of care than those on welfare? I believe it is important to get basic health care to those not covered, and not back away from that worthy goal if it contains an element (as it inevitably will) of two levels of health care.

To conclude: I am reminded of a story that came out of the Second World War when there was rationing of all kinds, when a man went into a restaurant and ordered a cup of coffee and then asked for more sugar. The waitress cast a cynical eye on him and said, "Stir what you have." I believe that is what America must do with its medical care expenses. We must stir between the over $1 billion a day that we already put into health care. There is not enough money, and we can buy an incredible amount of health if we in fact simply utilize our resources better.

Believe me—I understand I'm not even touching all of them. The great genius of democracy is that once you start asking the right questions, we can all get together to come up with the answers.

We can start off recognizing that our "health care system" has not too much to do with health, has little to do with caring, and clearly is not a system. That recognition of reality would be a giant step forward.

Then we must move simultaneously in many directions to reform our health care delivery mechanisms. We really do have to develop a concept of "appropriate" care or some sort of "cost-effective medicine." . . .

We can, in short, develop an ethic of restraint—not an ethic of "do more." Then, after we have done all those seemingly impossible things, we are going to have to discuss how we can fairly and compassionately "ration" medicine.

In summary, the issue is, What kind of world are we going to leave our kids and grandkids?

Health care is a very high social and public policy priority, but it isn't the only priority—it can't be a monopoly. We can, working together, find ways to deliver more health care to more people at an even lower cost.

CHAPTER SIX

Age-Based Rationing of Medical Care

Daniel Callahan

Daniel Callahan is a medical ethicist affiliated with the Hastings Center, a center for the study of biomedical ethics. He is a former drector of the Hastings Center and the author of several books on medical ethics, including *Setting Limits, What Kind of Life: The Limits of Medical Progress*, and *The Tyranny of Survival and Other Pathologies of Civilized Life*.

Callahan states that with unlimited medical need and limited medical resources, major changes must occur. He proposes the notion of a "natural life span" as a way of deciding upon an accepted cutoff point for expensive medical resources. He suggests that age is a good determinant because it is something that everyone must confront and because health care costs for the elderly are greater than those for any other group. This article is a response to critics of his book *Setting Limits*, in which he argues that in the future the scarcity of resources could make it necessary to resort to age limits on medical entitlements for the elderly.

Some six years ago, in the fall of 1987, I published *Setting Limits: Medical Goals in an Aging Society* (Callahan 1987). I argued that we would have to rethink once again the place of aging in the life cycle and that, in the future, scarcity of resources could force an age limit on medical entitlements for the elderly. That was not a popular thesis. I expected controversy and I got it, ranging from scholarly debates conducted with academic decorum to nasty public and media exchanges. Some six books of commentary and criticism, and an issue of a law review, were directly or indirectly inspired by *Setting Limits* (St. Louis University 1989; Homer and Holstein 1990; Binstock and Post 1991; Jecker 1991a; Barry and Bradley 1991; Winslow and Walters 1993; Hackler 1994).

The birth of *Setting Limits* came about because, beginning in the mid-1980s, I became aware of the striking demographic trends being reported, often accompanied by worries about their economic and social impact in the decades ahead (Preston 1984). I saw us moving—through no one's fault, and surely not the elderly—toward a potential tragic dilemma of the first order. Something would have to give somewhere. We could not possibly guarantee indefinitely to the growing number and proportion of the elderly all of the potentially limitless fruits of medical progress at public expense without seriously distorting sensible social priorities. Where and how could we set some sensible and fair limits?

WHAT I TRIED TO SAY

Setting Limits was the result of my effort to think through that problem. I argued that we should begin now, *before* the crisis is fully upon us, to change our expectations about elderly care in the future. I stressed in the book the *trend* in the development of expensive technologies, not their present costs, and the likely need for *future* change in entitlement policies, not at present. As a way into these likely changes, I said that we need to rethink two deeply imbedded ideas, widely if not universally held. The first is the cherished notion that we should try endlessly through medical progress to modernize old age, to turn it into a more or less permanent middle age. We should instead accept aging as a part of life, not just another medical obstacle to be overcome. The valuable and necessary campaign against ageism, highly individualistic in its premises, runs the risk of emptying age as a stage in life of meaningful content and, with the help of science, trying to turn it into a kind of repairable biological accident. The second idea I criticized was the view that there should be no limits to the claims of the elderly as a group to expensive life-extending medicine under *pub-*

lic entitlement programs, that only their individual needs should count, and count in an age-blind way.

After criticizing those two ideas, I offered a different picture of what a future health care policy for the elderly might look like, one designed to balance the new limits with some enriched entitlements. I was seeking a public policy that (1) would guarantee the elderly, along with everyone else, access to universal health care; (2) would help everyone to avoid an early, premature death; (3) would achieve a better balance of caring and curing to overcome the powerful bias toward the latter (whose effect is to undermine the former), and in particular to greatly strengthen long-term and home care support; and (4) would use age as a categorical standard to cut off life-extending technologies under the Medicare entitlement program—but using it as a standard *if and only if* the other reforms were put in place first.

I proposed the idea of a "natural life span" as a rough way of determining such a cutoff point. I would have been wise to have chosen a different word than "natural," since I meant by that concept a biographical not a biological standard, that is, a notion of when it might be said that most people will have lived an adequately full, if not necessarily totally full, life. I drew that notion from my own experience, and the traditions of most cultures, which perceive an important moral and social distinction between the sadness but fittingness of death in old age and the tragedy or outrage of an avoidable early, particularly childhood, death. I did not specify an exact age but suggested that the "late 70s or early 80s" would be an appropriate age range in which to look for it.

The great need is to find a type of limit that would dampen the potent trend to apply ever more expensive technologies to saving and extending the life of the elderly. That trend has seen a steady rise in the age of various surgical and other medical procedures, and in particular a rise often marked by successful results (Hosking et al. 1989; Latta and Keene 1989; Breidenbaugh, Sarsitis, and Milam 1990). But it is the success, I argued, that was creating the problem for us, not the failures, and I did not foresee us going backwards in care for the elderly, but radically slowing up and eventually plateauing the forward march of expensive medical progress.

I held, finally, that the needed changes should be effected, not by compulsion—the young imposing it by force on the unwilling old—but democratically, preceded by a decades-long period of changing our thinking, attitudes, and expectations about elderly health care. Those of us still reasonably young should be prepared in the future to impose an age limit on ourselves. As I noted in the preface to my book, in a passage often overlooked, "what I am looking for is not any quick change but the beginning of a long-term discussion, one that will lead people to change their thinking and, most important, their expectations, about old age and death" (Callahan 1987:10).

RESPONSES TO CRITICS

Let me take up, in turn, the major objections leveled at my argument. Since there were well over a hundred papers written about the book, and I was given the back of someone's hand in at least that many more, I will consolidate here the criticisms.

The use of age as a standard for limiting health care would be ageist and unjust. There are two discordant ways of thinking about the place and relevance of age from an individual and from a policy perspective. From an individual perspective, it is said, age as such should have no place in resource allocation. It is not a good predictor of health, mental or physical. True. Yet the difficulty here is obvious from a policy perspective: Age *is* a relevant and conspicuous variable in health care costs, and the elderly are more costly as a group than people of younger ages. The fact that many elderly people remain healthy most of their final years—and that there is a heterogeneous pattern of health care usage—does not change the fact that the average per capita costs of the elderly are significantly higher than for younger people. Public policy must take account of, and work with, those averages. They are what count in devising programs, in projecting future costs, and in estimating different health care needs. Age matters.

If age matters, how does it matter? It matters when, as we can now see, meeting the health care costs of the elderly as a group begins to threaten the possibility of meeting the needs of other age groups. In the nature of the case, moreover, there are no fixed boundaries to the amount of money that can be spent combating the effects of biological aging and attempting to forestall death in old age. It is an unlimited frontier. One could say exactly the same thing about trying to save the life of low birth weight infants. We can go from the present 450–500 grams and 24–25 weeks gestation to 400 to 300 grams, and 20–21 weeks gestation, and so on. There are no end of possibilities there as well, and thus some very good reasons to set limits to those efforts, using either weight or gestational age as a categorical standard (Callahan 1990). It is no more an anti-aging act than it is an anti-baby act to set limits (for instance, on neonatal care) in order to avoid pursuing unlimited, potentially ruinous possibilities.

Aging and death in old age are inevitable, and there should be no unlimited claim on public resources to combat them. But premature death, and bad schools, and blighted urban areas of great poverty, are not inevitable. The first health task of a society is that the young should have the chance to become old. That should always take priority over helping, at great cost, those who are already old [to become] still older. That is exactly what we can look forward to, as we throw more and more money into the fight to cure the chronic and degenerative diseases of aging, but not to care well for those who cannot be saved.

But if we set a limit on public entitlement for the elderly would this not be unfair and ageist? I believe we cannot achieve perfect equality in this world, much less in a health care system, without some harmful consequences. No country in the world, save the communist countries, has achieved any such goal, and the price they paid was rampant corruption and bribery; the wealthy and powerful still got better care. An age limit on entitlement benefits would of course perpetuate a two-tier system, with the rich able to buy health benefits not available to the poor, but that need not be the disaster many fear. The test should not be whether everyone receives exactly the same level of care. It should instead be whether the poorest and worst off receive decent health care. I believe the system I propose, guaranteeing universal care, a powerful effort to beat back premature death, a full range of health services through the late 70s or early 80s, a good range of social and caring services thereafter for one's entire life, and then (and only then) an age limit on expensive life-extending therapies, would be decent. If combined, moreover, with other kinds of limits in the health care systems for all groups, it would not be ageist even if it used age as a standard. It would use age as a standard simply because, as argued above, age does matter from a policy perspective.

It is unduly pessimistic to take seriously the projections that show a steadily increasing burden of elderly health care costs. "Callahan," one commentator said, "is overly alarmist about the relative burden of older persons" (Lawlor 1992:132). I have never known quite what to make of that charge. I have used the standard research available on demographic trends and projected health care costs. I have never been able to find *any* optimistic projections based on historical and current demographic and economic projections. Even the critic who said I was "alarmist" concluded that paragraph by criticizing the optimists for failing to note that "the arithmetic of compound growth is at work in the increase of health expenditures (prices, demographic change, and increasing intensity of care)" (Lawlor 1992:132). Since I wrote *Setting Limits*, moreover, the "pessimistic" data have continued to pour forth, even from those who are my critics on other grounds (Schneider and Guralnik 1990).

Since I have been unable to locate *any* optimistic data and reassuring projections, nor have any been cited in rebuttal, I can only observe that those who find me pessimistic rely on hopeful, but essentially still imaginary, scenarios about the future. One scenario is that in the future there will be a "compression of morbidity" and thus a decrease in the costs of elderly morbidity. That is a most invigorating hope, but the present evidence has moved in exactly the opposite direction, to greater not lesser morbidity, even if there is at least one recent report suggesting a slight amelioration of that trend (Manton, Corder, and Stallard 1993). The second scenario is that advances in medical research will find cures or inexpensive treatments for the degenerative diseases of aging (Schneider and Guralnik 1990). I hope that is true, but there is no evidence so far to support that hope as a likely outcome. The third scenario is that the elderly in the future will retire later and work longer, thus contributing more and much later to their health care costs. That could surely happen, and may by force happen, but it will as such not do a great deal about the disproportion of resources that could go to the elderly, although it surely might help. It is not likely to be helpful with the large number of people who live beyond 85, a rapidly growing group.

It is only because our health care system is wasteful, capitalistic, and paternalistic that we are even thinking of rationing and limits on care for the elderly. There is no doubt that ours is a wasteful, fragmented, and excessively costly system, and that we could spend more on the elderly if we reduced waste elsewhere (Estes 1988). The amount of money we spend in comparison with other developed countries, which get as good and often better outcomes for considerably less money, establishes that point well enough (though it does not establish that the money saved should go to the elderly as distinguished, say, from improving the schools). There are two points to consider here. The first is that, after more than twenty years of trying, we have not discovered in this country how, short of the universal health care and global budgeting we have been slow to embrace, to significantly control our costs; they just keep rising.

The second point is that, even if we can achieve those needed reforms, the problem will still not go away. The experience of other developed countries is already showing how an aging population can continue to push costs and demand up even in efficient, cost-effective, non-market health care systems (Hollander and Becker 1987; Loriaux 1990; Jouvenel 1989). Those countries, controlling the fees of health care workers, rationing technology, keeping a lid on drug and equipment costs, still have a growing age-related problem even so. Better health care systems can delay the problem, or ameliorate it; but they are not going to be a solution to it.

A popular proposal to reduce elderly costs is the promotion of "advance directives" to allow the elderly to voluntarily forgo expensive, useless, and undesired care at the end of life. Could that make a difference? The evidence is mixed on that point and still scanty. One study found that advance directives made no difference in the medical treatment or in the medical costs (Schneiderman et al. 1992), while another found evidence of dramatic savings (Chambers et al. 1994). My own guess is that advance directives will in the long run make some economic difference in relatively clear-cut cases of terminal illness for some classes of patients. There are two problems, however, which will make the greatest difference over time. One of them is the number of people who will execute advance directives, now still a significant minority. The other is the extent of expensive medical treatments that successfully avert the need to invoke advance directives, putting them off to another day; that's where the real bill is likely to add up, even if money can be saved in the last illness. To save money in the last days of life is not identical with saving money in the last years of life.

Even if it becomes necessary to set limits on public expenditures for elderly health care, that should be done on a case-by-case basis rather than categorically by age. Should rationing or limits be necessary, almost everyone's ideal would be a system that was simultaneously individualized, fair, and effective. Each patient would be considered on his or her medical merits, not on the basis of some categorical standard. Rejecting categorical standards, "the impersonal application of a rule to a faceless group," Dr. Norman G. Levinsky has written that "society must not insulate itself from the agony of each decision to forgo beneficial treatment as it is experienced by patients, families, and care givers" (Levinsky 1990:1815).

I can well understand the sentiment behind Dr. Levinsky's thinking, but I have simply never been able to understand how it would be possible to limit health care in general while individualizing it in particular. If the assumption is that people should receive care on the basis of its individual efficacy for them, then we will run afoul of what I would call the "efficacy fallacy," that is, the notion that those treatments that are individually efficacious are therefore socially affordable. But precisely the problem we are likely to face is this: It will be the efficacious, not wasteful, treatments that will cause us the most financial grief, simply because it will be all the harder to deny people such treatment. There is a related fallacy, what I will dub the "hidden hand fallacy," that is, the view that the aggregate impact of meeting individual needs will turn out to be identical with the available common resources. Why should that be the case?

My assumption, by contrast—using the available projections—is that we will be forced to limit some proven, efficacious treatments, of a kind that people will want and that would extend their lives. The choices we will have to make will then be genuinely tragic choices. The pain of such choices is that they allow us no happy way out. It is an easy exercise to measure age-limit proposals against the standard of unlimited resources and no hard choices; and, naturally, an age limit looks terrible by that standard. But if we understand that we may one day be faced only with nasty options, then our task will be to compare those options with each other, not compare them against a world where no unpleasant choices are needed.

The idea of using a "natural life span" as a basis for setting an age limit is too vague, and too controverted, to be useful. With great frequency I felt my proposal ran up against the individualism of our culture, not only in the repeated assertion about the heterogeneity of the elderly, but also in the rejection of a use of the life cycle as a place to look for an age limit. Yet I find it hard to know where else we might fruitfully look. If our standard is simply individual benefit, regardless of age, then there is no possible way we could effectively limit elderly health care costs; they will inexorably rise as technology improves. My alternative approach is to ask: How can we design a health care and entitlement system that would allow each of us to live a long and full life, but would not entail unlimited public support for whatever technology turned up at whatever cost?

I turned to the idea of a "natural life span" in order to capitalize on a common cultural sentiment, still alive in the United States. It is that, while all death is a cause for sadness, a death in old age after a long and full life is, given the inevitability of death, the most acceptable kind of death. Unlike the death of a child or a young adult, death in old age is part of our biology and part of the life cycle. It is no accident, I think, that there is less weeping at the death of a very old person than at the death of a child. Although the idea of a "natural life span" as a biographical notion was thoroughly assaulted by many of my critics, a recent survey indicates that the idea is still strong in our society, even if most people would at present probably resist using it for rationing purposes (Zweibel, Cassel, and Karvison 1993). Increased financial pressure, certain in the years ahead, may perhaps change the public bias against an age-based rationing standard.

I come back to a fundamental question. Do the elderly have an unlimited medical claim on public resources? No, they have only a reasonable and thus limited claim. What is a "reasonable" claim? I take it to be a claim to live a long life with public support, but not indefinitely long, and not at the price of potential harm to others. If we can agree with that proposition, then a "natural life span" is [an idea] that is highly useful—though admittedly not precise—allowing us a way of talking about what should count as a premature death, and as the basis for a claim on the public purse. It will surely work better than, say, "individual need," which is subject to technological escalation and intractable subjective desires. If we agree, for instance, that the preservation of life is a basic medical need, then in the nature of the case with the aging person there are no necessary limits at all, scientific or economic, to what can be done to achieve that goal. To be sure, any specific age to invoke as a limit will be arbitrary, but not necessarily capricious. That was true of age 65 when Medicare was established. It could have been 66 or 64. The point is that it was within a generally acceptable range of choices, and that is sufficient for fair public policy.

SOME TELLING POINTS

My response so far might indicate that I have been unwilling to give way to my critics or to admit any validity to what they say. Up to a point that is true. Nonetheless, on the old principle that much of life and policy lies in the details, some telling points have been made against me. They are worth further thought.

The most powerful criticism is political: Whatever the rational arguments in its favor, neither the public nor legislators would ever accept an open, explicit use of age as a criterion for cutting off life-extending medical care. One critic called this assumption on my part a "blunder," and (in some sympathy with my general argument about the need for limits) said that we might be forced to covertly have an age standard (Moody 1991). I have no doubt that an age limit would, politically, be obnoxious to politicians, at least at present. Even those countries known for using age as a norm (such as England and Switzerland) have done so tacitly and quietly, out of the public eye. Yet, if it is true that an explicit age standard is now and will remain for some time politically unacceptable as public policy, then we will be left with another dilemma. We will either have to come up with some other standard, bound to be unwanted also if it has any bite, or resign ourselves to euphemism and evasion, using age privately but never admitting it publicly.

There is a telling scientific criticism also. One of my goals with an age limit is to discourage the kind of scientific "progress" that endlessly generates new, almost always expensive, ways of extending the lives of elderly people. If those modalities were not going to be reimbursed, that would be a powerful disincentive to developing them in the first place. The problem here, as many noted, is that most of the technologies now used with the elderly were first developed with younger people in mind; few life-extending technologies are created for the elderly as such.

I cannot deny the force of those contentions. But that leaves us with another dilemma: If scientific progress moves along in an unchecked fashion, generating still more expensive ways of saving life, our tragic dilemma will become all the more painful. The gap between what we know we can or could do to save life will all the more harshly and conspicuously clash with our economic limitations. My own preference would be for a sharp increase in research designed to decrease morbidity and disability, discouraging, when possible, explicit efforts to develop more life-extending technologies.

Still another criticism might, for lack of a better name, be called the repugnance argument. It takes a number of forms. One of them is that we would find it repugnant to deny reimbursement to someone for a form of care that would clearly save that person's life; we could not just stand by and let the person die for lack of money. Another form is that, however nice my theory of justice between age groups, it would *look* like we were devaluing the worth of the elderly if we used age as an exclusive standard for denying care; we would find that hard to stand.

I agree that most people would find these consequences of an age limit repugnant. But again we are left with a dilemma, indeed more than one. What will we do about the repugnance that could well result from seeing a larger and larger, and even more disproportionate, share of resources going to the elderly while the needs of younger groups are going unmet? Or placing heavier and heavier economic burdens on the young to sustain the old? If we leave all choices about resource allocation to doctors and families at the bedside, what will we do about the repugnance regarding the variations in treatment that method will bring, with some getting too much treatment and others getting too little? If we find the open use of an age limit repugnant, will we feel any better about a covert use, one that could be forced by a shortage of money?

Another telling point, in some ways the most fundamental, leaves me with a deep and unresolved problem. In an unpublished paper Per Anderson suggests that the "high quality aging that Callahan wants medicine and society to support will serve to make the idea of the life cycle increasingly implausible . . . one can wonder whether Callahan would have us adopt an ethic of limits because it is the human good or because it is the grim necessity to which we must be resigned" (Anderson 1991:3). On this point, a profound one for medicine in general and not just for care of the aged, I am deeply ambivalent.

My own reading of history is that those people and cultures who live with some sense of intrinsic limits, whether natural or culturally inspired, better adapt to the human situation, and to aging and mortality, than do those who want to carry out endless warfare against human finitude. Yet I cannot ignore the other side of that coin, which is that we have enormously benefited from many efforts to transcend what earlier generations took to be fixed limits. I might not now be alive but for those efforts. How do we find the right balance here, between acceptance and acquiescence and the desire to struggle against our human condition? It is open to my critics to make a good case for fighting the ravages of age and to seek to further postpone death. I will respond by asking: Why should we believe that will necessarily increase our human satisfaction and sense of well-being? We will, I am sure, go back and forth on that point—and no doubt so will future generations.

WHAT ABOUT THE FUTURE?

There were three reasons why I was drawn to the use of an age limit as a likely way to eventually control health care allocation to the elderly. One reason was that it seems to me better in general for human beings to live with a strong sense of their mortality and to be willing to understand that their lives must come to an end. A second reason is that it seems to me merely the prejudice of an affluent, hyper-individualistic, technologically driven society to think that a denial of reimbursement for life-extending care beyond a certain point is tantamount to a denial of value and dignity to the elderly. The third reason for being drawn to age was that I simply could not imagine—and still cannot imagine—any other way of decisively and effectively and uniformly drawing a clear policy line than the use of age. It is precisely because it cuts through, and transcends, our individual differences that it is attractive for policy purposes.

That of course is precisely its greatest liability in the eyes of my critics, and I am more persuaded than I was initially that, for both symbolic and practical reasons, an age-based policy will appear, and well could be, obnoxious. Yet, having conceded that, I must then add: Show me an equally decisive alternative, one that will work to hold down costs, that does not depend upon variable bedside judgments, and that takes with full seriousness the need to find a solution—and a solution that does not depend on evading the problem altogether by invoking some yet-to-be-seen hopeful scientific or economic miracle.

If we agree on the eventual need for limits, does it follow that only an age limit would work? Not at all, and it may well be that the various repugnances I noted above will stand forever in the way of using an age limit. But in that case it will be necessary to come up with some plausible alternatives. Robert Veatch and Norman Daniels have suggested some interesting and alternative ways of using age, less stark than mine. They can be debated. Nancy S. Jecker and Robert A. Pearlman, after criticizing Harry R. Moody, Norman Daniels, and myself for our willingness to consider an age limit, conclude their article with a brief review of some possible alternatives—and find them full of problems as well!

(See Jecker and Pearlman 1989.) No doubt anyway, as they say, we will have to explore those alternatives. I offer a simple test as we try to think about one alternative or another: If it seems to avoid the need for nasty choices altogether, or seems painless and congenial (like just cutting out unwanted treatment), we should have a hard time taking it seriously. In the best of all possible worlds, what the elderly want and need would fit perfectly with the available resources. Ours is not, nor is it likely to be, such a world. Any solution that seems to imply such a world merits the same suspicion as offers of free trips to Europe or Florida just by placing a phone call.

Time and again I was accused of "blaming the elderly" for our present allocation problems. How nice it would be to find identifiable villains here, but I see no fault here *at all* with the elderly. Instead, we are only now beginning to see some of the costs and pitfalls of the great medical advances that have been made in recent decades, and some of the unforeseen and probably unforeseeable hazards of pursuing medical progress. It is the success of medicine, not its failures, that has created the problem of sustaining and paying for decent health care for the elderly. It is the success of the campaign against ageism, increasing the expectations of everyone for a medically and socially transformed old age, that have added to that problem. If there is any blame to be apportioned it should be directed at our dreams, some of which have come true. It is just that we did not know what that would mean. Now we are finding out.

REFERENCES

Anderson, P. (1991). On the "ragged edge" of medical progress: Daniel Callahan and problems of limits. Unpublished paper.

Barry, R. L., and Bradley, G. V. (Eds.). (1991). *Set no limits: A rebuttal to Daniel Callahan's proposal to limit health care for the elderly*. Urbana: University of Illinois Press.

Binstock, R. H., and Post, S. G. (Eds.). (1991). *Too old for health care: Controversies in medicine, law, economics, and ethics*. Baltimore: The John Hopkins University Press.

Breidenbaugh, M. Z., Sarsitis, I. M., and Milam, R. A. (1990). Medicare end-stage renal disease population, *Health Care Financing Review, 12*, 101–104.

Callahan, D. (1987). *Setting limits: Medical goals in an aging society*. New York: Simon and Schuster.

Callahan, D. (1990). *What kind of life: The limits of medical progress*. New York: Simon and Schuster.

Callahan, D. (1993). *The troubled dream of life: Living with mortality*. New York: Simon and Schuster.

Chambers, C. V., Diamond, J. J., Perkel, R. L., and Lasch, L. A. (1994). Relationship of advance directives to hospital charges in a Medicare population. *Archives of Internal Medicine, 154,* 541–547.

Estes, C. L. (1988). Cost containment and the elderly: Conflict or challenge? *Journal of the American Medical Association, 36,* 68–72.

Hackler, C. (ed.). (1994). *Health care for an aging population: Planning for the twenty-first century*. Albany: State University of New York Press.

Holahan, J., and Palmer, J. L. (1988). Medicare's fiscal problems: An imperative for reform. *Journal of Health, Politics, Policy and Law, 13,* 53–81.

Hollander, C. F., and Becker, H. A., (Eds.). (1987). *Growing old in the future*. Dordrecht: Martinius Nijhoff Publishers.

Homer, P., and Holstein, M., (Eds.). (1990). *A good old age: The paradox of setting limits*. New York: Simon and Schuster.

Hosking, M. P., Warner, M. A., Lobdell, C. M., Offord, K. P., and Melton, J. L. (1989). Outcome of surgery in patients 90 years of age and older. *Journal of the American Medical Association, 261,* 1909–1915.

Jecker, N. S. (1991a). Age-based rationing and women. *Journal of the American Medical Association, 266,* 3012–3015.

Jecker, N. S. (ed.). (1991b). *Ethics and aging*. Clifton, N.J.: Humana Press.

Jecker, N. S., and Pearlman, R. A. (1989). Ethical constraints on rationing medical care by age. *Journal of the American Geriatrics Society, 37,* 1067–1073.

Jouvenel, H. de. (1989). *Europe's ageing population: Trends and challenges to 2025*. Special co-publication of *Futures* and *Futuribles*. Guildford, U.K.: Butterworth.

Latta, V. B., and Keene, R. E. (1989). Leading surgical procedures for aged Medicare beneficiaries. *Health Care Financing Review, 11,* 99–100.

Lawlor, E. F. (1992). What kind of medicine? *The Gerontologist, 32,* 131–133.

Levinsky, N. G. (1990). Age as a criterion for rationing health care. *New England Journal of Medicine, 322,* 1813–1815.

Loriaux. (1990). Il Sera une fois . . . la revolution gruse jeux at enjeux autour d'une profunde mutation societale [Someday it will happen . . . the revolution of aging and the profound social change at stake]. Université Catholique de Louvain, Louvain-la-Neuve, Claco: Institut de Démographie.

Manton, K. G., Corder, L., and Stallard, S. (1993). Changes in the use of personal assistance and special equipment from 1982 to 1989: Results from the 1982 and 1989 NLTCS. *The Gerontologist, 33,* 168–176.

Moody, H. R. (1991). Allocation, yes; Age-based rationing, no. In R. H. Binstock and S. G. Post, (Eds.). *Too old for health care*. Baltimore: The Johns Hopkins

University Press, pp. 180–203.

Preston, S. (1984). Children and the elderly: Divergent paths for America's dependents. *Demography, 21*, 455–491.

St. Louis University. (1989). Health care for the elderly. Symposium in the *St. Louis University Law Journal, 33*, 557–710.

Schneider, E. L., Guralnik, J. M. (1990). The aging of America: Impact on health care costs. *Journal of the American Medical Association, 263*, 2335–2340.

Schneiderman, L., Kronick, R., Kaplan, R. M., Anderson, J. P., and Langer, R. D. (1992). Effects of offering advance directives on medical treatment and costs. *Annals of Internal Medicine, 117*, 599–606.

Winslow, G. R., and Walters, J. W. (Eds.). (1993). *Facing limits: Ethics and health care for the elderly*. Boulder, Colo.: Westview Press.

Zweibel, N. R., Cassel, C. K., and Karvison, T. (1993). Public attitudes about the use of chronological age as a criterion for allocating health care resources. *The Gerontologist, 36*, 74–80.

PART III

The Generational Interdependence Frame

CHAPTER SEVEN

America *Can* Afford to Grow Old

Alicia H. Munnell

Alicia H. Munnell is the Peter F. Drucker Professor in Management Sciences at Boston College's Carroll School of Management. She served as a member of the President's Council of Economic Advisers from 1995 to 1997 and as assistant secretary of the Treasury for Economic Policy from 1993 to 1995. She spent most of her professional career at the Federal Reserve Bank of Boston, joining the staff of the Boston Fed's Research Department as an economist in 1973 and becoming senior vice president and director of research in 1984. She was cofounder and the first president of the National Academy of Social Insurance. She has written extensively on tax policy, Social Security, public and private pensions, and productivity, publishing many articles, books, and edited volumes on these topics.

Munnell suggests that critics of Social Security are exaggerating the program's financing problems. As part of a strategy to promote and justify radical change (i.e., privatization, means-testing, and large benefit reductions), the critics are making unwarranted claims about intergenerational conflict and the negative effects of Social Security on the economy. A financing problem does exist, but she argues that it can be addressed through modest changes, involving some compromise between lowering benefits and increasing revenues. In her view policymakers should consider some prefunding of Social Security and investing of a portion of the trust funds in equities. Such changes would increase returns on payroll tax contributions and reduce the need to increase the payroll tax rate.

The cacophony created by critics of today's Social Security system has gotten so loud that it has begun to drown out the facts. One can argue for a bigger Social Security program or a smaller program, for individual accounts or investing the trust funds in equities, for trimming the cost-of-living adjustment (COLA) or developing a COLA for the elderly, but these arguments have to be based on a realistic assessment of the system's finances and on a clear understanding of the program's impact on the economy.

The critics have exaggerated the problems in order to justify dramatic solutions. They claim that entitlements are unsustainable and will push the economy to the breaking point. They are wrong. They claim that transfers to the elderly are undermining saving, investment, and economic growth. They are wrong. They claim that generational accounts are out of balance and unfair. They are wrong.

Although dramatic change is unnecessary, this is the time to make some decisions about the future of the program. The system has matured, so the full cost of providing current levels of benefits has become apparent. We can afford this level of protection, but should make the choice whether or not to maintain current benefits. Second, the system's long-term financing gap, though manageable, should be closed as soon as possible. Finally, many observers have argued that Social Security may be a logical vehicle for raising the nation's saving rate. If so, then we should reevaluate exclusive reliance on the payroll tax and consider some alternative revenue sources such as the higher returns on trust fund assets that would come from investment in equities, or an infusion of general revenues.

America *can* afford to grow old without placing an enormous burden on future generations of workers. The task that we face is to make responsible policy decisions based on sound economics.

HOW BIG IS THE PROBLEM?

The basic flaw in the analysis of many Social Security critics is that they tend to lump together the costs of Social Security and Medicare and treat them as a single, overwhelming crisis.[1] In fact, these are two separate programs; they are financed separately; and they face distinct problems. However, only by including the projections for Medicare can critics generate alarming projections for entitlement spending. But two-thirds of the projected cost increase is due to higher spending on health care; only one-third is due to Social Security.

When considering how to eliminate Social Security's projected long-term deficit, it would be a mistake to ignore completely the fact that the aging of the population will also place increased demands on the Medicare program. But only a fraction of Medicare's rising costs comes from demographics; the bulk comes from the growth in health care costs per person. This is a problem that affects medical care throughout the economy and one that policymakers are going to have to solve. The spread of managed care has provided some encouraging statistics, but reformers of the health care system are far from victory. Thus both the Medicare and Social Security problems are going to have to be solved, but they have to be solved separately. When devising solutions for the Social Security program, the right numbers to look at are the costs and revenues for Social Security alone.

When Social Security is examined as a separate program—as it should be—the figures are far from alarming. Every year, the system's Trustees publish an actuarial report that includes three sets of projections based on alternative assumptions about futures rates of population growth, future rates of economic growth, and interest rates. The intermediate projection from the 1998 report shows that between now and 2013, the Social Security system will bring in more money than it pays out. From 2013 through 2021, adding interest on trust fund assets to tax receipts produces enough revenues to cover benefit payments. After that, if no action is taken, total income will fall short of benefit payments, but the shortfall can be covered by drawing down trust fund assets until the funds are exhausted in 2032.

Critics talk about this 2032 date as if the whole Social Security system implodes in that year and nothing is left. This is simply not correct. Even if no tax or benefit changes were made, current payroll taxes and benefit taxation will provide enough money to cover roughly 75 percent of benefits in 2040 and nearly 70 percent in 2075. In other words, even if no reforms were introduced between now and 2032, the government would still be able to send out checks worth three-quarters of today's benefits to all retirees for most of the next century without increasing taxes.

The debate, therefore, is over how to close the gap between the 100 percent of benefits payable today and the 75 percent for which financing is already available in the future. One way to think of this gap is to consider the amount by which taxes would have to increase today to pay full benefits for the next seventy-five years, the planning horizon in the Trustees' projections. Even though, such a tax increase should not be necessary, it provides a useful way to gauge the size of the problem. According to the Social Security Trustees, the retirement system's projected long-run deficit over the next seventy-five years is equal to

2.19 percent of total payroll earnings over that period. The figure means that if the payroll tax rate were raised immediately by 2.19 percentage points—roughly 1.1 percentage points for the employee and 1.1 percentage points for the employer—the government would be able to pay for the current package of benefits, adjusted for rising future wages and for inflation after retirement, for everyone who reaches retirement age until 2075.

A tax increase of 2.19 percentage points is a serious matter, but it hardly qualifies as a "demographic time bomb."[2] The economy survived an increase of roughly the same magnitude between 1980 and 1990, when the combined employer-employee tax rate went from 10.16 percent to today's 12.4 percent. Moreover, no one proposes that the entire deficit be closed by raising payroll taxes. As members of the 1994–96 Social Security Advisory Council recommended, extending coverage to state and local employees, eliminating overstatement of the cost-of-living adjustment, extending the averaging period for the calculation of benefits, increasing the taxation of benefits, and perhaps raising the retirement age beyond that already included in the law are reasonable steps to meet a substantial part of the shortfall. In short, the financing hole is relatively small and policymakers have compiled a wide range of possible solutions.

ARE THE UNDERLYING ASSUMPTIONS REASONABLE?

Are these Trustees' projections based on sensible economic and demographic assumptions? After all, projecting costs for the next seventy-five years is equivalent to having made estimates for today in 1923. Forecasters in 1923 would have had no idea about the Great Depression, World War II, or a host of other demographic, economic, and social developments.

On the demographic side, the key variables are fertility and mortality rates. With regard to fertility, currently the average woman can be expected to have 2.0 children over her lifetime. Demographers agree almost unanimously that fertility rates will remain low. The Trustees' Report assumes that the fertility rate will decrease slightly to 1.9 percent. Some experts view this as a little pessimistic, and predict that future fertility patterns may cause costs to be somewhat lower. The consensus is that mortality will also decrease. This is important because the longer people live, the more years over which benefits have to be paid after retirement. The question is how fast mortality will decrease.[3] Some people believe that the Trustees' projections do not fully account for future improvements in mortality and that costs may be somewhat higher as a result. In all probability, the biases in the fertility and mortality assumptions balance out.

On the economic side, a key variable is the difference between the rate at which benefits once awarded increase—namely, the rate of increase in the consumer price index (CPI)—and the rate at which taxes rise—namely, the rate of growth in wages. During the twenty-year period before 1973, when productivity growth was high, this "real-wage differential" averaged 2.2 percent. Since 1973, it has averaged 0.3 percent. The question is how much weight to put on recent years as compared with the pre-1973 period. The Trustees have split the difference and adopted an assumption of 0.9 percent. What if they are wrong? By how much would a real-wage differential of 0.3 percent, rather than the assumed 0.9 percent, raise the seventy-five-year deficit? Sensitivity analysis shows that such a miscalculation would increase the seventy-five-year deficit by roughly 0.6 percent of taxable payroll.[4] In other words, a relatively large error in this assumption, taken in isolation, would worsen long-term Social Security financing by a relatively modest amount during the next seventy-five years.

How do other experts view the reasonableness of the assumptions? A 1994–95 Technical Panel to the recent Social Security Advisory Council concluded that "the 'intermediate' projection . . . for the OASDI program provide[s] a reasonable evaluation of the financial status. Although the Panel suggests that modifications be considered in various specific assumptions, the overall effect of those suggestions would not significantly change the financial status evaluation." More recently, Alan Greenspan in his October 8, 1997, testimony before the House Banking Committee characterized the Trustees' economic and demographic assumptions as "conservative." In short, one can quibble with any particular economic or demographic assumption, but taken as a whole they provide a reasonably realistic picture of the future.

WHY THE 1983 FIX DIDN'T STICK

Even if the projected deficit is relatively small and is based on reasonable economic and demographic assumptions, critics might still argue that we fixed Social Security before, and it did not stay fixed. Specifically, in 1983 Congress enacted legislation based on the recommendations of a commission chaired by Alan Greenspan. At that time, it was asserted that those recommendations would be sufficient to keep the Social Security system solvent for seventy-five years, with positive trust fund balances through 2060. Only a year after Congress enacted the legislation, however, the Trustees began to project a small deficit. The deficit has grown more or less steadily since then. How did this happen?

Interestingly enough, worsening economic and demographic assumptions have not—on balance—been responsible for the currently projected deficit. Since 1983, the demographic developments have been positive—at least from the program's perspective. Life expectancy assumptions have been lowered slightly, thereby reducing long-run costs. The positive impact on long-run costs from changing demographic assumptions was roughly offset, however, by changing economic assumptions. In particular, the Trustees lowered the assumed rate of real wage growth as it became clear that the productivity slowdown was here to stay. On balance, the economic and demographic changes have roughly offset one another.

Where did the deficit come from? About a third of the problem came from the fact that as time passes the seventy-five-year valuation period ends in a later year, so more high-cost future years are included in the projections. Including more deficit years raises the seventy-five-year deficit. Another third came from the disability caseload: disability cases grew much faster than anticipated, primarily because of legislative, regulatory, and judicial action that made it easier for individuals to qualify for disability benefits. The final third involved one-shot changes in the methodology used to project the future. For example, the large increase in the deficit from 1993 to 1994 was due mainly to new data suggesting that workers have more years of covered employment than previously had been thought and are therefore entitled to higher projected benefits.

Will the same thing happen again? Although Social Security actuaries will continue to incorporate improvements in data and methods, one would expect that, as experience piles up and methods are tested and retested, the need for major reassessment would decline. Demographic and economic assumptions may have to be revised, but it is easier to think of revisions that would lower costs—improvements in the CPI and more immigration—than to think of ones that would raise costs. Finally, most Social Security reform proposals contain provisions intended to prevent the system from drifting out of balance because of the inclusion of an additional deficit year. In short, the system is not facing a financial crisis, and a series of moderate program changes should be able to restore balance.

SOCIAL SECURITY DOES NOT HARM THE ECONOMY

Even if Social Security is not facing a financing crisis, critics charge that the program is harming the economy. They say that the program undermines saving, investment, and growth and that the payroll tax discourages people from working. Any such impact would be of great importance because economic growth depends on growth in labor and capital and on increases in the productivity of these resources. But the critics are wrong. There is no evidence that Social Security has reduced saving or significantly distorted labor supply decisions; it does not harm the economy. Let us look at the saving and labor supply issues separately.

SOCIAL SECURITY DOES NOT HURT NATIONAL SAVING

When thinking about the impact of the Social Security system on national saving, it is useful to divide the issue into three time periods: the start-up, the current mature system, and the future.

The start-up.
Congress enacted the Social Security system in 1935. Payroll taxes were first collected in 1937, and the first monthly benefits were paid in 1940. In 1939, Congress made a series of decisions that slowed the buildup of reserves, and the system has operated pretty much on a pay-as-you-go basis since then.

That beginning meant that the first generation of retirees received benefits far in excess of their tax payments. According to economists' life-cycle model, whereby individuals or households plan to consume all their income and wealth over their expected lifetimes, an increment to lifetime income would increase consumption and reduce saving. That is, workers are assumed to perceive that they have received a wage increase in the form of a future annuity, and to choose to consume part of that increase. To increase their current consumption, they would have to either reduce saving or increase borrowing. Lower personal saving, without any offsetting accumulation of reserves within the Social Security system, would be expected to reduce national saving and leave future generations with a lower capital stock than they would otherwise have had.

A thorough review of the empirical literature shows no compelling evidence of a sharp decline in saving in the wake of the introduction of Social Security. One reviewer summarized his findings as follows:

> For a variety of reasons, ranging from introspection and personal experience to the analysis of statistics on saving, people have developed hunches about how Social Security affects saving. Economists, who are no more immune to hunches than anyone else, have applied the tools of their discipline to try to determine which of these hunches is correct. The evidence is conclusive that

so far they have failed. Using the best that economic theory and statistical techniques have to offer, they have produced a series of studies that can be selectively cited by the true believers of conflicting hunches or by people with political agendas that they seek to advance.[5]

Ten years later, after a careful review, the World Bank reached much the same conclusion:

> Numerous empirical investigations (most of them based on U.S. data) have been unable to prove conclusively that saving did, indeed, drop once pay-as-you-go programs were established. . . . Analyses of saving rates in other countries yield similar conflicting results. Studies of the saving impact of old-age security programs in Canada, France, the Federal Republic of Germany, Japan, Sweden, and the United Kingdom found no significant impact, except for a slightly positive effect in Sweden where the pension program is heavily funded.[6]

Several explanations are possible. The first is that Social Security may have changed retirement expectations as well as increased lifetime income. That is, before Social Security workers may have expected to work until they died, but after Social Security age 65 became the normal retirement age. To the extent that Social Security encouraged people to retire earlier, they would have been forced to save over a shorter working life for a longer period of retirement. This retirement effect would have served to increase personal saving. Similarly, before Social Security, most elderly people lived with their children; after Social Security they were in a position to maintain their own households. The increased demand for independent living in old age would also have led to increased saving. Finally, many individuals save little or nothing at all, so that the only way to increase current consumption would be through borrowing. But these same individuals are likely to have low or moderate incomes; as such, they probably would be unable to borrow enough to achieve their ideal distribution of consumption over time. For such individuals, the introduction of Social Security would leave savings unaffected, dampening the effect on aggregate saving.

In short, the life-cycle model suggests a decline in saving in the wake of the introduction of the Social Security system, and a lower capital stock as a result. Several factors, however, mitigate this result. Empirical studies cannot document a significant decline in national saving from the introduction of the Social Security system.

The mature pay-as-you-go system.

Once the Social Security system has matured, the fact that it is financed on a pay-as-you-go rather than a funded basis has relatively little further impact on the nation's saving rate. The simplest way to think about the saving effect is to consider a closed economy with no population growth, no income growth, and no uncertainty. Under a funded system, individuals would accumulate saving over their working lives, but the elderly would draw down accumulated assets in retirement. The result would be zero aggregate net saving. With pay-as-you-go financing, the buildup of assets during the working years does not occur, but then neither does the drawing down of assets in retirement. The result would be altered somewhat by introducing income growth into the analysis; but basically, for any desired level of capital stock, saving would be similar.

The permanent effect of a pay-as-you-go system on saving is determined primarily by its initial effect during the "start-up" on saving and the capital stock. The intuition is that if the capital stock were cut sharply by the introduction of Social Security then less saving would be required over time to maintain that reduced level. But if the initial effect was negligible or zero, as suggested by a review of the evidence, then the effect on steady-state saving would also be negligible or zero. Thus, the pay-as-you-go Social Security program is probably not currently having any adverse effect on saving, investment, or economic growth.

The future.

Although the introduction of a pay-as-you-go Social Security system may not have had a discernible effect on national saving or the capital stock because of a variety of mitigating factors, moving toward a funded system could lead to some increase in saving. Studies suggest that the increase in saving would be less than the gross accumulation of assets in the fund because individuals tend to reduce their other saving in response to the accumulation of pension reserves.[7] The increase in saving that did occur would reflect the lowered consumption of the workers in the "transition generation," who pay the taxes to support the benefits of the elderly while also saving for their own retirement. The desirability of moving from pay-as-you-go to some prefunding will be discussed later in this chapter in the context of intergenerational equity.

SOCIAL SECURITY DOES LITTLE TO "DISTORT" LABOR SUPPLY DECISIONS

National pension programs like Social Security are established precisely to change the outcomes from unfettered labor markets. They are designed to allow earlier retirement or higher retirement incomes than individuals would have enjoyed otherwise. To the extent that they succeed, with minimal other distortions, any reduction in labor supply should be viewed as increasing the nation's welfare. Economic costs arise only when taxes or other provisions cause *unintended* changes in labor supply.

Social Security taxes would be expected to have little effect on labor supply of younger workers for two reasons.[8] First, economists believe that labor supply generally is not all that sensitive to changes in after-tax wages. Thus, to the extent that Social Security is viewed as a tax, the "substitution effect," by which the lower after-tax wage discourages work in favor of leisure, is roughly offset by the "income effect," whereby lower after-tax wages require individuals to work more to maintain their consumption. Second, to the extent that individuals view their Social Security taxes as a form of forced saving, Social Security has very little of even the modest incentive effects usually associated with a tax. Studies find that employment taxes have virtually no effect on work effort of so-called primary earners—that is, those workers whose earnings are the prime source of support for themselves and their families. The same studies, however, tend to show some modest reduction in labor supply from workers who have alternative sources of support, such as students, married women, or potential welfare recipients. In total, however, the distortions caused by the effects of payroll tax contributions on workers are small.

On the other hand, Social Security, in combination with private pensions and nonpension wealth, encourages individuals to retire at age 62, the age of first eligibility. Economists have found little evidence to suggest that even substantial changes in the structure of Social Security would have much effect on retirement at age 62 as long as benefits continued to be available at that age. But the goal of introducing Social Security was to enable workers to have higher retirement incomes and to retire at an earlier age. It is impossible to say whether or not the program has achieved the optimal amount of early retirement, but it would be incorrect to view all the reduction in labor force activity due to benefit availability as a distortion.

In summary, the impacts of Social Security on saving and labor supply have been hotly debated and intensively studied for the last twenty-five years. Several serious scholars have reviewed the studies and found no evidence that the pay-as-you-go Social Security system in the United States has reduced national saving.[9] With regard to labor supply, the evidence is mixed. Little support exists for the proposition that the Social Security tax discourages people from working, but the availability of benefits does encourage individuals to retire. It is difficult to characterize the latter effect as negative, however, because the system was designed to facilitate retirement.

THE QUESTION OF FAIRNESS AND INTERGENERATIONAL EQUITY

Even if critics could be persuaded that Social Security is not going broke and that it is not having a deleterious impact on the economy, they would still argue that it is unfair. It is unfair, they claim, because early generations received high returns on their benefits, and today's generations will receive low returns. It is unfair because this generation will leave future generations trillions of dollars of unfunded liabilities. It is unfair because the number of workers per retiree will decline dramatically and future workers will bear an intolerable burden of support. It is unfair because the elderly are getting all the money and the nation's children are getting little. Each critique contains a kernel of truth, but the conclusion drawn from the kernel is misleading at best. Let's go through them one by one.

A DECLINE IN RETURNS IS INEVITABLE WITH A PAY-AS-YOU-GO SYSTEM

Assessing the "high returns–low returns" issue requires a review of the history of the program. Social Security was established during the Great Depression, in part as a response to economic turmoil and in part as a response to industrialization.[10] The question facing policymakers was whether to prefund the program, such that the trust funds would accumulate assets for, say, thirty years before paying benefits, or to pay out benefits to the retiring workers who had just suffered ten years of economic depression.

Both the politics and the economics argued against prefunding. On the political side, some worried that a large trust fund might lead to pressure for more government spending or for government control of private industry. Others argued that it was unlikely that taxpayers would be willing to pay more to the government for decades than they would get back in benefits. On the economic front, supporters of early payment claimed that the elderly had been particularly harmed by the depression: the elderly were the first to lose their jobs, and the depression had strained the traditional family support system. Others worried that prefunding could have a contractionary effect on the economy. The decision was made to pay benefits to the first generation of retirees. That decision—to put the system on a pay-as-you-go basis—determined the pattern of returns over time.

The projected decline in the returns (commonly referred to as "money's worth") is primarily the consequence of the maturation of a pay-as-you-go system. Workers retiring early on in the program had only a few years of wages subject to the Social Security payroll tax. Over time, retirees had more and more years of wages subject to taxation, and the additional tax payments sharply reduced the rate of return.[11] The situation is actually somewhat more complicated, because benefit levels and tax rates were raised several times over the period. Increases in benefits and taxes can be seen as introducing new pay-as-you-go programs on top of the old, temporarily boosting returns. But the essence of the story is the maturation of a pay-as-you-go system. If one agrees with the initial decision to pay benefits to the first generation of retirees, then it is difficult to describe subsequent developments as unfair.

AGING OF THE POPULATION MUST BE PUT IN CONTEXT

The number of retirees per one hundred workers has increased from two in 1950 to thirty today and is scheduled to rise to fifty in 2040. That is true. But this trend has been well understood from the beginning of the program, has been fully factored in to the financial planning for the system, and will not create an intolerable burden.

An increase in the ratio of retirees to workers is inevitable during the start-up of a contributory retirement program. In the beginning no one has contributed and no one is eligible for benefits. Very gradually the numbers increase as more and more workers accumulate earnings records. Thus, it is not a surprising or disturbing phenomenon that the number of beneficiaries per hundred workers has risen from two to thirty. This was anticipated in the financing of the program.

It has also been recognized for a long time that the ratio will start rising once again as the baby boomers retire. The projections used in the 1998 Trustees' Report are very close to those used at the time of the 1983 Amendments, which were designed to put the system in long-range balance. In fact, as discussed earlier, demographic changes since 1983 have improved, not worsened the financial outlook. Thus, critics are wrong when they treat the demographic tends as new and unexpected.

Critics are also wrong when they suggest that the rising ratio of beneficiaries to workers will create an intolerable burden. The real financial burden facing future workers depends not just on the number of Social Security beneficiaries but on the total number of people that they will have to support, including children. As shown in figure 7.1, the number of nonworking persons per one hundred workers reached a long-term high in 1960 and has since declined by about

60 percent to a long-term low. The main reason for the decline is a sharp drop in the number of children. A secondary factor has been an increase in the number of women working.[12] Over the next forty-five years, the number of elderly will rise sharply as baby boomers retire, but the number of children per worker will stay low and even decline a bit. As a result, the total burden per hundred workers will increase by only 15 percent.[13] It would be hard to characterize 15 percent as an unbearable burden.

USING LARGE DOLLAR LIABILITY FIGURES DOES NOT MAKE SENSE

Critics often charge that the current generation is leaving the future generation with a large unfunded liability. That liability is usually stated in terms of a figure like $2.9 trillion dollars[14] and compared to national debt held by the public of $4 trillion. Those are indeed alarming numbers. The question is, What do they mean? The answer is that they are simply a dramatic way of restating the financial deficit discussed earlier in this chapter. If the present discounted value of future payroll taxes is subtracted from the present discounted value of future benefits for the next seventy-five years, the difference is $2.9 trillion. But, it does

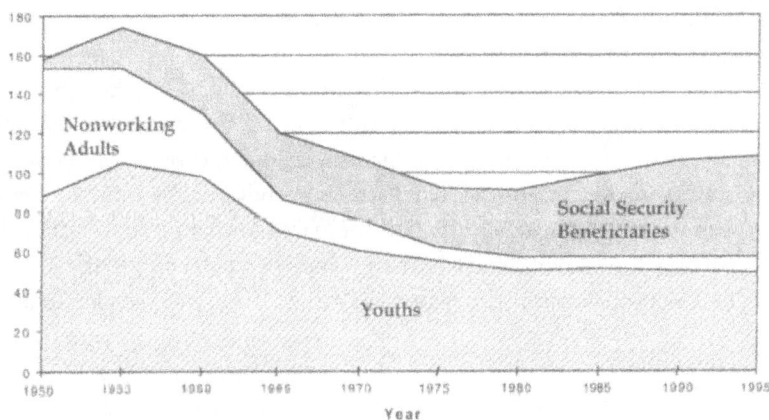

FIGURE 7.1
Nonworking Population per 100 Workers
Note: "Youths" refers to population under 20 years of age.
Source: Author's calculations.

not make sense simply to add up dollar figures over a seventy-five-year period; they should be expressed as a percentage of economic activity. Dividing that $2.9 trillion by the present discounted value of payrolls for the next seventy-five years yields the number 2.19 percent. This 2.19 percent is the financial deficit described in the first section. It sounds very large in dollar terms, but, as discussed earlier, is manageable when placed in the context of a growing economy and expanding payroll tax base.

All observers agree that the deficit in the Social Security program should be eliminated as soon as possible, both to restore confidence in the program and to take advantage of the fact that the required adjustments will be much smaller if done early. Closing the seventy-five-year financing gap is the same as eliminating the unfunded liability over that period. No one is arguing for leaving that burden to future generations.

THIS COUNTRY SHOULD SPEND MORE ON ITS CHILDREN

The state of this nation's children is shocking. More than 20 percent live in poverty.[15] And government spending on children is far below that for other groups. Part of the explanation is that for the most part parents pay for the care of the children, whereas much of the support for the elderly is funneled through the federal government. As a result, looking solely at government accounts provides a misleading picture of relative levels of aid. Nevertheless, the outcome is unacceptable and the call for more government assistance is understandable. Other countries have children's allowances and other provisions that help parents support their young families.

The mistake in the analysis comes when the reason for our lack of spending on children is said to be our spending on the elderly. It is possible to do both. Government spending in the United States is among the lowest of developed countries. Federal, state, and local government spending in the United States in 1995 amounted to 35.8 percent of GDP compared to 50.9 percent for France, 46.7 percent for Canada and Germany, and 42.3 percent for the United Kingdom. For some reason, this nation has chosen not to spend on its children.

CHOICES FOR THE FUTURE

Although the critics are wrong about the size of the financing hole, the impact of the program on the economy, and the fairness of the system, the time is ripe for making some choices about the future of Social Security. The questions are really quite simple. How big a slice of the pie do we want the elderly to receive in 2040? Can steps taken now influence how big the pie will be?

SOCIAL SECURITY HAS BEEN A VERY SUCCESSFUL PROGRAM

Even most critics of Social Security agree that to date the program has done a good job. For sixty years, Social Security has provided individuals with a basic level of retirement security. Although the benefit schedule is progressive and benefits are subject to taxation, Social Security is not subject to an explicit means test. The lack of means-testing allows many people to add other resources in order to achieve a level of income not too far below what they had when they were working.

Currently, about 90 percent of "aged units"—married couples one of whom is aged 65 or older and nonmarried persons aged 65 and over—are receiving Social Security benefits. These benefits are the only form of retirement benefit for about half of those units. Social Security is particularly important for the low-income elderly. For example, more than three-quarters of the money income of units in the bottom two income quintiles comes from Social Security benefits. Social Security benefits keep some 15 million people above the poverty line and millions more from near poverty. As recently as 1959, when data began to be collected, the poverty rate for the elderly was twice that for the rest of the population. Since that time the rate of poverty among the elderly has decreased, and it is now near the level for other adults. Social Security has been a key factor in that decline.

Social Security also provides protection against loss of family income due to disability or death. Roughly 5 million disabled adults and 3 million children, about half of them children of deceased workers, receive monthly benefits. In short, Social Security is an extremely valuable program that has raised the living standards of millions of Americans and markedly increased their sense of economic security.

HOW BIG A SLICE SHOULD THE ELDERLY GET?

The major reasons for the current controversy are that the Social Security system has slipped out of long-term balance and that at the same time the full cost of providing current benefits in a mature system to an aging population has become apparent. The earlier discussion of the system's finances put that cost in terms of percentage of taxable payrolls; it is also useful to consider the cost as a percentage of GDP. Social Security retirement and disability benefits are now equal to 4.6 percent of GDP. The Trustees' intermediate projections show that Social Security outlays will rise to 6.9 percent in 2040 and remain at roughly that level throughout the seventy-five-year forecast period.[16] This is clearly a manageable increase—defense spending has declined by a similar amount during the last six years; the question is whether we as a nation want to maintain current benefit levels and maintain the current definition of elderly. For, in the end, the only way to reduce the share of the pie going to the elderly is to cut the average benefit or cut the number of people receiving benefits.

The Social Security Administration calculates benefits and replacement rates for individuals and families with hypothetical earnings histories (see table 7.1). Although these numbers are far from a perfect representation of actual outcomes, they provide an indication of the level of protection.[17] (Benefits at age 62 are probably the more relevant numbers, because more than two-thirds of all benefits are reduced for early retirement.) Whether these benefits are too high or too low is clearly in the eye of the beholder. It would be difficult, however, to argue for cutting benefits for the low-wage worker, because current payments are very close to the poverty line, even if a couple is eligible for the additional 50 percent benefit for a nonworking spouse. Some have suggested means-testing as a way of reducing benefits to higher-income retirees, but most reject this route.[18]

The more conventional way of talking about reducing the slice of the pie is in terms of raising the age at which people are eligible for full benefits. This sounds like a logical proposal: life expectancy has increased; so should the length of the work life. After all, the increase in the number of years over which people receive benefits is a major reason for the increase in costs to date and will add to costs in the future.[19]

TABLE 7.1

Hypothetical Monthly Benefit Amounts and Replacement Rates, January 1997

	AGE 62		AGE 65	
Worker	Benefit	Replacement Rate	Benefit	Replacement Rate
Low earner	$450	44.4%	$565	55.7%
Average earner	$742	33.2%	$933	41.5%
Maximum earner	$1,056	22.0%	$1,326	27.5%

Source: Social Security Administration, "Fast Facts and Figures About Social Security, 1997," and Marilyn Moon, "Are Social Security Benefits Too High or Too Low?" in Eric R. Kingson and James H. Schulz, eds., Social Security in the 21st Century (New York: Oxford University Press, 1997), table 4.1, p. 65.

The problem is that to date the extension of longevity has not been accompanied by an increase in work; indeed, people are retiring earlier and earlier. If people do not alter their current retirement patterns, raising the retirement age is equivalent to an across-the-board benefit cut. This occurs because proposals are usually formulated in terms of maintaining 62 as the age of first eligibility and increasing the actuarial reduction for benefits claimed before the normal retirement age. The law already provides an actuarial reduction in benefits of 20 percent for those who retire at age 62, and this reduction will rise gradually to 30 percent with the scheduled increase in the normal retirement age to 67. Increasing the retirement age beyond 67 would hurt those who are forced—either because of poor health or lack of employment opportunities—to continue to retire early. The policy question is how many people who retire at age 62 would find it a serious hardship to extend their work life.[20]

The previous discussion does not mean that some reduction in benefits is out of the question. With an aging population some compromise between reducing benefits and raising revenues may be warranted. But given the level of current benefits, sweeping reductions could put families, particularly low-wage families, at risk.

One final note. It does not matter from an economic perspective whether the elderly's claim on the pie in 2040 is in the form of accrued rights under Social Security or in the form of purchasing power gained through the sale of accumulated assets.[21] Given the size of the pie, the question is simply how much the working population in 2040 will have to reduce its own consumption below that justified by current earnings in order to allow the elderly to increase its share beyond that justified by current earnings. The only difference between the two approaches is that the claims are probably more predictable if they are provided through a national pension system than if they depend on individual investment decisions. In short, proposals to introduce individual accounts for Social Security will have no impact on the future costs. Those costs are simply the amount of consumption that the working-age population will have to forgo in 2040, and they are determined by average benefit levels and the number of people entitled to benefits.

HOW BIG CAN THE PIE BE?

The size of the pie is not fixed, but depends to some extent on saving and investment decisions that are made in the interim. The bigger the capital stock and the better educated the workers, the larger will be the pie. Most observers believe that we are saving too little, and many have concluded that the Social

Security system is a good mechanism for increasing national saving. All three 1994–96 Social Security Advisory Council plans include a substantial accumulation of reserves. From an economic perspective, it does not matter whether that accumulation occurs in the existing trust funds or in individual accounts.

Moving from pay-as-you-go finance to the buildup of reserves within either the Social Security system or individual accounts is designed to increase national saving. For this effort to be meaningful, the current generation of workers will have to forgo some additional current consumption. That means that they will in effect pay twice: they already have to reduce their consumption to cover promised benefits for the retired and those about to retire; now they will also have to reduce consumption to build up assets either collectively or individually. This is an inescapable outcome of the decision to move from a pay-as-you-go system to prefunding.

Policymakers generally view some prefunding as desirable, either to maintain support for the program by holding down the ultimate contribution rate or to increase national saving. Although no compelling argument exists for increasing national savings through Social Security, the program may provide a useful vehicle. The difficulty is that prefunding can place a very large burden on the transition generation, whose members must continue to pay benefits for current retirees as well as accumulate reserves for their own retirement. Nevertheless, increasing national saving now will mean that the pie in 2040 will be larger. One study showed that even relatively modest advanced funding, if really saved and invested, could raise future aggregate income—that is, increase the size of the pie—sufficiently to offset the added Social Security costs on future workers due to the aging of the population.[22]

If the decision is made to prefund and the current generation must pay twice, the question arises whether it makes sense to continue to rely exclusively on the payroll tax. This is a regressive levy: it provides no deductions or exemptions, taxes only income from wages, and caps taxable income (at $68,400 in 1998). Payroll tax rates are already quite high; the majority of families pay more in payroll taxes than they do in federal income taxes. Further reliance on the payroll tax to increase national saving is hard to justify. It is time to consider introducing some other source of revenue. This could be general revenues, which would come primarily from the progressive income tax, or it could be higher returns on trust fund investments, which would result from investing a portion of the Social Security trust funds in equities. Either source of additional money would reduce the need to raise payroll tax rates.

None of the traditional criticisms of Social Security have much persuasive force on close examination: the system is not facing a financial crisis; it is not discouraging saving, investment, labor supply, or economic growth; and it is not unfair. Nevertheless, the current financing shortfall and the maturation of the system make this a propitious time for some fundamental decisions about the future of the system.

The financing gap should be closed as soon as possible in order to restore confidence in the program, to allow individuals time to adjust their private saving arrangements, and to avoid bigger changes down the road.

Closing the gap requires either cutting benefits or raising revenues. It is difficult to argue for cuts in benefit amounts given current levels and replacement rates. Extending the retirement age has some logic, but will produce permanently lower benefits unless people change their retirement patterns. Provision would be required for those who, because of illness or lack of employment opportunities, cannot remain working. Some compromise will be required between lowering benefits and raising revenues.

Increasing the amount of prefunding also makes sense and is incorporated in almost all reform proposals. The prefunding can be accomplished either through accumulations in the trust funds or individual accounts. To be meaningful and raise national saving, however, requires real sacrifice in the form of reduced consumption. Reducing consumption through further reliance on the regressive payroll tax is difficult to justify. The time has come to think about introducing new revenues into the system. Almost all the reform proposals have suggested investment in equities through either the trust funds, government-sponsored accounts, or mandated individually managed investments.

In short, the problems facing Social Security that result from the maturation of the program and the aging of the population can be solved without radical change in the system. To do so, however, will require a careful analysis of the underlying economics. Exaggerated claims about impending catastrophe and intergenerational conflict simply make deciding on solutions more difficult.

NOTES

The author would like to thank Henry J. Aaron, Robert M. Ball, and the editors of this volume for useful comments.

1. See, for example, Peterson 1996.

2. See Peterson 1996, p. 21.

3. For a discussion of alternative methods of projecting mortality, see Tuljapurkar and Boe 1998.

4. See the *1997 Trustees' Report*, table II.G4, p. 139.

5. See Aaron 1982, p. 51.

6. See World Bank 1994, p. 307. These quotations were also cited by Thompson (1998, ch. 4, p. 9.)

7. For a summary of the empirical literature on the impact of pensions on saving, see Munnell and Yohn 1992.

8. For a discussion of the evidence, see Quadagno and Quinn 1997.

9. Gramlich (1997) reaches a similar conclusion.

10. The United States was late in establishing its system; most other developed countries had already established similar programs as their economic base started to shift from agriculture to manufacturing.

11. In a mature pay-as-you-go system financed by a fixed tax rate on wages, the amount by which workers as a group can increase their transfer to retirees depends on the rate of growth of aggregate real wages. Slower growth in aggregate real wage income, due to slower population and productivity growth, has reduced the return that can be obtained from a pay-as-you-go system. Looking forward, with a constant or slowly growing population at working ages, the rate of growth of aggregate wages will depend primarily on the rate of growth of productivity. Productivity growth is likely to average between 1 and 2 percent; hence, the rate of return for cohorts as a whole will be in the range of 1 to 2 percent in real terms. See Samuelson 1958.

12. The major decline in the number of people classified as "nonworking adults" shown in figure 7.1 is the result of the big increase in the proportion of adults eligible for Social Security retirement and disability benefits. The increase in the proportion of women working in the paid labor force is another contributing factor.

13. Aaron (1997) presented a similar chart, but separated the nonworking population into nonworking elderly, nonworking nonelderly, and children.

14. For a description of unfunded liability numbers and for historical data, see Goss 1997.

15. U.S. Bureau of the Census 1997, p. v.

16. Costs as a percentage of taxable payrolls are scheduled to increase from 11.5 percent in 1997 to 17.9 percent in 2040 and to continue rising to 19.4 percent in 2075. These *rates* are higher because worker compensation is only two-thirds of GDP and taxable payrolls today are only 60 percent of compensation. The *increase* in these rates is greater, because the Trustees project that the ratio of taxable payrolls to compensation will continue to decline as employees receive an increasing share of their compensation in tax-preferred fringe benefits.

17. The concept of average earnings is based on a composite of earnings for all workers at all stages of their careers and does not reflect the fact that the earnings of retiring workers are usually higher than those of their younger counterparts. Thus, the earnings of the average retiring worker are higher and the replacement rate lower than shown in table 7.1. On the other hand, the benefits and replacement rates do not reflect the fact that spouses with no earnings or low earnings are eligible for benefits up to 50 percent of the worker's.

18. Means-testing sets up perverse incentives for people not to save, increases administrative costs, introduces stigma and take-up problems, and creates instability in that means-tested programs become politically unpopular during periods of budget stringency.

19. Since Social Security was enacted in 1935, life expectancy at age 65 has increased 3 years for men and 6 years for women. These life expectancies are projected to rise a further 3 years for both men and women by 2070.

20. A preliminary analysis of the age-62 retirees shows them falling into two groups. One consists of relatively prosperous individuals with some wealth and an employer-provided pension. The other is made up of lower-income, less healthy individuals with irregular preretirement work histories. Raising the retirement age for the first group creates few problems; raising it for the other group may well produce hardship.

21. This point was made by Thompson (1998).

22. See Aaron, Bosworth, and Burtless 1989.

REFERENCES

Aaron, Henry J. 1982. *The Economic Effects of Social Security*. Washington, D.C.: Brookings Institution.

Aaron, Henry J. 1997. "A Bad Idea Whose Time Will Never Come." *Brookings Review* (Summer): 7–23.

Aaron, Henry J., Barry Bosworth, and Gary Burtless. 1989. *Can America Afford to Grow Old?* Washington, D.C.: Brookings Institution Press.

Advisory Council on Social Security Reform. 1997. *Report of the 1994–1996 Advisory Council on Social Security*. Washington, D.C.: Department of Health and Human Services.

Ball, Robert M., with Thomas N. Bethell. 1997. "Bridging the Centuries: The Case for Traditional Social Security." Pp. 259–294 in *Social Security in the 21st Century*, edited by Eric R. Kingson and James H. Schulz. New York: Oxford University Press.

Board of Trustees of the Federal Old Age and Survivors Insurance and Disability Insurance Trust Funds. 1997. *1997 Annual Report*. Washington, D.C.: U.S. Government Printing Office.

Bosworth, Barry P. 1996. "Fund Accumulation: How Much? How Managed?" Pp. 89–115 in *Social Security: What Role for the Future?* edited by Peter A. Diamond, David C. Lindeman, and Howard Young. Washington, D.C.: National Academy of Social Insurance.

Committee on Economic Security. ([1935] 1985). Report to the President of the Committee on Economic Security. Reprinted in *Fiftieth Anniversary Edition of the Report of the Committee on Economic Security and Other Basic Documents Relating to the Development of Social Security*. National Conference on Social Welfare. Washington, D.C.: U.S. Government Printing Office.

Goss, Stephen C. 1997. "Measuring Solvency in the Social Security System." Working paper series PRC WP 97–12, Wharton School, University of Pennsylvania, October.

Gramlich, Edward M. 1997. "How Does Social Security Affect the Economy?" Pp. 147–155 in *Social Security in the 21st Century*, edited by Eric R. Kingson and James H. Schulz. New York: Oxford University Press.

Kotlikoff, Laurence J. 1993. "Justice and Generational Accounting." Pp.77–93 in *Justice Across Generations: What Does It Mean?* edited by Lee K. Cohen. Washington, D.C.: American Association of Retired Persons.

Moon, Marilyn. 1997. "Are Social Security Benefits Too High or Too Low?" Pp. 62–75 in *Social Security in the 21st Century*, edited by Eric R. Kingson and James H. Schulz. New York: Oxford University Press.

Munnell, Alicia H., and Frederick O. Yohn. 1992. "What Is the Impact of Pensions on Savings?" Pp. 115–139 in *Pensions and the Economy*, edited by Zvi Bodie and Alicia Munnell. Philadelphia: University of Pennsylvania Press.

Peterson, Peter G. 1996. *Will America Grow Up Before It Grows Old?* New York: Random House.

Quadagno, Jill, and Joseph Quinn. 1997. "Does Social Security Discourage Work?" Pp. 127–146 in *Social Security in the 21st Century*, edited by Eric R. Kingson and James H. Schulz. New York: Oxford University Press.

Samuelson, Paul A. 1958. "An Exact Consumption-Loan Model of Interest with and Without the Social Contrivance of Money." *Journal of Public Economics* 66 (December): 467–482.

Thompson, Lawrence. 1998. *Older and Wiser: The Economics of Public Pensions*. Washington, D.C.: Urban Institute Press.

Thurow, Lester. 1996. *The Future of Capitalism*. New York: Morrow.

Tuljapurkar, Shripad, and Carl Boe. 1998. "Mortality Change and Forecasting: How Much and How Little Do We Know?" Working paper series PRC WP 98–2, Wharton School, University of Pennsylvania, January.

U.S. Bureau of the Census. 1997. Current Population Reports. Series P60–198. *Poverty in the United States: 1996.* Washington, D.C.: U.S. Government Printing Office.

World Bank, 1994. *Averting the Old-Age Crisis.* New York: Oxford University Press.

CHAPTER EIGHT

Social Security and the Myth of the Entitlement "Crisis"

Jill Quadagno

Jill Quadagno holds the Mildred and Claude Pepper Eminent Scholar's Chair in Social Gerontology at Florida State University. She has been president of the American Sociological Association. She is a member of the National Academy of Social Insurance. Her books include *The Transformation of Old-Age Security*, *States and Labor Markets and the Future of Old-Age Policy*, and *The Color of Welfare*.

In this article Quadagno argues against means-based Social Security and Medicare programs because she believes they would stigmatize the needy. She explains that the redistributive nature of Social Security unites and binds communities. She asserts that there is not an entitlement crisis and that with manageable adjustments Social Security and Medicare can be stabilized.

Although public opinion surveys indicate high support for Social Security, confidence in the viability of the program has declined continuously. A 1986 survey by Cook and Barrett found that 96.7 percent of respondents favored maintaining (40 percent) or increasing (56.7 percent) Social Security benefits (Cook and Barrett 1992). Similarly, 84 percent of the respondents to a 1994 poll by the American Association of Retired Persons (AARP) said Social Security benefits were "very important," and 88 percent opposed cutting benefits to reduce the federal deficit (AARP 1994). By 1993, however, only 30 percent of the public felt confident that Social Security benefits would be paid throughout their retirement. Lack of confidence is especially low among young people (Friedland 1994; Marmor, Mashaw, and Harvey 1990).

The disparity between support and confidence partly reflects a pervasive distrust of government. Trust in government has steadily eroded from 75 percent in 1958 to only 19 percent by 1994 (Skocpol 1995). According to a 1993 Gallup survey, 88 percent of the public believe that the federal government routinely mismanages money, 80 percent that many elected officials are dishonest, and 70 percent that government employees are dishonest. If people believe that government is incompetent and government officials corrupt, it's not surprising that 81 percent believe that "fraud and waste in the Social Security system will reduce [their] retirement benefits" (Friedland 1994).

Public apprehension about Social Security's long-range viability reflects more than general distrust in government. It also reflects confusion generated by a public dialogue about such technocratic issues as the integrity of the trust fund as well as broader ideological questions about equity between generations. This dialogue has undermined public faith in social insurance and made tenable discussion of such radical options as means-testing and privatization.

The most recent debate concerns an entitlement "crisis." The entitlement crisis combines the theme of generational equity with dire predictions about the deficit, the erosion of family income, and the future of the economy. This article first identifies two core themes of the entitlement crisis, that entitlement spending is crowding out discretionary spending and that current trends cannot be sustained. It questions the substantive basis of these themes and then critically evaluates two proposals for the restructuring of Social Security, means-testing and privatization.

SOCIAL SECURITY AND THE ENTITLEMENT "CRISIS"

In the summer of 1994, the American public was bombarded with news of an entitlement crisis. It began in the House of Representatives with an "A to Z" spending cut plan for across-the-board cuts in all entitlement programs. It gathered momentum with media reports of progress by the Bipartisan Commission on Entitlement and Tax Reform. Yet, until 1994, few knew what an entitlement was.

Part of the confusion arises from the range of definitions associated with the term *entitlement*. It has a legal meaning, a theoretical meaning, and a budgetary meaning. The concept of an entitlement grew out of the "new property" movement in legal thought in the 1960s when the courts ruled in regard to Aid to Families with Dependent Children that social welfare benefits were not gratuities that could be denied at will. Rather, according to the court decision, "beneficiaries have something akin to property rights in them and therefore have a right to due process in their distribution" (Weaver 1985:308). In the legal sense, then, the term *entitlement* confers a right to benefits.

The theoretical definition of entitlements emphasizes their distinction from means-tested programs in regard to how benefits are distributed and in terms of what their objectives are. Social Security is an entitlement because people obtain eligibility based on prior work history and because it is designed to maintain preretirement living standards. This differentiates it from means-tested programs where eligibility is determined by income and where the objective is to provide a minimal income floor (Marmor et al. 1990). . . .

In the purely budgetary sense, however, what distinguishes entitlements from other programs is that they are governed by formulas set in law and not subject to annual appropriations by Congress (Congressional Budget Office [CBO] 1994a). This latter meaning has become the sole definition in the construction of the entitlement "crisis." Entitlements stand in distinction to two other federal budget categories, discretionary spending, which includes domestic and defense spending, and net interest on the debt. In the federal budget there are more than a hundred programs defined as entitlements, the three largest being Social Security, Medicare, and Medicaid.

The entitlement crisis conveys a range of messages about federal spending. These messages were condensed into two distinct problems by the Bipartisan Commission on Entitlement and Tax Reform. The first is that entitlement spending is consuming a disproportionate share of the federal budget and crowding out funds for other social needs (Bipartisan Commission 1994). The second is that current trends are not sustainable and that entitlements will consume all federal revenues by 2030.

GREEDY ENTITLEMENTS

[According to data provided by the Bipartisan Commission on Entitlement and Tax Reform (1994)], the share of federal spending devoted to entitlements increased from 22.7 percent in 1963 to 47.3 percent by 1993. This message—that entitlements are crowding out spending for domestic programs—derives from the rising deficit, which doubled from 1981 to 1985 from $784 billion to $1,499 billion (U.S. House of Representatives 1994). A recent *Fortune* magazine article (Dowd 1994) illustrates how Social Security has been linked to the deficit:

> Want to pin a face on America's persistent deficit and savings crisis? Forget those hoary cliches—the welfare queen, lazy bureaucrat, greedy business-man, weapons-crazed general or rich Third World potentate living off U.S. aid. Reach instead for a photograph of your mom and dad. That's because the main engine driving federal spending ever upward is the explosive growth in entitlements, programs that churn out benefits aimed mostly at older mid-dle- and upper-middle-[income] Americans. Indeed, you could eliminate all discretionary spending right now—shut down Congress, the federal agen-cies, the national parks, the Pentagon; wipe out waste, fraud and abuse—and thanks to the spending programmed to pour automatically through the enti-tlement spigot, the budget would be gushing red ink again by 2012. (p. 191)

The implication is twofold. First, both entitlements and discretionary spending cannot continue to increase because they will drive up the deficit. Second, even if discretionary spending is drastically cut, no deficit reduction will occur because of wasteful entitlement spending.

There are two problems with the [commission's] "finding." The first is that entitlement spending has not experienced explosive growth, but rather has been stable for more than a decade. The second is that shrinking discretionary spending is not the result of entitlement growth, but rather of tactics by con servatives to reduce the welfare state.

Is not an increase from 22.7 to 47.3 percent in entitlement spending explo-sive growth? As the Interim Report of the Bipartisan Commission on Entitlement and Tax Reform states, "To ensure that funds are available for essential and appropriate government programs, the nation cannot continue to allow entitlements to consume a rapidly increasing share of the federal budget" (Bipartisan Commission 1994:11). The problem with this message is that the bulk of the growth occurred between 1965 and 1975, a result of the start-up costs associated with Medicare, which was passed in 1965. A closer look illustrates that, in the decade between 1983 and 1993, entitlement spending increased by just 2 percent of federal expenditures from 45.2 percent to 47.3 percent.

The more valid measure of expenditure growth, that used by most economists and in all government documents, is the percentage of gross domestic product (GDP). By this measure, entitlement spending has shown almost no growth; it was 11.3 percent of GDP in 1976 and 11.9 percent in 1994 (CBO 1995). Social Security, the real target of this charge of rampant growth, has also remained steady at just over 4 percent of GDP since 1975. It will remain at this level until 2010, when it will rise by 2 percent of GDP as the baby boom generation retires. If there is an entitlement crisis due to rapid growth, it ended in 1975.

What is real is the decline in discretionary spending. It declined from 43.7 percent of federal spending in 1983 to just 38.6 percent by 1993. If entitlement spending growth is not the cause of declining funds for discretionary programs, then what is the cause? The lack of funding is the result of two measures, President Reagan's Economic Recovery Tax Act of 1981 (ERTA), which substantially cut taxes for individuals and corporations, and the Budget Enforcement Act (BEA) of 1990, which placed caps on spending for discretionary programs (CBO 1994b). These measures weakened the revenue base for discretionary social spending.

ERTA's major provisions included cumulative across-the-board reductions in individual income tax rates of 1.25 percent in 1981, 10 percent in 1982, 19 percent in 1983, and 23 percent in 1984 and a reduction in the top marginal rate from 70 percent to 50 percent. ERTA also reduced the maximum tax rate on long-term capital gains to 20 percent and indexed income tax brackets to increases in the consumer price index. Corporate tax rates declined from 17 percent on the first $25,000 of taxable income to 16 percent in 1982 and 15 percent in subsequent years. Taxes on the next $25,000 were reduced by 2 percent (Joint Committee on Taxation 1981).

Discretionary spending includes domestic programs and defense spending. As general revenue funds declined, the costs were borne solely by domestic programs. Defense spending rose. . . . Domestic spending declined from 22 percent of federal expenditures in 1980 to 14.8 percent in 1988. Nearly all the decline occurred in social programs for the poor. Reagan's Omnibus Budget Reconciliation Act of 1981 eliminated the entire public service jobs program, removed 400,000 individuals from the food stamp program, and reduced or eliminated AFDC and Medicaid benefits for the working poor. Residents of public housing were now required to pay 30 instead of 25 percent of their income toward rent (Quadagno 1994). As a result of these cuts, domestic spending declined from 4.9 percent of GDP in 1980 to 3.3 percent of GDP by 1987 (CBO 1995).

In that same period, defense spending more than doubled from $144 billion to $295 billion, and from 22.9 percent of federal expenditures to 27.3 percent (CBO 1994a). By 1991, defense spending was $319 billion.

Discretionary spending caps control annual appropriations decisions made by Congress by placing caps on the amount of discretionary appropriations that can be enacted each year (Kee and Nystrom 1991). If these caps are exceeded, automatic across-the-board cuts in appropriations are supposed to reduce aggregate spending. The BEA also included "pay-as-you-go" (PAYGO) rules mandating that any increased spending in one program be offset by cuts in other programs. Thus, domestic spending growth has been halted by the combination of the 1981 tax cut and the budget caps and PAYGO rules, not because of rising entitlements.

To summarize, a 1981 tax cut weakened the revenue base for discretionary programs, and mandatory spending caps strengthened the hands of budget cutters. These tactics increased the vulnerability of Social Security to charges that it was devouring an unfair share of federal revenues.

A puzzle remains. Yearly federal revenues did not decline following ERTA but remained stable. The explanation is that revenues from the payroll tax increase enacted as part of the Social Security Amendments in 1983 replaced revenues lost from ERTA. Following the 1981 tax cut, *general revenues* did drop sharply, but payroll tax revenues began rising. It was payroll tax revenues that financed the defense buildup and that are presently paying for a significant share of domestic programs.

The payroll tax hikes were intended to restore solvency to the Social Security trust fund, not to build up a reserve. As [the staff director] of the National Commission on Social Security Reform recalls, "The building up of a huge fund that would peak in the midst of the baby boomers' retirement was a coincidence—or at most, an unintended byproduct of the recommendations" (Myers 1988). Nonetheless, the reserve grew, providing an alternative source of revenues for discretionary programs.

This reserve buildup has allowed critics to expound the message that the trust fund is full of worthless IOUs and burdening future generations. According to one critic of Social Security, former commissioner Dorcas Hardy, "There are no real dollars in the Social Security trust funds. . . . The trust funds are, in effect, merely a growing stack of IOUs that will need to be redeemed in the future in order to meet program obligations" (Hardy 1993). . . .

To protect Social Security against such claims, program advocates have adopted a counterstrategy, that of declaring the trust fund "off-budget." The 1983 National Commission on Social Security Reform recommended removing Social Security from federal budget calculations "in order to insulate this trust fund from budgetary politics" (Chambers and Rotherham 1994:7). The 1983 amendments to the Social Security Act specified that beginning in 1993, income and expenditures from Old Age Survivors and Disability Insurance (OASDI) and Medicare would be *excluded* from the budget totals of the President and Congress. In the interim, the act specified that income from these trust funds be prominently displayed in the Presidential and Congressional budgets as *separate* categories (Koitz 1993).

Then in 1985, the Balanced Budget and Emergency Deficit Control Act further altered Social Security's budget treatment. The act specified two contradictory measures. On the one hand, it accelerated the off-budget treatment of Social Security, moving it up from 1993 to 1985. On the other hand, it specified that Social Security trust funds be counted in calculating budget deficits and in enforcing the deficit reduction goals established under the act (Koitz 1993). As a result, federal budget calculations began showing what the figures would be with and without Social Security. Then, in 1990, the Omnibus Budget Reconciliation Act removed all calculations of the Social Security trust funds from the federal budget. The purpose was to prevent the surplus in the Social Security trust fund from masking the extent of the deficit (Koitz 1995). Although Social Security became off-budget in 1990, payroll taxes continued to be deposited in the general treasury, with the appropriate crediting of securities to the trust funds, and benefits continued to be paid out of the general treasury.

Proponents of Social Security have sought to protect the program by weakening possibilities for program cuts. Programmatically, this tactic has succeeded; but ideologically, it has provided critics with a new critique. The ensuing debate has contributed to public confusion over the status of the trust fund and further undermined confidence in the program.

THE UNSUSTAINABLE FUTURE

A message with widespread public appeal is that of preserving the American dream for future generations. As outlined by a Republican pollster ("Attention" 1995):

> Your challenge is to create "The New America," the post–welfare state vision as powerful to Americans as the New Deal was 60 years ago. . . . Remember

that many Americans perceive the key challenge ahead in moral terms rather than economic terms. . . . Put the budget debate in terms of the "American Dream" and "our Children's Future." (section 4, p. 7)

With no immediate crisis in sight, conservative critics of Social Security have used the salable message of protecting the American dream for the next generation to describe a future crisis. This crisis is depicted with the [commission] "finding" that "current trends are not sustainable." The "finding" is based on thirty-year projections for Social Security, Medicare, Medicaid, federal employees' retirement benefits, and more than a hundred other entitlements. The accuracy of the finding depends on the validity of the projections.

The model for such long-term projections is Social Security, which itself is subject to a variety of inevitable inaccuracies as well as political manipulation. The Social Security actuaries yearly make projections about the long-range solvency of the Social Security trust fund (Board of Trustees 1994). These projections are based on assumptions about future economic and demographic trends. Their purpose is to estimate whether the system's resources and expenditures are somewhat aligned (Koitz 1986).

According to present projections, the Social Security trust fund will be insolvent by 2031 (Koitz and Kollmann 1995). These long-term projections have now become the grist for a new crisis, which combines fears about the economy with concern for future generations. As the National Taxpayers Union warns, we face "a huge financing gap that must be closed if tomorrow's promised benefits are to be paid at all" (Howe and Jackson 1994, chart 4-30). The problem with this message is that a crisis thirty years in the future may undermine confidence in the program, but it is unlikely to create sentiment for change, especially when experts explain that modest changes would restore the Social Security system to long-range actuarial balance. With a Social Security crisis as a dubious political weapon, critics have instead used the estimates as a base for a larger entitlement crisis, an unsustainable future. The severity of the crisis depends on the accuracy of the projections.

The commission's entitlement spending growth estimates are modeled after actuaries' predictions for Social Security and Medicare. Social Security is predicted to increase by less than 2 percent of GDP by 2030, a matter of concern but hardly a crisis. Health care costs have been rising rapidly, so the "crisis" must be in the two health care programs, Medicare and Medicaid. However, the Medicaid projections were based on a set of assumptions that have no programmatic or economic basis. . . .

Medicaid is projected to rise in concert with Medicare even though the two programs cover different population groups, pay for different services, and have different patterns of past growth. Medicare is a federal program that pays for inpatient hospital services and physician services for people over age 65, the disabled, and victims of chronic kidney disease. Medicaid is a federal-state health insurance program for low-income persons who are aged, blind, disabled, members of families with dependent children, and pregnant women and children. Medicaid eligibility is linked to eligibility for two means-tested welfare programs, AFDC and SSI. It also pays for nursing home care for the elderly and disabled (U.S. House of Representatives 1994). In the past there has been no correlation in growth between the two programs. From 1966 to 1993, Medicare spending increased much more rapidly than Medicaid spending. During the 1980s, Medicaid spending remained stable at 0.6 percent of GDP, while Medicare spending rose from 1.4 to 2.0 percent of GDP (CBO 1995). If program costs were not correlated in the past, why should they be correlated in the future?

Even if the Medicaid projections rested on programmatically plausible assumptions, which they do not, there is reason to question the validity of any thirty-year estimates. The Congressional Budget Office (1994a) provides numerous warnings regarding the accuracy of even ten-year projections:

> Great uncertainties surround such long-range extrapolations. The economy's performance is a big question mark; these projection[s] are predicated on continued growth in real GDP of 2.3 percent annually in 2000 through 2004, on inflation of 3.1 percent, and on short-term and long-term interest rates (specifically, rates on three-month Treasury notes and ten-year Treasury notes) of 4.7 percent and 6.2 percent, respectively. The economy is bound to deviate from these assumptions in ways that cannot be anticipated. And other major uncertainties abound, most notably about future trends in health care spending and about other open-ended commitments. (p. 28)

The warning is well taken. The 1993 budget projections made by the General Accounting Office (GAO) for President Clinton's 1994 budget were off by 23 percent in less than two years (GAO 1995a). How much faith can one place in thirty-five-year projections that combine all entitlement spending in one category? The answer is none.

Although the entitlement crisis lacks a factual basis, the charts and measures used to define it have not only become embedded in public debates, they have also become accepted estimates in official government documents. A 1995 report by the General Accounting Office makes the following disclaimer regarding Medicaid projections: "The Medicaid program presents a major estimating challenge. Each state makes different program choices. Further, eligibility is hard to predict, benefits are not cash, implementation and financing are shared among multiple parties and levels of government, and interactions with other programs are complex" (GAO 1995a:14).

Nonetheless, the GAO used the Entitlement Commission's Medicaid estimates unquestioningly for its long-term simulation model of future mandatory spending (GAO 1995b).

Through most of the twentieth century, the image of a trust fund ensured beneficiaries that their payroll tax contributions were held in a separate account, autonomous from other less trustworthy government activities. Over the past twenty years, this image has withered. Long-term projections of trust fund insolvency have become a potent symbol in the entitlement crisis.

PROPOSALS FOR RETRENCHMENT

Although the entitlement "crisis" has thus far had no programmatic impact, it has undermined further confidence in Social Security. As a result, critics have been able to make proposals for radical cuts that would have been unheard of even five years ago. Proposals now receiving serious attention include means-testing benefits and privatization.

MEANS-TESTING

Recently, means-testing Social Security benefits has been proposed as a way to reduce the deficit and relieve younger workers of an unfair tax burden. Advocates of means-testing argue that paying benefits to wealthy older people can no longer be justified when the tax burden is borne by low-income young workers. Means-testing is fair, they contend, because it would target benefits to those most in need.

The Final Report of the Bipartisan Commission on Entitlement and Tax Reform includes a proposal by commission member Peter Peterson to means-test all entitlements. The means test or "affluence test" would be

administered through the tax code with all taxpayers with incomes above the U.S. household median required to report all their estimated combined federal benefits for the coming year. . . . Households with incomes under $40,000 would not lose a penny in benefits. . . . Higher income households would lose 10 percent of all benefits that cause their incomes to exceed $40,000 plus 10 percent for each additional $10,000 in income. (Bipartisan Commission 1995:58)

Social insurance advocates have used two arguments to counter means-testing proposals. The first invokes the theoretical definition of entitlements as distinct from poverty-based programs. Invoking Americans' historical aversion to welfare, Eric Kingson (1994) explains: "As an earned right, social insurance benefits are not subject to a means test, a process that nearly all citizens consider demeaning" (p. 737). Similarly, according to the National Council of Senior Citizens (1994), "by denying or seriously reducing benefits to the middle class and well-to-do, Social Security and Medicare would be transformed from popular 'earned right' programs into 'welfare' programs that would benefit only the poor and lower-income" (p. 1).

The problem with this response is that it defines means-testing in the traditional sense, as a way of targeting benefits to the poor. The affluence test is not designed to target the poor, however, but rather to exclude the upper end of the middle-class income distribution. In this regard, it shares many of the characteristics of the income taxation of benefits already in place. As Peterson asks, "How does an affluence test differ in principle from progressive benefit taxation?" (Bipartisan Commission 1995:59). In fact, the distinction between means-testing and taxation of benefits is ambiguous. These complexities undermine the political argument against means-testing.

Because it is difficult to argue that a plan that excludes only the more affluent elderly is stigmatizing and demeaning, advocates have been forced to depend on a political argument. The political argument draws upon "middle-class universalism" as a justification for maintaining Social Security in its present form. Skocpol (1991), for example, contends that "while targeted programs generate forces that undo their aims, social policies that deliver benefits across classes and races generate broad, cross-class political coalitions that sustain and protect the policies" (p. 413). Similarly, Kingson (1994) asserts that "means-testing would undermine the political support, the legitimacy, and ultimately the financing of Social Security" (p. 740). The implication of these arguments is clear. Means-tested benefits cannot sustain public support if high earners are alienated from the program. Massive cuts in benefits will be inevitable.

Increasingly, liberal advocates of young, working families disagree with this logic. They point to programs such as the Earned Income Tax Credit (EITC) as "overwhelmingly popular and non-stigmatizing despite being means-tested" (Kaus 1994:120). They also contend that means-tested programs do not invariably alienate the public and are not invariably subject to cuts. Robert Greenstein (1994), director of a liberal think tank, for example, notes that even during the Reagan administration, when many social programs experienced large cuts, food stamps, the EITC, and Medicaid remained intact. Since 1980, other means-tested programs have expanded, and many, like the EITC, Women, Infants, and Children Program (WIC) or the Child Assistance Program Demonstration in New York state, provide benefits with dignity (Greenstein 1994). Present proposed cuts in the EITC undermine this argument, however.

PRIVATIZATION

Another option is the privatization of a portion of payroll taxes. In 1995, two prominent senators, Robert Kerrey (D-Nebr.) and Alan Simpson (R-Wyo.), introduced the Personal Investment Plan Act of 1995. As a revised version of a proposal in the *Final Report* of the Bipartisan Commission on Entitlement and Tax Reform, the act would allow workers the option of diverting 2 percent of their payroll taxes to their own personal investment plans. Employees would be allowed to invest their contributions either into an investment fund or into an Individual Retirement Account (IRA). The objective is to increase the national savings rate.

Proponents of Social Security respond to these charges by calling upon the social insurance characteristic of redistribution. Social Security is not strictly an annuity system, they contend. If it were, each worker's potential return on contributions would be the same, and the program could be evaluated against other methods of saving for retirement. But Social Security has social as well as insurance goals. The system was designed to give a better rate of return to some workers than to others, and to provide noncontributory dependents' benefits. As the AARP (1994) explains, "Social Security is different from a private pension. It is an almost universal social insurance program established by the government to provide income protection to workers and their families if the wage earner retires, becomes disabled or dies" (p. 17).

The debate over privatization has forced program advocates to respond in the language of private annuities and to contend that Social Security contributions represent an investment. According to Kingson (1994) "Even the well-off should have a reasonable return on their Social Security investment" (p. 740).

But if Social Security represents an investment with calculable rates of return, then it loses its moral legitimacy as a social insurance program.

Presently, there is no evidence that privatization of benefits would increase savings, and no evidence that private investments would provide an adequate substitute for Social Security benefits, at least for lower-income workers. Rather, past experience suggests that, unless these funds were highly regulated, people would be likely to withdraw them and use them as family needs arose. Further, if opting out of payroll taxes were voluntary, then one must consider how the entire system would be affected. Presently, the taxes of higher-income workers subsidize the benefits of low-income workers. One likely scenario is that high-income workers would opt out, but low-income workers would remain under the present system. That's what happened in Great Britain because the set-up costs of the optional plans made opting out too costly for low-income workers (Daykin 1994).

Both means-testing and privatization would fundamentally alter the core feature that makes Social Security a program of social insurance—the redistribution of income—by providing higher-income workers an alternative set of incentives. In the case of means-testing, higher-income workers would no longer view their payroll taxes as contributions because they would receive no benefits. In the case of privatization, higher-income workers, especially younger workers, would be most likely to opt out, and it is their taxes that subsidize the higher replacement rates of lower-income workers. Both options would further undermine the moral framework that has sustained public support for Social Security by fracturing solidarity along lines of class and generation.

In an era of mass-mediated political change, power struggles are not merely a matter of who gets what, but also of who defines what. The United States is presently engaged in a power struggle over the parameters of welfare state restructuring. Thus far, the battle has been waged at the ideological level. Although public support for Social Security remains high, confidence has declined, because discussion of options for reform have been narrowly circumscribed around budgetary issues. Other definitions of Social Security, as a program that provides an earned benefit, as a program that maintains pre-retirement living standards, and as a program that protects families over the life course have become extraneous to ongoing debates.

This is not to imply that the budgetary issues have no relevance. The debate over entitlements does have a material base, which is grounded in declining economic growth and declining family incomes. For a hundred years, from 1870

to 1972, the American economy grew at an annual rate of 3.4 percent after inflation. Then between 1973 and 1994, it grew only 2.3 percent a year. Recent estimates of the cost of slow growth is a $12 trillion dollar loss of goods and services
produced by the economy (Maddison 1991).

The causes of declining economic growth are complex and subject to much
debate among economists. Among the explanations proposed are that foreign
competition has reduced the domestic market for mass-produced goods, that
the offshore growth of U.S.–owned multinational corporations has helped to
erode the domestic wage base and reduce employment, and that rising deficits
have increased interest rates and reduced investment capital. Regardless of the
cause, the consequences have been damaging to workers and families. In the
past twenty years, average wages have fallen for most categories of workers; the
poverty rate, even for those who work full time, has increased; and incomes for
even the best educated have grown more slowly than in the past (Maddison
1991:50–53).

These trends are not distinct to the United States but are occurring in most
Western, capitalist democracies. They raise legitimate issues about how to protect vulnerable families and how to enhance economic growth. Yet, when discussion of these issues becomes absorbed into an entitlement "crisis," possibilities for rational problem solving dissipate. As *Washington Post* columnist
Robert Samuelson (1996) recognizes, "In politics words do matter. They help
create a climate of opinion. The abuse of language subverts reasoned debate.
Exaggeration, simplification and distortion are normal parts of political
debate. But the more these excesses are compounded, the harder discussion
becomes" (p. 5). Social constructions like an entitlement crisis thwart reasoned
public discussion of social needs and legitimate options for responding to
those needs.

NOTES

This article is based on a Distinguished Scholar lecture presented to the Section on
Aging, American Sociological Association, Washington, D.C., in August 1995. This
research was supported by a John Simon Guggenheim Memorial Fellowship, an
American Council of Learned Societies Fellowship, and a Congressional Fellowship
from the American Sociological Association. John Myles, Chris Howard, Theda
Skocpol, Hans Reimer, Eric Kingson, and James Schulz made helpful comments on
a previous version of this article.

REFERENCES

American Association of Retired Persons. (1994). *Public opinion on entitlement programs* (Research Report from AARP Research Division). Unpublished manuscript.

Attention! All sales reps for the Contract with America. (1995, February 5). *New York Times*, section 4, p. 7.

Balanced Budget and Emergency Deficit Control Act of 1985. (1985). Gramm-Rudman-Hollings Act, 101st Congress; Public Law 99-177. Washington, D.C.: U.S. Government Printing Office.

Bipartisan Commission on Entitlement and Tax Reform. (1994). *Interim report to the President.* Washington, D.C.: Superintendent of Documents.

Bipartisan Commission on Entitlement and Tax Reform. (1995). *Final report to the President.* Washington, D.C.: U.S. Government Printing Office.

Board of Trustees of the Federal Old Age and Survivors Insurance and Disability Insurance Trust Fund. (1994). *Annual report.* Washington, D.C.: U.S. Government Printing Office.

Budget Enforcement Act of 1990. (1990). *Title XIII of the Omnibus Budget Reconciliation Act of 1990.* Washington, D.C.: U.S. Government Printing Office.

Chambers, L., and Rotherham, J. A. (1994). *Social Security financing.* Washington, D.C.: National Committee to Preserve Social Security and Medicare.

Congressional Budget Office. (1994a). *The economic and budget outlook: Fiscal years 1995–1999.* Washington, D.C.: U.S. Government Printing Office.

Congressional Budget Office. (1994b). *Reducing the deficit.* Washington, D.C.: U.S. Government Printing Office.

Congressional Budget Office. (1995). *The economic and budget outlook: Fiscal years 1996–2000.* Washington, D.C.: U.S. Government Printing Office.

Cook, F. L., and Barrett, E. J. (1992). *Support for the American welfare state: The views of Congress and the public.* New York: Columbia University Press.

Daykin, C. (1994, May 5–6). *Occupational pension provision in the United Kingdom.* Paper presented at the 1994 Pension Research Council Symposium, "Security Employer-Based Pensions: An International Perspective." Wharton School, University of Pennsylvania.

Dowd, A. R. (1994, November 14). Needed: A new war on the deficit. *Fortune*, pp. 191–192.

Economic Recovery Tax Act of 1981. (1981). H.R. 4242, 97th Congress; Public Law 97-34. Staff of the Joint Committee on Taxation. Washington, D.C.: U.S. Government Printing Office.

Friedland, R. (1994). *When support and confidence are at odds: The public's under-*

standing of the Social Security program. Washington, D.C.: National Academy of Social Insurance.

General Accounting Office. (1995a). *Fiscal year 1994 budget estimates and actual results* (Report to the Chairman, Committee on the Budget, House of Representatives). Washington, D.C.: General Accounting Office.

General Accounting Office. (1995b). *The deficit and the economy. An update of long-term simulations* (Report to the Chairman, Committee on the Budget, U.S. Senate and the Chairman, Committee on the Budget, House of Representatives). Washington, D.C.: General Accounting Office.

Greenstein, R. (1994). Comments. In R. Friedland, L. Etheredge, and B. Vladeck (Eds.), *Social welfare policy at the crossroads: Rethinking the roles of social insurance, tax expenditures, mandates, and means-testing*. Washington, D.C.: National Academy of Social Insurance.

Hardy, D. (1993, August). The Social Security trust funds: Myth or reality? *United Seniors Association Newsletter*, pp. 1–7.

Howe, N., and Jackson, R. (1994). *Entitlements and the aging of America*. Washington, D.C.: National Taxpayers Union Foundation.

Joint Committee on Taxation. (1981). *General explanation of the Economic Recovery Tax Act of 1981, H.R. 4242, 97th Congress; Public Law 97-34*. Washington, D.C.: U.S. Government Printing Office.

Kaus, M. (1994). The case for means-testing. In R. Friedland, L. Etheredge, and B. Vladeck (Eds.), *Social welfare policy at the crossroads: Rethinking the role of social insurance, tax expenditures, mandates, and means-testing*. Washington, D.C.: National Academy of Social Insurance.

Kee, J. E., and Nystrom, S. V. (1991, Spring). The 1990 budget package: Redefining the debate. *Budgeting and Public Finance*, 3–24.

Kingson, E. (1994). Testing the boundaries of universality. *The Gerontologist, 34*, 733–740.

Koitz, D. (1986). *Social Security: Its funding outlook and significance for government finance*. Washington, D.C.: Library of Congress.

Koitz, D. (1993). *Social Security: Its removal from the budget and procedures for considering changes to the program*. Washington, D.C.: Library of Congress.

Koitz, D. (1995). *Social Security's treatment under the federal budget: A summary*. Washington, D.C.: Library of Congress.

Koitz, D., and Kollmann, G. (1995). *The financial outlook for Social Security and Medicare*. Washington, D.C.: Congressional Research Service.

Maddison, A. (1991). *Dynamic forces in capitalist development*. New York: Oxford University Press.

Marmor, T., Mashaw, J. L., and Harvey, P. (1990). *America's misunderstood welfare state*. New York: Basic Books.

Myers, R. (1988, October). Two current widespread myths about Social Security financing. *Generational Journal*, 3–8.

National Academy of Social Insurance. (1994). *Social Security: Public support and public confidence*. Seventh Annual Conference, National Academy of Social Insurance, Washington, D.C.

National Council of Senior Citizens. (1994). *A crash course on the entitlement debate*. Washington, D.C.: National Council of Senior Citizens.

Omnibus Budget Reconciliation Act of 1990. (1990). H.R. 5835, 106th Congress; Public Laws 101–403. Washington, D.C.: U.S. Government Printing Office.

Personal Investment Plan Act of 1995. (1995). Introduced May 18, 1995. U.S. Senate: Washington, D.C.

Quadagno, J. (1994). *The color of welfare: How racism undermined the War on Poverty*. New York: Oxford University Press.

Samuelson, R. J. (1996, January 8). You call this a revolution? *Washington Post National Weekly Edition*, p. 5.

Skocpol, T. (1991). Targeting within universalism: Politically viable policies to combat poverty in the United States. In C. Jencks and P. E. Peterson (Eds.), *The urban underclass* (pp. 411–436). Washington, D.C.: Brookings Institution.

Skocpol, T. (1995, January 24). *Why it happened: The rise and resounding demise of the Clinton Health Security Plan*. Paper presented at the Brookings Institution, conference on The Past and Future of Health Reform, Washington, D.C.

Social Security Amendments of 1983. (1983). H.R. 1900, April 21. Washington, D.C.: U.S. Government Printing Office.

U.S. House of Representatives. (1994). *Overview of entitlement programs, 1994 green book*. Committee on Ways and Means, 103d Congress, 2d Sess.

Weaver, K. (1985). Controlling entitlements. In J. Chubb and P. E. Peterson (Eds.), *The new direction in American politics* (pp. 307–341). Washington, D.C.: Brookings Institution.

CHAPTER NINE

Scapegoating the Old: Intergenerational Equity and Age-Based Health Care Rationing

Robert H. Binstock

Robert H. Binstock, a political scientist, is the Henry R. Luce Professor of Aging, Health, and Society at Case Western Reserve University School of Medicine. He is a former president of the Gerontological Society of America and co-editor of the *Handbook of Aging and the Social Sciences* now in its fourth edition. Among his other books are *The Future of Long-Term Care: Social and Policy Issues*, *Dementia and Aging: Ethics, Values, and Policy Choices*, and *Too Old for Health Care?*

Binstock asserts that intergenerational conflict does not exist and that issues which are framed in terms of conflicts between age groups are based on spurious assumptions. Binstock suggests that the elderly have been unfairly stereotyped as self-interested, and he suggests that rising health care costs do not necessarily hurt the global position of the American economy.

In 1984 the National Institute on Aging launched a major research initiative focused on the oldest old, persons aged 85 years and older (U.S. Department of Health and Human Services 1984). The initiative has proven to be a timely measure for better understanding the implications of population aging because it has generated valuable studies of a swiftly growing group in which the prevalence of chronic illnesses and disabilities is very high compared with that of other age groups within the older population.

This focus on the oldest old, however, is highly susceptible to familiar mechanisms of distortion that may generate unwarranted stereotypes of persons in this older age range. In turn, such stereotypes may exacerbate the implications of contemporary issues of so-called intergenerational equity, in some instances with pernicious implications for older persons and our society in general.

This chapter analyzes the emergence of issues of intergenerational equity, showing that they are spuriously constructed on the basis of inaccurate old-age stereotypes, superficial reasoning, and unrealistic extrapolations from existing public policies. It suggests how stereotypes of the oldest old may fit into the scenarios framed by these issues. Further, it illustrates how artificial issues of intergenerational equity—such as "justice between age groups" in the allocation of health care—divert our attention from seeking more useful alternative issues to confront in dealing with our domestic social-policy dilemmas.

THE PUBLIC POLICY CONTEXT

Studies of the oldest old are emerging in a climate of American politics and public discourse that is increasingly hostile to older persons in general. As we begin the 1990s, public resources are perceived as scarce. The need to "reduce the deficit" is a rhetorical mainstay of domestic politics. "Containing health care costs" is widely considered to be one of the major problems of our day.

Population aging is commonly perceived as worsening each of these problems, and others as well. Many issues of domestic policy portray "the aged" as in conflict with other groups of Americans or as a growing and unsustainable burden that will undermine our national well-being. How did this political hostility to older persons develop?

COMPASSIONATE AGEISM AND THE "OLD-AGE WELFARE STATE"

From the Social Security Act of 1935 through the 1970s, American policies toward older persons have been adopted and amended in substantially different social,

economic, and political contexts. Interpretations of the original goals of such policies vary widely (Achenbaum 1983; Campion 1984; Cohen 1985b; David 1985;
Derthick 1979; Graebner 1980; Harris 1966; Holtzman 1963; Marmor 1970).

Regardless of the original intent of various policies toward aging, by the late
1960s and early 1970s a common theme was taking shape: Through the cumulative impact of many disparate legislative actions, American society had adopted
and financed a number of age-categorical benefit programs and tax and price
subsidies for which eligibility is not determined by need. Through Social
Security, Medicare, the Older Americans Act, and a variety of other measures,
older persons were exempted from the screenings that are customarily applied to
other Americans in order to determine whether they are worthy of public help.

This theme was strengthened as a number of old-age-based interest groups
articulated compassionate stereotypes of older persons (Binstock 1972; Pratt
1976). These advocates for the aged told us repeatedly that the elderly are poor,
frail, socially dependent, objects of discrimination, and, above all, *deserving*
(Kalish 1979).

Through this compassionate ageism—the attribution of the same characteristics, status, and just deserts to the elderly—advocates managed to artificially
homogenize, package, label, and market a heterogeneous group of older persons as "the aged" (Binstock 1983). However, ageism, in contrast with racism,
has provided many benefits to older persons (Kutza 1981).

Because older persons came to be stereotyped as the "deserving poor," programs for the aged have not been subject to the disdain and stigmatization
attached to other welfare programs in American political culture. In truth, of
course, any of the "deserving" needs for collective assistance that have been
symbolized by compassionate old-age stereotypes can be found among persons
of all ages. Yet, the great bulk of our social-welfare and health expenditures is
for benefits to the aged.

THE EMERGENCE OF THE AGED AS SCAPEGOAT

Since 1978, however, the long-standing compassionate stereotypes of older persons have been undergoing an extraordinary reversal (Binstock 1983). Older
persons have come to be portrayed as one of the more flourishing and powerful groups in American society and have been attacked as a burdensome
responsibility. These new stereotypes, devoid of compassion, are:

1. The aged are relatively well off—not poor, but in great economic shape.
2. The aged are a potent political force because there are so many of them and

they all vote in their self-interest; this "senior power" explains why more than one-quarter of the annual federal budget is spent on benefits to the aged.

3. Because of demographic changes, the aged are becoming more numerous and politically powerful, and will claim even more benefits and substantially larger proportions of the federal budget. They are already costing too much, and in the future will pose an unsustainable burden for the American economy.

Even as the earlier compassionate stereotypes of older persons were partially unwarranted, so are these current stereotypes. They are generated by applying simplistic assumptions and aggregate statistics to a group called "the aged" in order to gloss over complexities. If one chooses to compare changes in the median or average income of all older persons with changes in the income of other groups, one can conclude that the aged are relatively well off and ignore millions of older persons who are in dire economic circumstances (Smeeding 1990). If one wishes to ignore abundant evidence to the contrary (Hudson and Strate 1985; Jacobs 1990), one can assume that the votes of older persons are determined by issues, and one particular issue above all others, which they will respond to with self-interest, and that their self-interests will be common. If one pretends that outlays for Medicare, Old Age Insurance, and other policies are mechanistically determined by demographics rather than by legislative and administrative decisions, one can conclude that benefits to the aged constitute an unsustainable burden for the American economy. Certainly, the enactment of the Medicare Catastrophic Coverage Act of 1988 and its speedy repeal in 1989 (Findlay 1989; Tolchin 1989) should remind us that extrapolation from existing policies and institutional arrangements is a poor mode of prediction.

The new stereotypes of older persons began to appear in the late 1970s during a so-called crisis in the cash flow of the Social Security system, within the larger context of a depressed economy during President Carter's administration (Estes 1983). Although this cash-flow problem may have been an immediate precipitating factor, two more fundamental elements seem to account prominently for the reversal of stereotypes.

One element was a tremendous growth in the amount of federal funds expended on benefits to the aging, which journalists (Samuelson 1978) and academicians (Hudson 1978) began to notice and publicize in the late 1970s. By 1982 an economist in the U.S. Office of Management and Budget (Torrey 1982) had reframed the classical trade-off metaphor of political economy from "guns versus butter" to "guns versus canes." By the late 1980s, the proportion of the annual federal budget being spent on benefits to the aging had remained at about 26 percent for more than a decade (U.S. Senate 1988) and had been widely recognized as one of the few large expenditure categories in the federal budget (along with national defense and interest on the national debt).

Another element in the reversal of old-age stereotypes was dramatic improvement in the aggregate status of older Americans, in large measure due to the impact of federal benefit programs. . . .

Regardless of specific causes, the reversal of stereotypes continued throughout the 1980s to the point where the new stereotypes can now be readily observed in popular culture. Typical of contemporary depictions of older persons was a "cover story" in *Time* Magazine entitled "Grays on the Go" (Gibbs 1988). . . . Older persons were pictured as America's new elite—healthy, wealthy, powerful, and "staging history's biggest retirement party."

A dominant theme in such portrayals of older persons is that their selfishness is ruining the nation. The *New Republic* highlighted this motif early in 1988 with a cover displaying "Greedy Geezers" (Fairlie 1988). . . . Or, as a *New York Times* "Op-Ed" article was headlined: "Elderly, Affluent—and Selfish" (Longman 1989).

In serious forums of public discourse these new stereotypes have bolstered the use of the aged as a scapegoat for an impressive list of American problems. As social psychologist Gordon Allport observed in his classic work the *ABC's of Scapegoating*: "An issue seems nicely simplified if we blame a group or class of people rather than the complex course of social and historical forces" (1959:13–14).

Advocates for children and demographer Samuel Preston (1984) have blamed the political power of the elderly for the plight of youngsters who have inadequate nutrition, health care, and education and lack supportive family environments. Former secretary of commerce Peter Peterson (1987) has suggested that a prerequisite for the United States to regain its stature as a first-class power in the world economy is a sharp reduction in programs benefiting older Americans. . . .

Perhaps the most serious scapegoating of the aged—in terms of the vulnerability of older persons, the oldest old, and, maybe, of all persons in our society—has been in the area of health care. A widespread concern about high rates of inflation in health care costs has been refocused in the past few years from health care providers, suppliers, administrators, and insurers—the parties that are responsible for setting the prices of care—to the elderly patients for whom health care is provided and who pay for more than 40 percent of their aggregate care (U.S. House of Representatives 1989:8).

Americans aged 65 and older, about 12 percent of our population, account for one-third of the nation's annual health care expenditures, over $175 billion in 1988 (U.S. House of Representatives 1989:4). Because the elderly population is growing, absolutely and proportionately, health care costs for older persons have been depicted as an unsustainable burden, or as ethicist Daniel Callahan has put it, "a great fiscal black hole" that will absorb an unlimited amount of our national resources (1987:17). Indeed, because of concerns for health care costs of the old, in 1984 the then Governor of Colorado, Richard Lamm, was widely reported to have pronounced that terminally ill old people have a "duty to die and get out of the way" (Slater 1984).

AMERICANS FOR INTERGENERATIONAL EQUITY

Parallel to this emergence of the aged as scapegoat for a number of societal problems were the activities of a new organization, Americans for Generational Equity (AGE). Established to propound issues of "intergenerational equity," it had solid financial backing from the corporate sector as well as political support from selected members of Congress (Quadagno 1989)....

Each year AGE organized conferences focused on themes suggesting that public expenditures on older persons were wasteful and should be reallocated to younger age groups. For example, at a conference entitled "Medicare and the Baby Boom Generation," one of the organization's prominent board members espoused the view that "in the interest of doing the greatest good for the greatest number, some forms of medical intervention should be denied, as a matter of government policy, to elderly or terminally ill patients" (Lamm 1987:77).

Central to AGE's credo was the proposition that the large aggregate of public transfers of income and other benefits to today's cohorts of older persons, financed through burdensome taxes on the contemporary labor force, were unlikely to be available in the future as old-age benefits (e.g., Social Security and Medicare) when the present cohort of workers becomes elderly retirees (Longman 1987). Moreover, AGE contrasted the relatively prosperous circumstances of the elderly with those of other groups such as disadvantaged children and an estimated 37 million Americans who lack health insurance....

Some members of Congress, like Senator David Durenberger of Minnesota, were among the founding members of Americans for Generational Equity, and they recruited former Governor Lamm, demographer Preston, biomedical ethicist Callahan, and others of like mind to their organization....

AGE's basic approach—framing public policy questions as issues of inter-generational conflict—seemed to reflect and/or to capture successfully the mind-set of the media and of powerful members of Congress. For example, as the Medicare Catastrophic Act of 1988 was repealed in November 1989, Congressman Dan Rostenkowski, Chairman of the House Ways and Means Committee, observed: "One of the most unhappy results of our ongoing bud-get gridlock has been an uneven contest between the very young and the very old." He said that "the sad story of the 1980s" was that "the old have gotten more while the young have gotten less" (Tolchin 1989).

THE OLDEST OLD AND "INTERGENERATIONAL EQUITY"

The oldest old are receiving attention at a time when issues of intergenerational equity have become axioms of public rhetoric. In this context it is more than possible that the subgroup of persons aged 85 and over will become subject to stereotyping on the basis of multiple old-age categories. "The oldest old," in contrast with "the aging," could well become a common label for extreme con-ditions of frailty, disease, disability, and social dependency among the elderly.

A notable precedent in such a stratification of old-age stereotypes took place in the 1980s through, ironically, a distortion of Bernice Neugarten's (1974) effort to break down age-based stereotypes. It became a widespread practice to label persons 65 to 74 years of age as the "young old" and to perceive all persons in this age group as healthy and capable of earning income. If retired, they were seen as a rich reservoir of resources to be drawn upon for providing unpaid social and health services and fulfilling a variety of other community roles (Kieffer 1986). In contrast, persons aged 75 and older became commonly termed the "old old" and tended to be saddled with the traditional compassionate stereotypes of older persons as poor and frail.

These age-stratified conventions that developed in the 1980s staked out—in effect—a high ground in the politics of compassionate ageism. They served politically to legitimate marginal changes in the traditional ages used for old-age categorical policies, without the need to confront the basic issue of whether it makes sense to continue policies that utilize old-age categories, rather than need, for determining eligibility (Neugarten 1982). For example, due to the Social Security Reform Act of 1983, the age of initial eligibility for full Old Age Insurance benefits is scheduled to rise gradually from age 65 to 67 early in the next century. Furthermore, many suggestions have been made for moving the age of Medicare eligibility up to age 67, 70, or even 75. In short, a multiplication of strata for old-age stereotypes has made it easier politically to effect minor changes in the ages that are used as very crude markers in public policies for approximating those among the elderly who may need collective assistance of one kind or another.

Today the label "oldest old" may breed a new level in the stratification of old-age stereotypes. In turn, stereotypes of the oldest old may shape political issues and policy choices. Such stereotypes may be inaccurate, based on misinformation and misconceptions. But, nonetheless, they may have important consequences for how America copes with the challenges of population aging.

The term "intergenerational equity" has already become a sweeping conventional label for describing trade-offs in health and social-welfare allocations. In turn, it has spawned a series of metaphors to describe dilemmas in particular sectors of American life: a perceived need for new principles by which to allocate acute health care resources; challenges of providing adequate long-term care for the elderly; macroeconomic burdens of supporting a large, dependent older population; and "the inevitability" of political conflict between a powerful bloc of self-interested seniors and the rest of us.

It is easy enough to envision how a stereotyped oldest-old group might fit into the scenarios framed by these issues. In some scenarios the casting of roles for the oldest old may be relatively benign, but in others it may be extremely pernicious.

JUSTICE BETWEEN AGE GROUPS

"Justice between age groups" (Daniels 1983) has become a metaphor for concerns that ever-increasing health care costs in the United States will bring about far more rationing of acute health care than we have thus far experienced informally (Blank 1988). Such concerns appeared well founded in 1989 as Alameda County, California, and the state of Oregon became the first governments in this country to begin a process of explicitly rationing health care among patients in their jurisdictions who are paid for by Medicaid, the federal-state health insurance program for "the medically indigent" (Garland 1989; Gross 1989). Both governments ranked medical procedures, with descriptions of age categories and sex as well as health care need.

There is no inherent reason, of course, why issues of justice in allocating health care resources need to be framed on the basis of age. One can frame trade-offs just as easily within age groups or without regard to age. In fact, health care resources—like most other goods and services in the United States—have long been allocated on the basis of social class and ability to pay

(Churchill 1987). Many procedures—even relatively low-cost ones, such as immunization—are not readily available to persons of low economic and social status (Hiatt 1987).

Nonetheless, old age came sharply into focus as a prime target for stepped-up acute-care rationing in the past decade. In a 1983 speech, economist Alan Greenspan, now chairman of the Federal Reserve Board, stated that 30 percent of Medicare is annually expended on 5 to 6 percent of Medicare eligibles who die within the year. He pointedly considered whether it is worth it. (Schulte 1983). Richard Lamm says that he was misquoted in 1984 when he was reported as urging older persons to die in order to make room for the young (Slater 1984), but he has been delivering the same message repeatedly since then, in only somewhat more delicately worded fashion (e.g., Lamm 1987, 1989a).

During the last half of the 1980s, this focus spread to a number of forums. Philosophers generated principles of equity to undergird "justice between age groups" in the provision of health care (e.g., Daniels 1988) rather than, for instance, justice between rich and poor. Conferences and books explicitly addressed the issue of "Should Health Care Be Rationed by Age?" (e.g., Smeeding et al. 1987), and biomedical ethicists turned to examining the economics of terminal illness (Veatch 1988) and "assisted suicide" in old age (Battin 1987).

In the context of this ongoing dialogue on old-age-based health care rationing, the swiftly increasing oldest-old population may well develop as the leading symbol for "runaway" health costs. Persons aged 85 and older, for instance, stand out—even among elderly persons—as high users of health care resources.

For instance, persons aged 85 and older presently use days of care in "short-stay" (as opposed to chronic disease) hospitals in the United States at a rate that is 123 percent higher than that of those aged 65 to 74 and 83 percent higher than that of those aged 75 to 84 (National Center for Health Statistics 1987). Similarly, about 1 percent of Americans aged 65 to 74 years are in nursing homes, compared with 6 percent of persons 75 to 84 years of age and 22 percent of persons aged 85 and older (Hing 1987). The greater numbers of persons who will be in the oldest-old category, combined with their current high rates of health care use, lead to projections that Medicare costs for the oldest old may increase six-fold by the year 2040, as estimated in constant, inflation-adjusted dollars (Schneider and Guralnik 1990).

Even in the mid-1980s, as issues of health care costs and allocations began to be framed as trade-offs between age groups, it did "not take much imagination to envision that a stereotyped group termed the 'oldest old' will be assembled in the front row of the trading block" (Binstock 1985:433). And indeed, they have been by ethicist Daniel Callahan, who is willing to transcend the bounds of traditional Judeo-Christian morality (Post 1991) regarding the sanctity of human life.

In a book entitled *Setting Limits: Medical Goals in an Aging Society*, Callahan proposes that life-saving health care should be officially forbidden to all American citizens who are of an advanced age category. He depicts the elderly as "a new social threat" and a "demographic, economic, and medical avalanche . . . that could ultimately (and perhaps already) do great harm" (1987:20). Callahan's remedy for this threat is to use "age as a specific criterion for the allocation and limitation of health care" (23), by denying life-extending health care—as a matter of public policy—to persons who are aged in their "late 70s or early 80s" and/or have "lived out a natural life span" (171).

Although Callahan's arguments are seriously flawed (Binstock and Kahana 1988), his proposal received a great deal of national attention. It was reviewed in national magazines, the *New York Times*, the *Washington Post*, the *Wall Street Journal*, and almost every relevant professional and scholarly journal and newsletter. Callahan himself was and continues to be invited to present and/or debate his proposal in a number of public forums throughout the country, and he has reiterated his viewpoint in a recent book (Callahan 1990). It appears that his proposal to forbid lifesaving care to the oldest among us has come to be rather firmly embedded in public discourse concerning health care policies in the United States.

Such proposals are likely to persist, albeit with refinements. And they will probably stay focused on very old persons because of preoccupations with financing and outlays for the Medicare program, the biggest single source of payment for health care in America (Health Care Financing Administration 1987). Moreover, Medicare, widely perceived as the "health program for the elderly," is a prime target for cost-containment reforms because its approaches to paying for care affect the financial incentives of a very high percentage of American hospitals, nursing homes, physicians, and other health care providers and suppliers.

LONG-TERM CARE

"Long-term care" has become a metaphor for health care and social supports for chronically ill and disabled elderly persons. But long-term care, and the costs of providing it, are issues very pertinent to persons of all ages. Consider, for example, that in the United States the number of severely disabled adults aged 18 to 64 who live outside institutions is more than twice the total of all chronically ill and severely disabled persons aged 65 and older who reside in nursing homes and elsewhere (Gornick et al. 1985:22–23).

Here again the issue is framed myopically to emphasize the enormous economic, social, and familial burdens of caring for the needs of older persons, without granting comparable public attention to the implications of such needs and burdens generated within other population groups. To the extent that attention is given to such needs within younger populations, however, rehabilitation—whether focused on the goals of compensation for, or restoration of lost functional capacities—receives a reasonable amount of attention. However, only a few (for example, Brody 1984–1985; Williams 1984) have given attention to rehabilitation as a dimension of treatment for the chronically disabled elderly, even with the modest goal of *maintenance* of existing functional capacities.

Stereotyping of the oldest old would likely reinforce current tendencies to perceive the challenges of chronic illness and disabilities in terms of care, *without rehabilitation*, for elderly residual human entities as their functional capacities gradually erode or precipitously decline just before death. Indeed, this perspective has already been propounded by philosophers (e.g., Daniels 1988) and ethicists (e.g., Callahan 1987). They view long-term care as a hospicelike palliative measure, as relatively inexpensive, and as a desirable public-funding alternative to (what they incorrectly perceive as) more costly health care measures that can preserve, improve, or at least maintain the quality of an older individual's life. . . .

INCREASING DEPENDENCY RATIOS

"Increasing dependency ratios," conventionally expressed as the size of the retired population relative to the working population, has become a metaphor for anxieties about the economic burdens of population aging. This construct grossly distorts the issues involved because it is largely an artifact of an existing policy, Social Security, that finances benefits to retirees through a tax based on the paychecks of workers. It does not capture the range of major elements that determine whether a society is economically capable of supporting dependents within it.

The most fundamental problem with this construct lies in using the number or proportion of workers in a society in order to assess the productive capacity of the economy. Productive capacity is a function of a variety of factors—including capital, natural resources, balance of trade, and technological innovation—as well as number of workers. Hence, issues involving productive capacity and number of workers should be expressed in terms of "productivity per worker" in order to take account of an appropriately full range of macro-economic variables (Committee on an Aging Society 1986; Habib 1990).

More specific flaws in common usage of dependency ratios express the ubiquitous impact of ageism in the framing of issues. Age categories are used to estimate the numbers of workers and retirees—rather than actual and projected labor-force participation rates—even though the two approaches can yield substantially different results. In addition, the focus on retirees as the "dependent population" ignores the fact that many retired older persons are economically independent. It also ignores children and unemployed adults of any age who are economically dependent; for instance, research has indicated that a decline in "youth dependency" during the decades ahead may well moderate or even dominate the economic significance of projected increases in "elderly dependency" (Crown 1985; Habib 1990).

Nevertheless, discussions of increasing dependency ratios have generated several assumptions that may be unwarranted: First, we will need a far greater number of workers in the decades ahead than is projected from current age norms for entering and retiring from the labor force. Second, older persons who retire in the context of contemporary policies, many of whom engage in unpaid productive activities (Committee on an Aging Society 1986), will want to and be able to work for pay in the future if incentives to retire and the ages associated with them are marginally adjusted. Third, it is assumed that there will be employer demand for such workers. . . .

THE POLITICAL POWER OF THE AGED

"The political power of the aged" is still another metaphor frequently used to misframe issues in terms of age-group conflicts (e.g., Chakravarty and Weisman 1988). Although older persons have constituted 16.7 to 21 percent of those who voted in national elections during the 1980s (U.S. Senate 1988:11), election exit polls have demonstrated repeatedly that the votes of older persons are distributed among candidates in about the same proportions as the votes of other age groups of citizens (*New York Times*/CBS News Poll 1980, 1982, 1984, 1986, 1988). Even in the context of a state or local referendum that presents a specific issue, rather than candidates, for balloting—such as propositions to cap local property taxes or to finance public schools—old age is not a statistically significant variable associated with the distribution of votes (Chomitz 1987).

These data should not be surprising because there is no sound reason to expect that a cohort of persons would suddenly become homogenized in self-interests and political behavior when it reaches the old-age category (Simon 1985). Diversity among older persons may be at least as great with respect to political attitudes and behavior as it is in relation to economic, social, and other characteristics (Hudson and Strate 1985).

Moreover, the scholarly literature indicates that organized demands of older persons have had little to do with the enactment and amendment of the major old-age policies such as Social Security and Medicare. Rather, such actions have been largely attributable to the initiatives of public officials in the White House, Congress, and the bureaucracy who have focused on their own agendas for social and economic policy (Cohen 1985a; Derthick 1979; Hudson and Strate 1985; Jacobs 1990; Light 1985). . . .

A number of public policy decisions that are conventionally perceived as adverse to the self-interests of older persons proved to be politically feasible in the 1980s through changes in Medicare, Social Security, and other programs. Medicare deductibles, co-payments, and Part B premiums have increased continuously. Old Age Insurance (OAI) benefits have become subject to taxation. . . . The Tax Reform Act of 1986 eliminated the extra personal exemption that all persons 65 years of age and older had been receiving in filing their federal income-tax returns. Most recently, the politics of enacting and repealing the Catastrophic Coverage Act clearly illustrated that older persons are not a homogeneous group, either politically or in terms of self-interests.

Despite these facts, the image of so-called senior power persists because it serves certain purposes. It is used by journalists as a tabloid symbol to simplify the complexities of politics. It is marketed by the leaders of old-age-based organizations who have many incentives to inflate the size of the constituency for which they speak, even if they need to homogenize it artificially in order to do so. It is attacked by those who would like to see greater resources allocated to their causes and who depict the selfishness of the aged as the root of many problems (Longman 1987). . . .

TRANSCENDING INTERGENERATIONAL EQUITY: PERSPECTIVES ON OLD-AGE-BASED HEALTH CARE RATIONING

These examples of current metaphors in the politics of health and social-welfare allocations may be sufficient to illustrate that issues are being framed in terms of conflicts between age groups; that these issues are frequently constructed from spurious and unwarranted assumptions; and that the emergence of the oldest old within these scenarios tends to exacerbate the implications of the issues that have been framed.

The lesson to be drawn from this is *not* that research on the oldest old should cease or be muted. Indeed, multidimensional knowledge about persons who are in their late eighties and older will be essential for coping with the challenges posed by population aging. It is important to note, however, that the issues of intergenerational equity—although arbitrary and flawed— have focused the social-policy agenda and diverted attention from other ways of viewing trade-offs and options available to us that may be more accurate and propitious.

The lesson *is* that any description of the axis upon which equity is to be judged tends to circumscribe the major options available for rendering justice. If we can perceive issues that express equity in ways other than intergenerational trade-offs (Heclo 1988; Kingson, Hirshorn, and Cornman 1986; Neugarten and Neugarten 1986; Wisensale 1988), those alternative issues may generate a series of new practical choices for public and private institutional arrangements in the decades ahead. It is not within the scope of this discussion to set forth a blueprint for such arrangements. But it is feasible to illustrate the principle by briefly considering some of the ways in which issues of health-resources allocation, presently expressed in terms of old-age-based rationing proposals, can be viewed in other terms.

Many contemporary discussions about old-age-based rationing are laden with misperceptions of what is actually happening in the world of health care for elderly Americans. Physicians are viewed as blindly pursuing a "heroic model" of medicine (see Cassel and Neugarten 1991) in which no cost or form of intervention will be spared in attempting to extend the lives of persons who are already near the end of their natural life course. These expenditures and interventions are seen as largely futile and wasteful, especially when applied to the very old. And their elimination, through one means or another, is perceived as an important measure for reducing health care costs, particularly because of the swiftly increasing size of the oldest-old population.

But the decision processes through which physicians actually decide whether and how to treat elderly patients are not widely known. The benefits such patients receive from treatments are not understood, either in comparison with younger patients or in terms of cost effectiveness for society. Frequently quoted statistics concerning health care costs are often unexamined with respect to their significance.

THE MYTH OF OVERLY AGGRESSIVE, HIGH-TECHNOLOGY CARE
FOR THE ELDERLY

A central theme in most current discussions of whether American society
should deny or limit health care to older persons is that costly, high-technology
medicine is used too frequently and wastefully in treating elderly patients (e.g.,
Callahan 1987; Daniels 1988; U.S. Congress 1987). For some years the press has
provided dramatic accounts of organ transplants and other forms of surgery on
persons in their seventies, eighties, and nineties (e.g., Koenig 1986), as well as
reports of legal issues involving the extended ordeals of older patients who
linger on the edge of death in hospitals, sustained only by mechanical breathing ventilators or nutrition obtained intravenously or through tube feeding
(e.g., Kleiman 1985).

However, the popular conception that elderly persons are frequently subject
to "Faustian technologies" of intensive care (Lamm 1989a:6) against their wishes
is wrong (Schwartz and Reilly 1986). The majority of the funds expended on
health care for the aged in the United States are not for dramatic technological
interventions or even for hospitals. In 1988 nursing homes accounted for 21 percent of health expenditures on older persons, yet only a negligible proportion of
elderly nursing-home patients receive life-sustaining technologies (U.S.
Congress 1987:12). A wide range of nonhospital and nonphysician health services—such as prescription drugs, dental care, home health care, vision and hearing aids, and medical equipment and supplies—totaled 16 percent of expenditures, and outpatient and inpatient physician fees were 22 percent. The remaining 41 percent was for payments to hospitals (U.S. House of Representatives
1989:21).

Studies in both the United States (Scitovsky 1984) and Canada (Roos,
Montgomery, and Roos 1987) indicate that aggressive acute-care medical interventions are comparable across adult age groups in the last years of life,
although elderly persons are far more likely to incur expenses for nursing
homes and home-care services. In fact, a study of several hundred older persons
who died within a twelve-month period indicates that severely impaired geriatric patients who received only supportive care—and little of it from hospitals
and physicians—averaged only slightly fewer expenses for the year (amounting
to about 8 percent less) than the most expensive decedents, who were treated
aggressively with high-technology measures (Scitovsky 1988).

Old age, as a single factor or independent variable, is a poor predictor of
whether a medical intervention will be "wasted," even for highly technical and
aggressive medical interventions (see Jahnigen and Binstock 1991). Moreover,

experience with advanced medical technologies—such as those used in renal dialysis, liver transplantation, and heart transplantation—shows that those older patients who are selected for such procedures unquestionably benefit from them, sometimes more than younger patients (Evans 1991). In certain cases, even transplantations are the most cost effective mode of treatment. For example, kidney-transplant recipients whose new organs function satisfactorily incur far lower treatment expenses than dialysis patients (Evans et al. 1987; Evans, Manninen, and Thompson 1989).

At the same time, the caricature of contemporary physicians as Don Quixotes who will tilt at "death as an enemy," regardless of cost and prognosis, misses the mark badly. Transplantation specialists, for example, take great care to select older candidates for surgery who have outstanding prospects for survival and benefit (Evans 1991). Furthermore, it is clear that physicians generally recognize the futility of many interventions for older persons, depending on disease and level of function (Gillick 1988; La Puma et al. 1988; Miles and Ryder 1985; Scitovsky 1988; Youngner et al. 1985).

CAN WE SAVE MONEY ON ELDERLY PATIENTS WHO DIE WITHIN THE YEAR?

Even if health care treatment of older persons is not wasteful or overly aggressive, it is not always successful. Alan Greenspan's 1983 pronouncement (Schulte 1983) that a high proportion of Medicare expenditures is accounted for by a small proportion of Medicare enrollees who die within the year was basically correct. About 6 percent of Medicare enrollees who die within a year account for about 28 percent of Medicare's annual expenditures (Lubitz and Prihoda 1984). In 1987, when the total Medicare expenditure was $81 billion (Letsch, Levit, and Waldo 1988), this would mean that about $22.6 billion in Medicare funds was used to reimburse health care for about 6 percent of Medicare eligibles who died.

Suppose it were possible, both clinically and ethically, to identify prospectively those Medicare patients who were going to die within the year, and whose treatment would be *comparatively costly*, to choose not to undertake aggressive treatment of them, and thereby to save unnecessary health care costs? How much would be saved in terms of Medicare resources and the nation's annual health expenditures? To the extent that it is possible to estimate, not very much.

The best available nationwide study (Lubitz and Prihoda 1984) found that in 1978 only 3 percent of Medicare-eligible decedents had reimbursements of $20,000 or more, and they accounted for 3.5 percent of total Medicare expenditures that year. This $20,000 or more per capita figure for the high cost of Medicare decedents would undoubtedly be much larger today because health care costs have increased substantially in the ensuing years (U.S. House of Representatives 1989:10).

Placing these findings in the context of a more recent year, the 3.5 percent of Medicare spent on high-cost decedents in 1978 would have yielded a total of $2.84 billion for 1987. To be sure, changing medical practices such as the introduction of high-cost technologies and low-cost hospice programs may have had the net effect of increasing or decreasing the percentage of Medicare spent on high-cost decedents since 1978. Even an increase of 1 or 2 percent, however, would not substantially change the general picture.

In the context of 1987, when national health care expenditures were over $500 billion and Medicare expenditures were $81 billion, saving an estimated $2.84 billion seems negligible. . . .

Even if our nation were firmly resolved, as a matter of public policy, to eliminate all wasteful and unnecessary health care expenditures, and even if it was ethically palatable to do so, would it be possible to eliminate such "waste" by not treating Medicare patients who are likely to be expensive decedents? Only, apparently, if we are willing not to treat costly patients who will recover—to throw away those high-cost patients who would survive into the same "wastebasket" as costly decedents. The study by Lubitz and Prihoda (1984) found about the same numbers of survivors and decedents in the high-cost patient category and about the same amount of aggregate expenditures on them. Of 49,000 Medicare enrollees in the high-cost category, 25,000 survived and 24,000 died.

Prospective distinctions between high-cost survivors and decedents are usually problematic, especially in cases that are likely to involve high costs (Scitovsky 1984). In short, even for those who may feel that it was not worth it in 1987 to spend $2.84 billion—*or six-tenths of one percent of a national total of $500.3 billion*—on high-cost Medicare decedents, there is no practical way to operationalize a policy that would save such funds without deliberately cutting off successful treatment for an equal number of likely survivors as well.

IS MORE HEALTH CARE RATIONING NECESSARY?

Much of the public discourse about health care rationing has been explicitly undergirded by concerns about rising health care costs. These concerns flared up in the 1980s as a "cost-containment" fever that shows no sign of subsiding. From 1980 to 1988 consumer health care costs rose at an annual average rate of about 12 percent (U.S. House of Representatives 1989:11). . . .

During the first three-quarters of this century, the providers of health care, rather than those who paid for it, were largely able to control the prices and mechanisms for allocating health care resources (Starr 1983). However, at the outset of the 1980s the governmental and corporate entities that pay for an overwhelming proportion of American health care began attempting to limit their financial obligations (Thurow 1985). California, Massachusetts, and several other states enacted statutes—at the behest of insurance companies and large corporate employers—to curb hospital costs (Kinzer 1983). In 1983 the federal government limited Medicare reimbursements to hospitals by implementing a prospective payment system through which the size of payments were fixed in accordance with a "diagnosis-related group" (DRG) classification for each Medicare inpatient, rather than the length of hospital stay and the services received by the patient (Latta and Helbing 1988). By the end of the decade, executives of major corporations were breaking a long-standing taboo by announcing their support for the notion of national health insurance, as a means of cutting their firms' costs for employee health-insurance premiums, and redistributing the expense to taxpayers in general (e.g., Freudenheim 1989a, 1989b).

Health care costs: How much is "too much"?
As this cost-containment milieu has developed, it has been accompanied by a chorus of opinions that we are spending "too much" of our national resources on health care (e.g., Lamm 1989a). Health-policy analysts who want us to curb our national health care investment feel that larger health care expenditures will have adverse consequences for American economic competitiveness, government budgets, and a variety of other social and economic responsibilities (e.g., Mechanic 1985).

Although health care cost containment is a reasonable political objective, it is not supported by any "iron law" of economics. Advocates of cost containment warn, rhetorically, that we cannot sustain increasing health care expenditures. But no one has yet articulated the inevitable dire consequences that would ensue for our nation if such costs continue to increase and if we exceed a specific percentage of GNP in our annual health care expenditures. It is not at all clear, for instance, that escalating health care costs hurt the global position of the American economy. Despite present laments about the economic decline of the United States, our share of the world's GNP has held constant at 23 percent since the mid-1970s (Nye 1990), a period during which our health care costs increased annually at a rate ranging from two to three times our general rate of inflation.

An arbitrary but commonly used frame of reference for arguing that the United States spends too much is comparison with other countries. We spend far more of our national wealth on health care than does any other developed nation. For instance, the proportion of U.S. resources allocated to health expenditures is 74 percent greater than that of the United Kingdom and 27 percent greater than that of Canada (Waldo, Levit, and Lazenby 1986).

On the other hand, Americans might not be satisfied with the levels of care generally available in these other nations. The quality of health care provided by the smaller proportions of national wealth spent on it in the United Kingdom, Canada, and elsewhere has been increasingly questioned by both indigenous and foreign observers of those systems (for the United Kingdom, see Aaron and Schwartz 1984, Grimes 1987, and Smith 1989; for Canada, see Barber 1989, Iglehart 1986, and Walker 1989). . . .

As such comparisons indicate, there are no universal or scientific criteria for determining what is too much for a nation to spend on health care. The proportion of our national wealth that we can or ought to invest in health care (as opposed to other purposes) is not a technical issue but, of course, a value judgment that will be resolved through politics.

Costs and scarcity are separate issues.

Regardless of competing value judgments as to the appropriate amount of GNP to spend on health care, cost containment appears to have become an end in itself in the United States. However, anxieties that escalating costs must lead to acute health care rationing on a scale far greater than ever before, through public policy, may be unfounded. As Moody (1991) has observed, situations that justify "rationing," as opposed to allocation, are characterized by both a *scarcity* of supply and a widely shared sense of *crisis*.

Although there may be a sense of crisis about costs, health care resources are actually expanding (Gornick et al. 1985; Letsch, Levit, and Waldo 1988). The concern about containing health care costs has generated changes in the sources and mechanisms of payment for health care. One consequence of these changes is fierce competition among health care providers. For providers who are winning in the competition, resources are plentiful. For the providers who are losing, particularly those primarily dependent on public insurance reimbursement, resources are scarce; and it is for their customers—patients dependent upon public insurance—and for the 37 million Americans without any insurance that resources are scarce and for whom informal rationing takes place.

If we can put aside our preoccupation with Medicare and its age-category principle, perhaps we will see that it is the capacity of patients to pay for charges—out of pocket or through third-party reimbursements—that has a great deal to do with the allocation of care. It is not a scarcity of health resources that poses a problem, but an unwillingness and/or incapacity of our political system to allocate them through some means other than economic and social stratification.

"Justice between rich and poor" may be a better metaphor than "justice between age groups" for the dilemmas of equity we might confront in the allocation or rationing of acute care. With the issue framed on this axis, the specific policy options we might generate and consider would be rather different from those we are contemplating now, and would more likely reflect the true trade-offs that do take place in the allocation of health care resources.

As many qualified observers have pointed out (e.g., Schwartz and Aaron 1985), there is no inherent reason why 11, 12, 13 percent, or more of our GNP cannot be expended on health care. After two decades of socialization to the rights or entitlements provided through Medicare and Medicaid, it could well be that Americans—reassured that they are not paying for waste and excess profits—will not want to impose a ceiling on health care expenditures and/or will not be willing to acquiesce in rationing practices that such a ceiling might impose (Aaron and Schwartz 1984). After all, as Abel-Smith (1985) has noted, among the industrialized nations in the world, the United States is "the odd man out" in its approaches to the regulation, delivery mechanisms, and financing of health care.

Walzer (1983) has argued that notions of justice throughout history have varied not only among cultures and political systems, but also among distinct spheres of activities and relationships within any given culture or political system. Nothing requires us to devise or accept separate spheres of justice within the health care arena, either spheres separating age groups or spheres separating the relatively wealthy from the relatively poor. We may prefer to delineate the health care arena as a single sphere of justice within which no such distinctions are made. Uwe Reinhardt (1986:29) explains the choice very clearly: "If the American public, and the politicians who represent it, really cared about the nation's indigent, they ought to be able to exploit the emerging surplus of health care resources to the advantage of the poor."

This discussion of perspectives on old-age-based health care rationing represents but one example of how contemporary dilemmas can be perceived in terms that express neither compassionate and dispassionate ageism nor conflicts between age groups. Whether such perceptions are more accurate or even more propitious ways to frame issues is certainly open to debate. They have been offered to illustrate that preoccupations with stereotypes, conventional wisdom, and existing policies and institutional arrangements can divert us from seeking alternative ways to anticipate and deal with the implications of population aging and other societal challenges.

Even as we generate valuable knowledge about the oldest-old population to inform our choices for the future, it is especially important that we examine the principles of equity implicit in the choices that we frame. If we allow our thinking to be confined by an agenda of intergenerational equity issues, and by our current policies and the principles that they have come to reflect, we may very well find ourselves engaged in policy debates on issues of age-group conflict that are far worse than those we have experienced to date: trading off the value of one human life against another as a matter of official policy.

Ultimately, the principles of equity that we use to describe our choices will be far more important than data and policy analyses for shaping the quality of life and the nature of justice in our society, and for the oldest old among us.

REFERENCES

Aaron, H. J., and W. B. Schwartz. 1984. *The Painful Prescription: Rationing Hospital Care.* Washington, D.C.: Brookings Institution.

Abel-Smith, B. 1985. Who Is the Odd Man Out?: The Experience of Western Europe in Containing the Costs of Health Care. *Milbank Memorial Fund Quarterly/Health and Society* 63 (1): 1–17.

Achenbaum, W. A. 1983. *Shades of Gray: Old Age, American Values, and Federal Policies Since 1920.* Boston: Little, Brown.

Allport, G. W. 1959. *ABC's of Scapegoating.* New York: Anti-Defamation League of B'nai B'rith.

Barber, J. 1989. Sick to Death: Caught Between Rising Costs and More Restraints, Hospitals Are Cutting Services. *Maclean's* (February 13): 32–35.

Battin, M. P. 1987. Choosing the Time to Die: The Ethics and Economics of Suicide in Old Age. In *Ethical Dimensions of Geriatric Care*, ed. S. Spicker, 161–189. Dordrecht, Holland: Reidel.

Binstock, R. H. 1972. Interest-group Liberalism and the Politics of Aging. *The Gerontologist* 12: 265–80.

——. 1983. The Aged as Scapegoat. *The Gerontologist* 23:136–43.

——. 1985. The Oldest-Old: A Fresh Perspective or Compassionate Ageism Revisited? *Milbank Memorial Fund Quarterly/Health and Society* 63:420–51.

Binstock, R. H., and J. Kahana. 1988. An Essay on *Setting Limits: Medical Goals in an Aging Society*, by D. Callahan. *The Gerontologist* 28:424–26.

Blank, R. H. 1988. *Rationing Medicine*. New York: Columbia University Press.

Brody, S. J. 1984–1985. Merging Rehabilitation and Aging Policies and Programs: Past, Present, and Future. *Rehabilitation World* 8 (4): 6–9, 42–44.

Callahan, D. 1987. *Setting Limits: Medical Goals in an Aging Society*. New York: Simon and Schuster.

———. 1990. *What Kind of Life: The Limits of Medical Progress*. New York: Simon and Schuster.

Campion, F. D. 1984. *The AMA and U.S. Health Policy Since 1940*. Chicago: Chicago Review Press.

Cassel, C. K., and B. L. Neugarten. 1991. The Goals of Medicine in an Aging Society. In *Too Old for Health Care?: Controversies in Medicine, Law, Economics, and Ethics*, ed. R. H. Binstock and S. G. Post, 75–91. Baltimore, Md.: Johns Hopkins University Press.

Chakravarty, S. N., and K. Weisman. 1988. Consuming Our Children? *Forbes* 142:222–32.

Chomitz, K. M. 1987. Demographic Influences on Local Public Education Expenditures: A Review of Econometric Evidence. In *Demographic Change and the Well-Being of Children and the Elderly*, ed. Committee on Population, Commission on Behavioral and Social Sciences Education, National Research Council, 45–53. Washington D.C.: National Academy Press.

Churchill, L. R. 1987. *Rationing Health Care in America: Perceptions and Principles of Justice*. Notre Dame, Ind.: University of Notre Dame Press.

Clark, R. L. 1990. Income Maintenance Policies in the United States. In *Handbook of Aging and the Social Sciences*, 3rd ed., eds. R. H. Binstock and L. K. George, 382–97. San Diego, Calif.: Academic Press.

Cohen, W. J. 1985a. Securing Social Security. *New Leader* 66:5–8.

———. 1985b. Reflections on the Enactment of Medicare and Medicaid. *Health Care Financing Review* (Annual Supplement): 3–11.

Committee on an Aging Society, Institute of Medicine and National Research Council. 1986. *America's Aging: Productive Roles in an Older Society*. Washington, D.C.: National Academy Press.

Crown, W. 1985. Some Thoughts on Reformulating the Dependency Ratio. *The Gerontologist* 25:166–71.

Daniels, N. 1983. Justice Between Age Groups: Am I My Parents' Keeper? *Milbank Memorial Fund Quarterly/Health and Society* 61 (3): 489–522.

———. 1988. *Am I My Parents' Keeper? An Essay On Justice Between the Young and the Old*. New York: Oxford University Press.

David, S. I. 1985. *With Dignity: The Search For Medicare and Medicaid*. Westport, Conn.: Greenwood Press.

Derthick, M. 1979. *Policymaking for Social Security*. Washington, D.C.: Brookings Institution.

Estes, C. L. 1979. *The Aging Enterprise*. San Francisco: Jossey-Bass.

——. 1983. Social Security: The Social Construction of a Crisis. *Milbank Memorial Fund Quarterly/Health and Society*, 61:445–61.

Evans, R. W. 1991. Advanced Medical Technology and Elderly People. In *Too Old for Health Care? Controversies in Medicine, Law, Economics, and Ethics*, ed. R. H. Binstock and S. G. Post, 44–74. Baltimore, Md.: Johns Hopkins University Press.

Evans, R. W., D. L. Manninen, L. P. Garrison, Jr., and L. G. Hart. 1987. *Special Report: Findings from the National Kidney Dialysis and Kidney Transplantation Study*. Baltimore, Md.: Health Care Financing Administration (HCFA pub. no. 03230).

Evans, R. W., D. L. Manninen, and C. Thompson. 1989. *A Cost and Outcome Analysis of Kidney Transplantation: The Implications of Initial Immunosuppressive Protocol and Diabetes*. Seattle, Wash.: Battelle Human Affairs Research Centers.

Fairlie, H. 1988. Talkin' 'bout My Generation. *New Republic* 198 (13): 19–22.

Findlay, S. 1989. The Short Life of Catastrophic Care. *U.S. News and World Report* (December 11): 72–73.

Ford Foundation. Project on Social Welfare and the American Future, Executive Panel. 1989. *The Common Good: Social Welfare and the American Future*. New York: Ford Foundation.

Freudenheim, M. 1989a. A Health-Care Taboo Is Broken. *New York Times* (May 8): 23.

——. 1989b. Calling for a Bigger U.S. Health Role. *New York Times* (May 30): 29.

Garland, S. B. 1989. Health Care for All or an Excuse for Cutbacks? *Business Week* (June 26): 68.

Generational Journal. 1989. Untitled statement of organizational purpose and tax status of Americans for Generational Equity. 1 (4): 104.

Gibbs, N. R. 1988. Grays on the Go. *Time* 131 (8): 66–75.

Gillick, M. 1988. Limiting Medical Care: Physicians' Beliefs, Physicians' Behavior. *Journal of the American Geriatric Society* 36:747–52.

Gornick, M., J. N. Greenberg, P. W. Eggers, and A. Dobson. 1985. Twenty Years of Medicare and Medicaid: Covered Populations, Use of Benefits, and Program Expenditures. *Health Care Financing Review* (Suppl.): 13–59.

Graebner, W. 1980. *A History of Retirement: The Meanings and Functions of an American Institution, 1885–1978*. New Haven, Conn.: Yale University Press.

Grimes, D. D. 1987. Rationing Health Care. *Lancet* 1 (8533): 615–16.

Gross, J. 1989. What Medical Care the Poor Can Have: Lists Are Drawn Up. *New York Times* (March 27): 1.

Habib, J. 1990. The Economy and the Aged. In *Handbook of Aging and the Social*

Sciences, 3rd ed., ed. R. H. Binstock and L. K. George, 328–45. San Diego, Calif.: Academic Press.

Harris, R. 1966. *A Sacred Trust.* New York: American Library.

Health Care Financing Administration. 1987. National Health Expenditures, 1986–2000. *Health Care Financing Review* 8 (4): 1–36.

Heclo, H. 1988. Generational Politics. In *The Vulnerable*, ed. J. L. Palmer, T. Smeeding, and B. B. Torrey, 381–411. Washington, D.C.: Urban Institute Press.

Hiatt, H. H. 1987. *America's Health in the Balance: Choice or Change?* New York: Harper and Row.

Hing, E. 1987. *Use of Nursing Homes by the Elderly: Preliminary Data from the 1985 National Nursing Home Survey, Advance Data No. 135.* Hyattsville, Md.: National Center for Health Statistics, May 14.

Holtzman, A. 1963. *The Townsend Movement: A Political Study.* New York: Bookman.

Hudson, R. B. 1978. The "Graying" of the Federal Budget and Its Consequences for Old-Age Policy. *The Gerontologist* 18:428–40.

Hudson, R. B., and J. Strate. 1985. Aging and Political Systems. In *Handbook of Aging and the Social Sciences*, 2nd ed., ed. R. H. Binstock and E. Shanas, 554–85. New York: Van Nostrand Reinhold.

Iglehart, J. K. 1986. Canada's Health Care System. *New England Journal of Medicine* 313:202–8, 778–84, 1623–28.

Jacobs, B. 1990. Aging in Politics. In *Handbook of Aging and the Social Sciences*, 3rd ed., ed s. R. H. Binstock and L. K. George, 349–61. San Diego, Calif.: Academic Press.

Jahnigen, D. W., and R. H. Binstock. 1991. Economic and Clinical Realities: Health Care for Elderly People. In *Too Old for Health Care? Controversies in Medicine, Law, Economics, and Ethics*, ed. R. H. Binstock and S. G. Post, 13–43. Baltimore, Md.: Johns Hopkins University Press.

Kalish, R. A. 1979. The New Ageism and the Failure Models: A Polemic. *The Gerontologist* 19:398–407.

Kieffer, J. A. 1986. The Older Volunteer Resource. In *America's Aging: Productive Roles in an Older Society*, ed. Committee on an Aging Society, Institute of Medicine and National Research Council, 51–72. Washington, D.C.: National Academy Press.

Kingson, E. R., B. A. Hirshorn, and J. M. Cornman. 1986. *Ties That Bind: The Interdependence of Generations.* Washington, D.C.: Seven Locks Press.

Kinzer, D. M. 1983. Massachusetts and California: Two Kinds of Cost Control. *New England Journal of Medicine* 308:838–41.

Kleiman, D. 1985. Death and the Court. *New York Times* (January 19): 9.

Koenig, R. 1986. As Liver Transplants Grow More Common, Ethical Issues Multiply:

By Operating on the Elderly, Thomas Starzl Steps Up Patient Selection Debate. *Wall Street Journal* (October 14): 1.

Kutza, E. A. 1981. *The Benefits of Old Age*. Chicago: University of Chicago Press.

La Puma, J., M. Silverstein, C. Stocking, D. Roland, and M. Siegler. 1988. Life-Sustaining Treatment: A Prospective Study of Patients with DNR Orders in a Teaching Hospital. *Archives of Internal Medicine* 148:2193–98.

Lamm, R. D. 1987. A Debate: Medicare in 2020. In *Medicare Reform and the Baby Boom Generation*, edited proceedings of the second annual conference of Americans for Generational Equity, April 30–May 1, 77–88. Washington, D.C.: Americans for Generational Equity.

———. 1989a. Columbus and Copernicus: New Wine in Old Wineskins. *Mount Sinai Journal of Medicine* 56 (1): 1–10.

———. 1989b. Saving a Few, Sacrificing Many—At Great Cost. *New York Times* (August 8): 23.

Latta, V. V., and C. Helbing. 1988. Medicare: Short-Stay Hospital Services, by Leading Diagnosis-Related-Groups, 1983–1985. *Health Care Financing Review* 10 (2): 79–107.

Letsch, S. W., K. R. Levit, and R. Waldo. 1988. National Health Expenditures, 1987. *Health Care Financing Review* 10 (2): 109–22.

Light, P. 1985. *Artful Work: The Politics of Social Security Reform*. New York: Random House.

Longman, P. 1987. *Born to Pay: The New Politics of Aging in America*. Boston: Houghton Mifflin.

———. 1989. Elderly, Affluent—and Selfish. *New York Times* (October 10): 27.

Lubitz, J., and R. Prihoda. 1984. The Use and Costs of Medicare Services in the Last Two Years of Life. *Health Care Financing Review* 5 (3): 117–31.

Marmor, T. R. 1970. *The Politics of Medicare*. London: Routledge and Kegan Paul.

Mechanic, D. 1985. Cost Containment and the Quality of Medical Care: Rationing Strategies in an Era of Constrained Resources. *Milbank Memorial Fund Quarterly/Health and Society* 63:453–57.

Miles, S., and Ryder, M. 1985. Limited-Treatment Policies in Long-Term Care Facilities. *Journal of the American Geriatric Society* 33:707.

Moody, H. R. 1991. Allocation, Yes: Age-Based Rationing, No. In *Too Old for Health Care?: Controversies in Medicine, Law, Economics, and Ethics*, ed. R. H. Binstock and S. G. Post, 180–203. Baltimore, Md.: Johns Hopkins University Press.

Myles, J. F. 1983. Conflict, Crisis, and the Future of Old-Age Security. *Milbank Memorial Fund Quarterly/Health and Society* 61:462–72.

National Center for Health Statistics. 1987. Utilization of Short-Stay Hospitals, United States, 1985, Annual Summary. *Vital and Health Statistics*, series 13, no. 91.

Washington, D.C.: U.S. Department of Health and Human Services.

Neugarten, B. L. 1974. Age Groups in American Society and the Rise of the Young Old. *Annals of the American Academy of Political and Social Science* 415:187–98.

———. 1982. *Age or Need?* Beverly Hills, Calif.: Sage.

Neugarten, B. L., and D. A. Neugarten. 1986. Age in the Aging Society. *Daedalus* 115 (1): 31–49.

New York Times/CBS News Poll. 1980. How Different Groups Voted for President. *New York Times* (November 9): 28.

———. 1982. Party Choices of Voters, 1982 vs. 1978. *New York Times* (November 8): B11.

———. 1984. Portrait of the Electorate. *New York Times* (November 8): A19.

———. 1986. Portrait of the Electorate: The Vote for House of Representatives. *New York Times* (November 6): 15Y.

———. 1988. Portrait of the Electorate. *New York Times* (November 10): 18Y.

Nye, J. S., Jr. 1990. The Misleading Metaphor of Decline. *Atlantic Monthly* 265:86–94.

Peterson, P. 1987. The Morning After. *Atlantic* 260 (4): 43–69.

Post, S. G. 1991. Justice and the Elderly: Judeo-Christian Perspectives. In *Too Old for Health Care? Controversies in Medicine, Law, Economics, and Ethics*, ed. R. H. Binstock and S. G. Post, 120–37. Baltimore, Md.: Johns Hopkins University Press.

Pratt, H. J. 1976. *The Gray Lobby*. Chicago: University of Chicago Press.

Preston, S. H. 1984. Children and the Elderly in the U.S. *Scientific American* 251 (6): 44–49.

Quadagno, J. 1989. Generational Equity and the Politics of the Welfare State. *Politics and Society* 17 (3): 353–76.

Reinhardt, U. 1986. Letter of June 9, 1986, to Arnold S. Relman. *Health Affairs* 5 (2): 28–31.

Roos, N. P., P. Montgomery, and L. L. Roos. 1987. Health Care Utilization in the Years Prior to Death. *Milbank Memorial Fund Quarterly/Health and Society* 65:231–54.

Samuelson, R. J. 1978. Aging America: Who Will Shoulder the Growing Burden? *National Journal* 10:1712–17.

Schneider, E. L., and J. M. Guralnik. 1990. The Aging of America: Impact on Health Care Costs. *Journal of the American Medical Association* 263:2335–46.

Schulte J. 1983. Terminal Patients Deplete Medicare, Greenspan Says. *Dallas Morning News* (April 26): 1.

Schwartz, D., and P. Reilly. 1986. The Choice Not to be Resuscitated. *Journal of the American Geriatric Society* 34:807–11.

Schwartz, W. B., and H. J. Aaron. 1985. Health Care Costs: The Social Trade-offs. *Issues in Science and Technology* 1 (2): 39–46.

Scitovsky, A. A. 1984. "The High Cost of Dying": What Do the Data Show? *Milbank Memorial Fund Quarterly/Health and Society* 62:591–608.

———. 1988. Medical Care in the Last Twelve Months of Life: The Relation Between Age, Functional Status, and Medical Care Expenditures. *Milbank Memorial Fund Quarterly/Health and Society* 66:640–60.

Simon, H. A. 1985. Human Nature in Politics: The Dialogue of Psychology with Political Science. *American Political Science Review* 79:293–304.

Slater, W. 1984. Latest Lamm Remark Angers the Elderly. *Arizona Daily Star* (March 29): 1.

Smeeding, T. M. 1990. Economic Status of the Elderly. In *Handbook of Aging and the Social Sciences*, 3rd ed., ed. R. H. Binstock and L. K. George, 362–81. San Diego, Calif.: Academic Press.

Smeeding, T. M., M. P. Battin, L. P. Francis, and B. M. Landesman, eds. 1987. *Should Medical Care Be Rationed by Age?* Totowa, N.J.: Rowman and Littlefield.

Smith, T. 1989. BMA rejects NHS Review but . . . Doctors Must Develop Coherent Alternative. *British Medical Journal* 298:1405–6.

Starr, P. 1983. *The Social Transformation of American Medicine.* New York: Basic Books.

Thurow, L. C. 1985. Medicine versus Economics. *New England Journal of Medicine* 313:611–14.

Tolchin, M. 1988. New Health Insurance Plan Provokes Outcry Over Costs. *New York Times* (November 2): 1.

———. 1989. Lawmakers Tell the Elderly: "Next Year" on Health Care. *New York Times* (November 23): 10Y.

Torrey, B. B. 1982. Guns vs. Canes: The Fiscal Implications of an Aging Population. *American Economics Association Papers and Proceedings* 72:309–13.

U.S. Congress, Office of Technology Assessment. 1987. *Life-Sustaining Technologies and the Elderly.* Washington, D.C.

U.S. Department of Health and Human Services. 1984. Announcement: The Oldest Old. *National Institutes of Health Guide for Grants and Contracts* 13 (12): 29–33.

U.S. House of Representatives, Select Committee on Aging. 1989. *Health Care Costs For America's Elderly, 1977–88.* Washington, D.C.

U.S. Senate, Special Committee on Aging. 1988. *Developments in Aging, 1987.* Washington, D.C.: U.S. Government Printing Office.

Veatch, R. 1988. Justice and the Economics of Terminal Illness. *Hastings Center Report* 18 (4): 34–40.

Waldo, D., K. Levit, and H. Lazenby. 1986. National Health Expenditures, 1985. *Health Care Financing Review* 8 (1): 1–21.

Walker, M. A. 1989. From Canada: A Different Viewpoint. *Health Marketing Quarterly* (First Quarter): 11–13.

Walzer, M. 1983. *Spheres of Justice.* New York: Basic Books.

Williams. T. F. (ed.) 1984. *Rehabilitation and the Aging.* New York: Raven Press.

Wisensale, S. M. 1988. Generational Equity and Intergenerational Policies. *The Gerontologist* 28:773–78.

Youngner, S., W. Lewandowski, D. McClish, B. Juknialis, C. Coulton, and E. Bartlett. 1985. Do Not Resuscitate Orders: Incidence and Implications in a Medical Intensive Care Unit. *Journal of the American Medical Association* 253:54–57.

CHAPTER TEN

Social Security and the Politics of Generational Conflict

Theodore Marmor, Fay Lomax Cook, and Stephen Scher

Theodore Marmor is professor of public policy and management at Yale University and a member of the National Academy of Social Insurance. His books include *Understanding Health Care Reform, America's Misunderstood Welfare State,* and *The Politics of Medicare.* Fay Lomax Cook is professor of education and social policy at Northwestern University. Her books include *Who Should Be Helped? Public Support for Social Services* and *Support for the America Welfare State: The Views of Congress and the Public.* Stephen Scher is a lawyer who teaches ethics and public policy at the Yale School of Management. He is a mediator and consultant in health care, medical ethics, and public policy. He is the author of *The Divisive Legacy of Bioethics: Beyond Dogma and Distrust.*

Marmor, Cook, and Scher reject many of the assertions of those who frame the debate over Social Security policy in terms of generational equity. They argue that many of these claims misrepresent Social Security in an effort to make a case for cuts in spending and view this as part of an effort by political conservatives to reduce spending on social welfare programs more generally. The authors contrast the residualist view of social welfare programs with the social insurance conception and point out that a majority of Americans favor the latter view. They are critical of efforts by conservative residualists to portray themselves as defending the interests of children as they call for cuts in spending on the elderly; this is viewed as an effort to divide the young and the old in the name of generational equity so as to justify cuts in Social Security spending.

Social Security has been, and remains, one of the most popular and successful social programs in American history. . . . Polls consistently find that Americans of all age groups are nearly unanimous in their support for the maintenance of its pension benefits (Reno and Friedland 1997). Moreover, the retirement program has done precisely what its originators intended it to do: protect retirees and their families from income losses that would drastically reduce their economic well-being.[1] Against this backdrop of popularity and achievement, it is surprising to find so many policy elites fretting about the alleged unfairness of Social Security.

Is the United States allocating too large a proportion of its public resources to the elderly at the expense of the young?[2] This question, which has come to be framed as one of "generational equity," has prompted a considerable amount of comment since the mid-1980s. And it has also bred conflict between some groups and individuals claiming to represent either the young or the old. Our view is that the substantive claims underlying this conflict are largely fictive. The conflict is the product, instead, of a fundamental misunderstanding of Social Security, coupled with the broader political efforts of the most prominent critics to reduce the scope of, and public expenditures for, America's social insurance programs.

The controversy about the claimed conflict between young and old over Social Security pensions is very much a part of contemporary debate in American politics over social policy. As such, it can best be understood as an instance of a broader dialogue about the proper role and scope of the federal government. We begin then by considering the context of American political debate and continue by locating the disputes over Social Security and the welfare state within it.

THE AMERICAN POLITICS OF EXAGGERATION

Foreign observers from de Tocqueville to Thatcher have described American politics as unruly, combative, and feverish. Whether the question is support for cabinet nominees or the invasion of Haiti, tax increases or prayer in the schools, universal health insurance or welfare reform, disputants swat incessantly at each other. Particular constituencies and advocates obviously vary with the conflict, but there is a recurrent process. Claims of crisis are made to attract attention, followed by predictable countercharges of emotionalism and attention-grabbing. Statistical aggregates (deficit levels here and abroad, or estimates of the number of homeless, disabled, fearless, or fearful) are presented in speeches or in writing as if the mere statistics were sufficient to justify a single, inescapable policy response to a complex social or political problem.

Crisis-mongering and fact-throwing ensure that the supply of American public "problems" will be enormous; the simple citation of facts can always establish a gap between aspiration and actuality. Moreover, there are always compelling illustrations to demonstrate the character of the difficulties and, if appropriately crafted, to suggest the right remedy. There will, of course, be difficulties, audiences are told. But, with political will and a modicum of good luck, the nation can choose the right course and move toward whatever is claimed to be the desirable state of affairs: less infant mortality, better education for the young, more effective defense, less injustice, lower medical costs, more habitable cities, more readily available therapeutic drugs, control over Alzheimer's disease, reduced levels of cancer, fairness in Social Security, or whatever.

With an emphasis on unanalyzed statistics and with the goal of identifying yet another crisis, rhetoric and ridicule supplant reasoned analysis and discussion all too often within the political arena. Indeed, what Americans learn about politics and policy choices, particularly on television but also in the print media, gives enormous weight to the simplistic analysis of problems, to vivid images of allegedly straightforward remedies, to the confusion of anecdote with social fact, and to the purveying, alternately, of doom and delight. These are the materials out of which politicians create their own, often self-serving, myths of political or social problems and of how they must be remedied. We all may agree, of course, that genuine problems exist or that "there oughta be a law," but the real issue—and the real challenge—is to determine just what law should be enacted, just what can reasonably be achieved.

In this context, what is sometimes known as America's "politics of exaggeration" tends to obscure rather than address the sources of America's social and political problems and what must be done to ameliorate them. The complaint is not simply that reasoned debate is too rare in American politics, but that mythmakers and their calls of crisis play too prominent a role in defining what the policy debates are about. Open democratic politics must include clichés, slogans, rallying symbols, even myths of failure and of ready remedies. Nonetheless, the politics of exaggeration, when systematic, can paralyze as well as prod. All too often, elected politicians, appointed officials, pressure groups, and the media coalesce to produce a cacophony of proposal, commentary, and appraisal. Strident and superficial public debate tends to inhibit rather than enhance the formulation and implementation of effective public policy. In place of collective determination to ameliorate public problems, we end up with a deeply divided citizenry who cannot agree on either the sources of our problems or how to address them. And in place of ameliorative programs, we end up with heightened expectations and programmatic half-measures. The consequences are ineffective interventions, recurrent recriminations, and, increasingly, the political disillusionment of the American public.

THE CRISIS OF THE WELFARE STATE

Current political disputes over social welfare policies have been shaped by two decades of troubled economic circumstances and declining expectations in America. For much of the 1970s and 1980s the recurrent refrain in American commentary on social policy was that of crisis. Stimulated by the quadrupling of oil prices in 1973–74, the stagflation of the 1970s occasioned dire observations about the capacity of American government to improve social conditions. Some argued that diminished public revenues made it impossible to satisfy the expectations generated by the Great Society programs of the Kennedy-Johnson years. Others claimed that the programs themselves had helped to produce the economic mess we came to call stagflation. Whatever the cause, the malaise seemed palpable. A diminished sense of what was possible, a sad or angry reaction to the earlier aspirations, and a skeptical view of governmental capacities—all of these reactions constituted the basic claim that there was a crisis in America's welfare state.

Exacerbating this sense of crisis and disorientation was the fact that America's social welfare programs were themselves adopted in response to crises, and in times of great social need; they lack a deeply rooted, widely understood ideological foundation, a common social or political vision.[3] We live, for instance, with the legacy of the New Deal's social policies, a set of programmatic initiatives for providing relief, promoting economic security, and insuring against the devastating family consequences of unemployment, widowhood, industrial accident, and the like.... From this beginning came later adaptations of the original models, extensions of Social Security and related programs to the survivors of workers (in 1939), to disabled workers (in 1956), and to the medical expenses of the elderly and the poor (Medicare and Medicaid in 1965) (Berkowitz 1997). As a consequence, with a perceived crisis in these social programs themselves, the political consensus about the programs—their legitimacy, their viability, and their goals—is vulnerable to exaggerated fears.

Political discussions of social welfare policies have followed the same pattern of frenzied activity described in the preceding section. The facts presented, the standards invoked, the options considered—all are regularly riddled with misconception and much mischief (Marmor, Mashaw, and Harvey 1990). There are, to be sure, excellent descriptions of American conditions, and there is an abundance of social scientific work, much of it illuminating when understood properly. But as this scholarly work is used in political disputes over social welfare policies, the nuances and uncertainties of the social scientific literature are typically lost. Assisted by a large industry of analysts who provide the requisite factual foundation in reports and studies, elected officials, lobbyists, and other participants in political debate latch onto the "explanations" and "solutions" that best fit their own political goals. The results of this process are deeply unsettling, a kind of rationalistic fantasy where elements of reasoned argument and symbol-rattling coalesce into a muddle of intellectual confusion.

Amidst this confusion, however, there is a continuing and recognizable pattern, one that reflects two quite different, competing views of the goals of our social welfare programs: the residualist and the social insurance conceptions of the welfare state.[4] Each of these has its own attractions. Each has had an impact on public discussion. And each has the capacity to influence the character of America's social welfare programs, including the treatment of the young and the old.

The view of the welfare state as "residualist" characterizes social policies as a safety net. The "net" of social welfare programs is intended to rescue the victims of capitalism and to give subsistence-level relief to those unable to provide for their own needs. This view of purpose, originating as it did in the European poor laws, is found everywhere among capitalist nations. Though its popularity differs among those nations, the residualist conception has had a pervasive impact on public debates about social welfare programs. In the United States, and in Australia and Canada as well, the residualist conception is the staple not only of business and financial elites, but also of substantial proportions of middle- and lower-income populations.

Most of those who describe the welfare state as residual believe that social policy's aim should be temporary assistance, and its governance highly decentralized. In federal regimes the rallying cry of the residualists has been to diffuse authority for social programs to the states and provinces. American public assistance programs such as the federal-state Aid to Dependent Children (later Aid to Families with Dependent Children, AFDC), which was part of the original Social Security Act of 1935, exemplify the residual model. Advocates of decentralization presume that individual families will typically assure the welfare of their members. When that fails, institutions close to those families—

charitable groups, then local and state programs—constitute the appropriate protection against destitution.

The metaphor of the safety net suggests the key features of residualist welfare policy. The net is close to the ground and the benefits are accordingly modest—a subsistence that might vary widely in connection with community standards of adequacy. The clientele are the down-and-out; the eligibility criteria, whether tests of needs or means, are designed to sort out the truly needy from the rest. There is an implicit notion of avoiding potential waste; aid should go only to those who need the net to survive. Minimal adequacy, selectivity, localism, and tests of need—these constitute the residualist's controlling notions for evaluating the welfare state.

So stated, the conception of welfare as residualist differs sharply from what is known as the social insurance model. The basic purpose of social insurance is to maintain economic well-being amidst threats to or loss of family income. What links social insurance advocates is their rejection of the residualist conception of welfare as a mere safety net against destitution.

The central metaphor of social insurance is the insurance card. If the net of welfare is to catch those who have already failed, the card of social insurance symbolizes prevention against a radical decline of a family's living standards. The aim is simple: the universalization of the financial security presumed in the fringe benefits of higher civil servants and economic elites. The threats to economic security include some obvious ones—involuntary unemployment, widowhood, sickness, injury, or retirement—as well as less obvious ones such as a large family (child allowances). Welfare states have provided for these eventualities at different times, in different sequences, and with considerable variation in generosity and terms of administration. Yet, irrespective of form and levels of payment, social insurance programs have rejected as inferior the selective machinery of means-tested programs: the more universal the entitlement, the closer it is to the model. . . .

Contributions during working life, according to the orthodox theory of social insurance, "entitle" one to "protection" against large reductions in economic status. Sometimes the contributions are payments into the larger society's general tax revenues, as is the case in Canada. Or, as in Great Britain, contributions are in the form of weekly social insurance payments. These arrangements differ from the percentage-of-payroll taxes of the United States' Old Age and Survivors Insurance program, the familiar FICA tax. Yet the idea is the same: to contribute while working to future financial security. The overriding goal is to protect citizens, through a social insurance program, against the predictable risks of a modern industrial society.[5]

THE CONFLICT BETWEEN THE OLD AND THE YOUNG OVER
SOCIAL SECURITY

With this background in mind, we are in a position to turn to Social Security itself, with special attention to the much-touted conflict between old-age beneficiaries and younger Americans. Those younger Americans, according to the proponents of intergenerational inequity, face unfair prospects. They will either receive no Social Security retirement benefits at all, or obtain, in comparison with previous retirees, substantially reduced "rates of return" on their contributions to Social Security.[6] In the meantime, Social Security's current and projected expenditures appear to make other social programs for children and working Americans unaffordable.

What facts support this fearful picture? There is no dispute that America's older citizens receive the lion's share of the income, in cash and in services, that the nation's social programs distribute. In 1994, for example, expenditures on the elderly amounted to roughly a third of the entire federal budget.[7] Nor ... is there disagreement that a large proportion of younger Americans *fear* that Social Security pensions will not "be there" for them when they retire. Two-thirds of Americans aged 25 to 34 believe it is either very or somewhat likely that they will not receive their retirement pensions. The same proportion fears for the future of the entire Social Security program itself.[8] What underlies these fears and beliefs is fundamental uncertainty about the fiscal future of Social Security pensions.... Current projections are that pension payments will begin to exceed the Social Security payroll and benefits tax early in the twenty-first century, and that the resulting operating deficit will deplete the Social Security trust fund by 2030. Will substantial—and unaffordable—tax increases be the only means of maintaining reasonable benefit levels and of paying the promised pensions to retirees?

Before turning to the issue of future affordability, let us begin by discussing whether it is even appropriate to conceptualize Social Security issues in terms of the young versus the old, in terms of the supposedly threatened and the supposedly indulged. "Justice between age groups," as Norman Daniels has cogently argued, "is a problem best solved if we stop thinking of the old and the young as distinct groups. We age. The young become the old. As we age, we pass through institutions that affect our well-being at each stage of life, from infancy to very old age" (1988:18).

All young people anticipate, even if hazily, a time when they will be old. Their parents and grandparents are vivid examples of what it means to move through the life cycle. A social insurance system designed to deal with predictable changes in income is simultaneously a means of distributing income among particular age cohorts and a means of distributing income over the life cycle of particular people. As a normative matter, the justice of a program is a question of whether it treats people fairly as they move through stages. As a financial matter, the affordability of programs over time is [a question of] whether current promises can be kept. The first matter is one that ignores time, place, and particular facts. The second is very much a matter of whether, at some future time, promises can be kept. Keeping these two issues distinct is crucially important if problems concerning Social Security are to be properly understood and addressed. Unfortunately, much of the old-versus-young debate over Social Security has disregarded this distinction and consequently confused, rather than clarified, public discussion.[9]

The foregoing analysis is quite consistent with the available survey data. Americans do not see issues of Social Security as involving an irreducible conflict between the young and the old. For example, in a random survey of 1,209 Americans, Cook and Barrett (1992) found that an astounding 97 percent favored maintaining or increasing Social Security benefits. Four out of five respondents reported they were satisfied that a portion of every working person's income goes to support Social Security. Almost two-thirds said they would pay higher taxes if the program were threatened with cuts from its current pension levels (which provide retirees, on average, about 40 percent of their pre-retirement wage and salary income). As Reno and Friedland (1997) note, . . . other polls tell a similar story. The National Election Surveys and the National Opinion Research Center, which have monitored attitudes toward Social Security since 1982, provide cross-sectional data from two large national samples that substantiate high levels of support for Social Security (Cook 1996).

At least as far as public preferences are concerned, then, there is undeniably broad support for a Social Security pension program whose goals fall well within the social insurance, rather than the residualist, conception of the welfare state. The American public appears committed to a pension program that provides retirees with reasonable income security, and at a level above that of mere subsistence. Moreover, there is only marginal support for cutting back pensions to the minimal levels preferred by residualists.

Given this continuing public support for the present Social Security pension system, one might wonder why there has been such fearfulness about the retirement program's future, both its fairness and its future affordability. Here is where specters of the future—widely disseminated—have frightened so many contemporary citizens.[10] Upon examination, however, the facts are far less frightening than they may be made to appear at first glance. Since the reform amendments were enacted in 1983, for example, the surplus of revenues over benefits and administrative expenses has been substantial (Marmor, Mashaw, and Harvey 1990:140).[11] This obvious fact led Brookings Institution economists Henry Aaron and Robert Reischauer to characterize Social Security as an "island of budgetary surplus in the midst of an ocean of red ink" (Aaron and Reischauer 1987). In 1994 alone, the Social Security "surplus"—the excess of revenues over outlays—amounted to $44 billion.

With a cumulative surplus in 1994 of $436 billion in the Social Security pension program, the question of affordability depends only upon the prospects for maintaining current pension levels into the indefinite future. The demographic data are, in fact, already well known. The elderly of the twenty-first century have, for the most part, already been born, and their gross numbers can be estimated with considerable confidence. The elderly will almost surely constitute a larger share of the population than they do now (12.6 percent; see table 10.1). Nonetheless, the record of other industrialized countries provides grounds for cautious optimism. Many of these countries have been maintaining their retirement pension programs intact with proportions of the elderly far greater than the United States is projected to have in 2010 (12.8 percent).[12]

TABLE 10.1

Estimated Percentages of Population Age 65 and Older, 1970–2020, in Selected Countries

	1970	1980	1990	2000	2010	2020
Canada	7.9	9.5	11.5	12.4	13.3	16.7
France	12.9	14.0	14.0	15.6	16.0	19.5
Germany	13.7	15.6	14.6	15.5	18.4	19.1
Italy	10.9	13.1	14.1	17.0	18.9	20.9
Japan	7.1	9.0	11.7	16.2	20.1	24.2
United Kingdom	12.9	15.1	15.7	15.4	15.8	18.2
United States	9.8	11.3	12.6	12.3	12.8	16.3

Note: The projections for 2000, 2020, and 2020 are based on assumptions about future trends in fertility. In preparing these assumptions, the United Nations' statistical unit published high-, medium-, and low-fertility variants but says that the medium-fertility variant projections can be thought of as "most likely" (United Nations 1993:84). Therefore, we use medium-fertility variant projections in this table.

Source: Compiled by the authors from data in United Nations 1993:408–9, 462–63, 470–71, 510–11, 514–15, 660–61, 666–67.

In assessing the future affordability of Social Security pensions, it is also important to determine what other changes there will be in the demands upon both the income of workers and the public treasury. What else is happening to the population that will affect the affordability of Social Security pensions and other social welfare programs? In this context, one crucially important change concerns what is known as the "dependency ratio," the percentage of the population not available for productive work (children, the elderly, and the disabled). Although the number of elderly Americans is increasing and will continue to increase, the number of infants and school-age children is *decreasing* even more rapidly. By 2040, the dependency ratio is expected to be even lower than it was in 1960 (U.S. Congress 1989, p. 89, table 13). And insofar as the dependency ratio is decreasing, the total burden upon workers to support the young and the old may also decrease as well, despite the expected growth in the number of elderly Americans.[13]

This line of reasoning does not require any particular conclusion about whether the mix of future financial demands will be more or less acceptable to future taxpayers. But it does provide a context in which "affordability" can be more reasonably assessed. If we know that the proportion of one set of claimants on public support will grow in scale and that the proportion of another will fall, it places the shape of our public household in perspective. Then the question becomes a practical one of shifting expectations, adjusting flows of taxation, and the like. The available data simply do not support the vision of a society overrun by greedy geezers. Instead, what we can project is that reasonable adjustments will need to be made in Social Security pensions and taxation levels in order to achieve the consensual and morally appropriate goal of maintaining Social Security pension support for our retired citizens. Indeed, by one estimate (Ball 1996), a 1.9 percentage point increase in taxes on employees and employers would correct the shortfall projected for 2020.

THE DIVISIVE ISSUE OF GENERATIONAL EQUITY

We have just seen how helpful it is to distinguish between the normative desirability of, and public support for, Social Security pensions, on the one hand, and the affordability of those pensions, on the other. For example, with the goal of maintaining long-term pension levels threatened in the late 1970s and early 1980s by the retirement program's *projected* long-term deficits, Congress enacted the requisite reforms. By putting Social Security back on a firm financial foundation, the reforms of 1983 effectively ensured that the system's basic commitments would be protected for the foreseeable future.[14]

Once the 1983 reforms were enacted, one might have expected the public debate over Social Security to subside. Once again, Social Security was, or so it seemed, a politically popular, fiscally sound program with clear, broadly accepted purposes. Nonetheless, after a pause in the mid-1980s, the disputes returned and, indeed, grew increasingly strident by the end of the decade. Political conservatives remained deeply dissatisfied with the admittedly large expenditures to which Social Security is committed; motivated by residualist goals to reduce these expenditures, conservatives succeeded in re-opening the debate by changing the terms of the debate itself.

The issues raised in the 1970s and early 1980s had mostly to do with affordability. Could Social Security be maintained in an economic context of stagflation? Was "bankruptcy" its fate? The clear answer of 1983 was yes to the first question and no to the second. What, then, could be raised as a fundamental objection to a widely supported program, one regularly labeled a "sacred cow" by its critics? From the conservative perspective of welfare state residualists, a currently solvent Social Security program required reinterpretation. That reinterpretation, it turned out, involved the theme of "generational equity." And because this expression combined claims of unfairness with ones of affordability, it became a potent ideological symbol and weapon against the status quo.

The question of how this old-versus-young formulation took shape in the 1980s and 1990s is one on which future historians will expend ample energy. But, for our purposes, it is necessary only to outline the main features of the campaign and the policy issues they raise. Quite apart from the merits of their arguments, the purveyors of the conflict between old and young have played upon the consciousness of age within American culture. This became more politically salient when the federal government, constrained by stagflation, faced difficult allocational decisions in an environment influenced by an increasingly powerful, highly visible lobby of America's seniors.[15] In this context, residualist critics invoked the concept of generational equity, as it came to be defined in the early 1980s, as a means of creating conflict where previously there had been none: the current young should not be deprived of opportunities for economic and social well-being because of excessive allocations of resources to the old.[16]

This strategy of reinterpreting the affordability of social welfare programs for the elderly in terms of a supposed conflict between generations was very successful indeed. Even in the wake of the Social Security reforms of 1983, pundits received enormous attention and succeeded in making the conflict between young and old feel both real and pressing. In 1984, for instance, Senator David Durenberger (R-Minn.), founded Americans for Generational Equity (AGE) to "promote the concept [of generational equity] . . . among America's political, intellectual, and financial leaders." Claiming credit for calling "into question the prudence, sustainability, and fairness of federal old age benefit programs" (AGE 1990:2), AGE's impact was, according to scholarly evaluations, considerable. One scholar of American social policy maintains that AGE, despite going out of business in the wake of Senator Durenberger's financial scandal in the late 1980s, reshaped public discussion. "All future policy choices," according to Quadagno, "will have to take generational equity into account" (1989:364).

What political conservatives claimed, some academic figures supported. This was particularly true of the demographer Professor Samuel Preston. Preston was the best known of the academic experts to support the charge that conditions had deteriorated for children and improved dramatically for the elderly. Moreover, Preston claimed that "gains for one group . . . at least in the public sphere . . . come partly at the expense of another." It was but a short intellectual step from this position to the conclusion that huge "transfers from the working-age population to the elderly are also transfers away from children" (1984:450–52). This formulation remains at the core of the charge of generational inequity, and the source of deep conflict between the young and the old.

As well befits American politics and its tendency to abuse statistics for partisan purposes, it is worth mentioning that Preston is a distinguished demographer, with considerable expertise in the determinants of large-scale population shifts. But he has no expertise in public finance, social insurance, or public policy politics. His fearful formulation, substantiated with data from the 1970s, took no account of the reforms of 1983. None of this mattered, however, to residualists looking for the evidence they needed to support the charge of generational inequity. His views spread rapidly through both academic and journalistic circles.[17]

This disconnection between the realities of program finance and the rhetoric of generational conflict has, indeed, become standard since the mid-1980s. Whereas the doomsaying of the early 1980s was occasioned by the projected deficits of the Social Security system, criticism of the Social Security system took on an altogether different cast by the late 1980s. The facts were plain. By 1989, the system's reserves had reached $163 billion and were to increase to $226 billion by the end of 1990. Ironically, such surpluses were as worrying to the critics of the greedy aged as the projected deficits had been. They constituted what one congressman called a "catastrophe waiting" to happen. Even the *New York Times* came to regard Social Security surpluses as "a crisis in trillions . . . a crisis in slow motion" (*New York Times* 1988:A-18). This continuity of program-matic criticism and fearful forecasting, given the enormous change of fiscal facts, shows clearly the ideological character of the debate over old and young in social policy politics. When critics wring their hands whether a program is in deficit or surplus, one rightly suspects they are critical of the program's aims as such, and not simply of the program's performance.[18]

In the late 1980s political conservatives moved beyond their assault on Social Security toward a broader attack on America's welfare state. In *On Borrowed Time: How the Growth of Entitlements Threatens America's Future*, former secre-tary of commerce Peter Peterson and the political analyst Neil Howe launched a residualist critique of entitlement programs in general. The generational equity issue was again the battering ram used against the elderly. In addition to constituting an illegitimate transfer from the young to the old, excessive Social Security disbursements were, the authors argued, "a direct cause of our federal deficit" (Peterson and Howe 1988:43). After the unexpected demise of Ameri-cans for Generational Equity, Peterson himself helped to found a new group, the Concord Coalition, with the same conservative policy agenda. Nominally dedicated to the purpose of educating Americans about the hard financial choices the nation will be confronting, the coalition reiterates the conservative position that government spending favors older, more affluent Americans at the expense of a younger generation that is already under financial distress (Concord Coalition 1992). In addition to encouraging younger Americans to see themselves as needy and to see the elderly as an affluent group not deserv-ing of public support, the coalition is not beneath the use of scare tactics. It has warned, for example, that the failure to transform Social Security may bring on a generational war. And given their own residualist political agenda, Peterson and other coalition members have been ready to lead it.

Though Peterson, Howe, and other conservative residualists portrayed them-selves as defending the interests of America's children, many professionals dedi-cated to promoting just those interests have seen through this strategy. They rec-ognize it as a dangerous effort to divide the young and the old, and to undercut public support for important governmental programs such as Social Security.[19] Many advocates for the interests of children have therefore made a concerted effort to quell the intentionally divisive rhetoric of generational equity. Of special importance has been their role in founding Generations United, a group whose goal is to "dispel the myth of competition for scarce resources and reap the ben-efits of intergenerational collaboration . . . and interdependence" (Generations United 1990a, 1990b). According to David Liederman, executive director of the Child Welfare League of America, who helped to start Generations United, "What we are trying to say is that the fates of the generations are linked. Obviously, I want better programs for kids . . . but they should not come at the expense of seniors, especially the large number of seniors who are poor or near poor" (quoted in Pearlstein 1993).

No one can doubt that the Social Security retirement program needed the reforms enacted in 1983 or that more reforms will be needed in the future. The 1983 reforms put Social Security back on the track to fiscal balance, and there seems little reason to doubt that a nation dedicated to the continuance of the program will again find the means and the resolve to adapt it to changing circumstances. In this context, the shrill claims of generational inequity are substantively misguided and factually unfounded. Nonetheless, interpreted within the larger residualist political agenda of reducing the scope of the federal government and of rejecting the existing goals of the welfare state, the claim of generational unfairness has proven to be remarkably newsworthy. By invoking the seemingly high moral ground of generational equity, residualists have succeeded in launching a concerted and surprisingly resonant attack upon Social Security and other programs for the aged.[20] It is important to note, however, that advocates of generational equity, despite their alleged concern for the young, have almost never made demands that public expenditures for the benefit of children be increased.

The claim of generational unfairness has proven to be a deeply divisive element in the social policy politics of the last decade. Because reasoned public debate is so difficult to sustain in the United States, this conflict will surely remain a source of tension in future discussions of programs affecting elderly Americans.

NOTES

   1. For purposes of this essay, Social Security refers to the retirement, disability, and survivors pensions administered by the Social Security Administration. The SSA also administers public assistance programs (AFDC, SSI) that do not depend on social insurance principles. Certain programs (e.g., Medicare, Medicaid) are administered by other agencies (e.g., the Health Care Financial Administration). It is against this broader background of social welfare policy that we will assess the character, and the distortions, of the dispute over generational equity as it relates to Social Security pensions.

   2. It is not just the policy elites who are fretting. The issue of generational equity has become a prominent one in the mass media, which often stress the element of conflict between generations. . . .

3. This contrasts with Sweden, for example, where social security programs
were much more directly linked to social democratic ideological foundations
(William-son and Pampel 1993a, 1993b).

4. To avoid any possible confusion, it should be noted that some scholars refer
to this social insurance conception of the welfare state as the "institutional model"
of social welfare.

5. Because of its marginal impact on both public debate and public policy, we
are relegating to an endnote a third conception of the welfare state, namely, that of
the radical populist. From this radical perspective, the aims of help and compensation are themselves questionable, since they constitute adjustments to the harsh
realities of industrial society, not means of transforming society. The standard for
the radical theorist is equalization, not equitable insurance payments or adequacy
of cash payments. The aim is social change, not evening the distribution of income
over the life cycle. And the mechanisms are not ameliorative social programs for the
people, but income and power to the less privileged. What social insurance advocates count as generous provision is, for the radical populist, a token gesture, no
more than a way to gloss over the contradictions of modern capitalism. For others
on the radical left, social insurance and other social welfare benefits are a citizen's
rightful wage, a benefit that workers demanded and won through conflict with the
economic elite. This entire section draws liberally from Marmor, Mashaw, and
Harvey 1990, chs. 2–3.

6. The projection of substantial declines in the rate of return on Social Security
contributions creates an independent source for claiming generational inequity in
relation to Social Security and Medicare. The current generation of elderly
Americans has, according to this argument, received a much higher rate of return
than will apply to the current cohort of working Americans. . . .

7. That budget was approximately $1.53 trillion (U.S. Office of Management
and Budget 1995, table 6-1). The fact that a large share of the federal budget is for
programs affecting the elderly is a consequence of how the United States has structured its public household, not some sort of mistake. Medicare began as a program
for the elderly, the only example in the Western industrial world of public health
insurance for an age group. This has the effect of highlighting the medical costs of
the elderly when the fact is that elderly citizens are high utilizers of medical care in
every society. Likewise, the retirement program of the SSA assumes a more prominent place in federal expenditures because the United States funds primary and secondary education from largely local sources and, unlike Western Europe, does not
have a very large public housing program. In short, what should be no surprise—
the prominence of the elderly in American public finance—is inappropriately
treated as some sort of failure.

8. See Reno and Friedland 1997 for a detailed analysis of Social Security and public opinion.

9. By focusing exclusively on Social Security retirement pensions, critics invoking the conflict between young and old have effectively ignored the federal government's established commitment to provide economic protection over the entire course of the life span. For example, children already benefit, directly or indirectly, from a wide range of programs administered by the SSA and by other federal agencies.

10. See the later discussion of Americans for Generational Equity and the Concord Coalition, two of the most recently established groups that have resorted to crisis-mongering and manipulation of statistics in an effort to undercut public support for Social Security.

11. These included raising the eligibility age from 65 to 67 by some time in the twenty-first century, increasing payroll taxes, subjecting up to 50 percent of Social Security benefits to income taxation, and instituting a surplus revenue system.

12. The projected proportion of elderly Americans in 2020 (16.3 percent) is approximately the same as Great Britain has already experienced, and without having to drastically alter its pension benefits (see Williamson and Pampel 1993a, 1993b).

13. The image of elderly Americans as greedy geezers who are depleting the public treasury at the expense of the young is, in this context, a product of incomplete demography. There are, in fact, two measures of dependency. A narrow measure of dependency is the ratio of conventional retirees to workers. It is this ratio that is increasing and that, taken in itself, appears to support alarming projections. A broader and more helpful measure of dependency, however, is the ratio of Americans over 65 *plus* children under 18 *plus* other nonworkers such as the disabled, to workers. By taking the elderly, the children, and the disabled into account, this ratio provides a much more complete picture of those dependent upon the public treasury for support and services. It is this ratio that is decreasing and that undercuts projections that Social Security pensions will overrun the public treasury. . . .

14. For example, Social Security reserves totaled an estimated $226 billion in 1990, up from $163 billion just the year before.

15. This analysis follows that of Pierson and Smith (1994:22–23, 43–47), who also found that issues of age have little to do with the politics of social policy in Canada, where discussions are dominated by issues of class and federalism. Similarly, in an analysis of the salience of issues related to generational equity in Canada and the United States, Cook et al. found little attention given to generational equity in Canada (Cook, Marshall, Marshall, and Kaufman 1994).

16. With the American welfare state focusing so much on programs for the elderly (such as Social Security pensions and Medicare), some critics have blamed the nation's fiscal problems on its greedy geezers. This scapegoating was an unanticipated consequence of how America has structured its public household. Canada, with an equivalent proportion of the elderly and with similar rates of medical care use, experienced comparable economic strain in the 1970s and 1980s. But because Canada's universal medical program covers everyone who is sick, and not just the elderly, there has been no widespread hand-wringing there about the "greying of the federal budget" (Marmor and Beglin 1995).

17. Between 1985 and 1992, the *Social Science Citation Index* shows that Preston's writings in *Demography* and *Scientific American* were cited in 158 articles. This amount of attention classifies Preston's work as what some scholars call a "research front." Only 3 percent of all published articles in scholarly journals are cited fifty times or more (Garfield 1984).

18. This analysis is drawn from Marmor, Mashaw, and Harvey 1990, ch. 5.

19. For a discussion of how the conflict between young and old might be reframed, see Kingson and Williamson 1993.

20. For an analysis of the 1995 residualist assault on Medicare, see Marmor and Beglin 1995.

REFERENCES

Aaron, Henry J., and Robert D. Reischauer. 1987. "Bite the Deficit, Not Social Security." *Washington Post* (December 16).

Americans for Generational Equity. 1990. *Annual Report*. Washington, D.C.: Americans for Generational Equity.

Ball, Robert M. 1996. Personal communication.

Ball, Robert M., and Thomas N. Bethell. 1997. "Bridging the Centuries: The Case for Traditional Social Security." Pp. 259–294 in *Social Security in the 21st Century*, edited by Eric R. Kingson and James H. Schulz. New York: Oxford University Press.

Berkowitz, Edward D. 1997. "The Historical Development of Social Security in the United States." Pp. 22–38 in *Social Security in the 21st Century*, edited by Eric R. Kingson and James H. Schulz. New York: Oxford University Press.

Chen, Yung-Ping, and Stephen C. Goss. 1997. "Are Returns on Payroll Taxes Fair?" Pp. 76–90 in *Social Security in the 21st Century*, edited by Eric R. Kingson and James H. Schulz. New York: Oxford University Press.

Concord Coalition. 1992. *The Zero Deficit Plan*. Washington, D.C.: Concord

Coalition.

Cook, Fay Lomax. 1996. "Public Support for Programs for Older Americans: Continuities Amidst Threats of Discontinuities." Pp. 327–346 in *Continuities and Discontinuities in Adulthood and Aging*, edited by Vern Bengtson. New York: Springer.

Cook, Fay Lomax, and Edith J. Barrett. 1992. *Support for the American Welfare State: Views from Congress and the Public*. New York: Columbia University Press.

Cook, Fay Lomax, Victor W. Marshall, Joanne Gard Marshall, and Julie E. Kaufman. 1994. "The Salience of Intergenerational Equity in Canada and the United States." Pp. 96–101 in *Economic Security and Intergenerational Justice*, edited by Theodore R. Marmor, Timothy M. Smeeding, and Vernon L. Greene. Washington, D.C.: Urban Institute.

Daniels, Norman. 1988. *Am I My Parents' Keeper? An Essay on Justice Between the Young and the Old*. New York: Oxford University Press.

Garfield, Eugene. 1984. "The 100 Most Cited Papers Ever and How We Select Citation Classics." *Current Classics* 23 (4): 176–178.

Generations United. 1990a. *Strategies for Change: Building State and Local Coalitions on Intergenerational Issues and Programs*. Washington, D.C.: Generations United.

Generations United. 1990b. *Promoting Cooperation Among Americans of All Ages*. Washington, D.C.: Generations United.

Kingson, Eric R., and John B. Williamson. 1993. "The Generational Equity Debate: A Progressive Framing of a Conservative Issue." *Journal of Aging and Social Policy* 5 (3): 31–52.

Marmor, Theodore R., and Julie Beglin. 1995. "Medicare and How It Grew—To Be Confused and Misjudged." *Boston Globe* (May 7).

Marmor, Theodore R., Jerry L. Mashaw, and Philip L. Harvey. 1990. *America's Misunderstood Welfare State: Persistent Myths, Enduring Realities*. New York: Basic Books.

New York Times. 1988. "Trillions, Trillions All Around." Editorial (April 11), p. A-18.

Pearlstein, Steven. 1993. "The Battle Over 'Generational Equity': Powerful Spending, Tax Choices Have the Young Calling for the Old to Get Less." *Washington Post* (February 17).

Peterson, Peter G., and Neil Howe. 1988. *On Borrowed Time: How the Growth in Entitlement Spending Threatens America's Future*. San Francisco: Institute for Contemporary Studies.

Pierson, Paul, and Miriam Smith. 1994. "Shifting Fortunes of the Elderly: The Comparative Politics of Retrenchment." Pp. 21–51 in *Economic Security and Intergenerational Justice*, edited by Theodore R. Marmor, Timothy M. Smeeding, and Vernon L. Greene. Washington, D.C.: Urban Institute.

Preston, Samuel H. 1984. "Children and the Elderly: Divergent Paths for America's

Dependents." *Demography* 21 (4): 435–457.

Quadagno, Jill. 1989. "Generational Equity and the Politics of the Welfare State." *Politics and Society* 17 (3): 353–376.

Reno, Virginia P., and Robert B. Friedland. 1997. "Strong Support but Low Confidence: What Explains the Contradiction?" Pp. 178–194 in *Social Security in the 21st Century*, edited by Eric R. Kingson and James H. Schulz. New York: Oxford University Press.

Thompson, Lawrence H., and Melinda M. Upp. 1997. "The Social Insurance Approach and Social Security," Pp. 3–21 in *Social Security in the 21st Century*, edited by Eric R. Kingson and James H. Schulz. New York: Oxford University Press.

United Nations. 1993. *World Population Prospects: The 1992 Revision.* New York: U.N. Department for Economic and Social Information and Policy Analysis.

U.S. Congress, House Committee on Ways and Means. 1989. *Background Material and Data on Programs Within the Jurisdiction of the Committee on Ways and Means.* Washington, D.C.: U.S. Government Printing Office.

U.S. Office of Management and Budget. 1995. *Analytical Perspectives, Budget of the United States Government, Fiscal Year 1996.* Washington, D.C.: U.S. Government Printing Office.

Williamson, John B., and Fred C. Pampel. 1993a. *Old-Age Security in Comparative Perspective.* New York: Oxford University Press.

Williamson, John B., and Fred C. Pampel. 1993b. "Paying for the Baby Boom Generation's Social Security Pensions: United States, United Kingdom, Germany, and Sweden." *Journal of Aging Studies* 7 (1): 41–54.

CHAPTER ELEVEN

Why Privatizing Social Security Is a Bad Idea

Eric R. Kingson and John B. Williamson

Eric R. Kingson is professor of social work at Syracuse University's School of Social Work. He is a member of the National Academy of Social Insurance, and he served as professional staff to the 1982 National Commission on Social Security Reform and to the 1995 Bipartisan Commission on Entitlement and Tax Reform. His publications include *Social Security in the 21st Century, Ties That Bind: The Interdependence of Generations,* and *Social Security and Medicare: A Policy Primer.* See chapter 1 for biographical information about John B. Williamson.

Kingson and Williamson trace the evolution of proposals to privatize Social Security from their status as a right-wing fantasy during the early 1980s to what are considered mainstream policy options today. By challenging the legitimacy and widespread support of Social Security, the generational equity theme has done much to advance and legitimize the idea of privatizing Social Security. After discussing the pitfalls of privatization, the authors point out that there are many viable alternatives to privatization for addressing the Social Security financing problem. They argue that reform should proceed with an appreciation for the values at play in the debate. The moral basis of Social Security, they suggest, draws on the stake the citizenry has in the well-being of their families, neighbors, and communities.

Proposals to privatize Social Security are increasingly prevalent, having moved from the status of a right-wing fantasy during the early 1980s to serious policy consideration by the mid-1990s. What explains this change in the contemporary Social Security policy agenda, and what do policymakers and the public need to know to carefully assess various proposals to privatize or partially privatize Old Age Survivors and Disability Insurance (OASDI)? To answer these questions, we briefly trace the evolution of Social Security and the growing prominence of privatization proposals, emphasizing the role served by the generational equity theme as a vehicle for challenging the widespread public support for Social Security, thereby paving the way for possible radical reforms. Next, focusing much of our discussion on the report of the 1994–96 Advisory Council on Social Security, we discuss factors that need to be taken into account when considering privatization proposals. It is important to understand that much is at stake in this debate and that privatization proposals generally make it more difficult to address Social Security's projected financing shortfalls. We suggest that privatization proposals are consistent with the pattern that John Kingdon (1995) identifies, whereby policy entrepreneurs seek to attach their preferred "solutions" (i.e., privatization) to whatever problem (i.e., financing) is sufficiently large enough to open a window of opportunity for reform.

SOCIAL SECURITY: RATIONALES, ORIGINS, AND EVOLUTION

Social Security is the central institution in the American approach to social protection. It is the only pension protection available to six out of ten working persons in the private sector. For those who are relatively well off, say the roughly 4.8 million elderly households with incomes between $18,732 and $31,179 in 1994, Social Security provides nearly half of the total income going to their homes. For the 60 percent of the elderly households (14.6 million) with incomes under $18,731 in 1994, Social Security provides over 70 percent of all income (U.S. Department of Health and Human Services 1996). The main source of disability and survivors protection for America's families and employees, the program provides the equivalent of roughly a $300,000 life insurance policy and a $207,000 disability policy for a "typical" family with young children. Indeed, though known by few, the program provides the equivalent of $12.1 trillion dollars in life insurance protection, more than the entire value ($10.8 trillion) of all the private life insurance in force. Included among its 44 million beneficiaries are three million children under 18 who receive benefits each month.

Of course, it wasn't always this way. "Prior to the enactment of the Old Age

Insurance Program in 1935, economic security rested on the ability, discretion, and goodwill of families, charities, and government officials to supplement individuals' actions" (Kingson and Schulz 1997:42). And the county poorhouse, now little more than a historical footnote, stood as the most feared symbol of indigence in old age.

The rapid growth of an industrializing and capitalizing economy meant that the nation could afford more social protection. Simultaneously, a changed economy placed more workers at risk of loss of income due to economic cycles, age-related obsolescence, and disability (Berkowitz 1991). At the beginning of the twentieth century one group of social reformers, looking to the European experience, began to advance the social insurance approach to economic security. Rejecting the principle of "less eligibility" arising out of the nation's poor laws traditions—the idea that the circumstances of relief should be so unpleasant as to discourage all but the most needy from seeking public benefits—the social insurance approach sought to provide widespread protection against risks considered common to industrial societies, namely income loss due to old age, unemployment, disability, survivorship, and health care costs (Williamson and Pampel 1993).

Unlike private insurance, which protects those who can afford *and* choose to purchase coverage, the driving purpose behind social insurance is to provide broad protection against identifiable risks across all income groups. Private insurance emphasizes the principle of "individual equity"—that, all things being equal, rates of returns to beneficiaries should be proportional to premium payments. But social insurance—built on the belief that it is in society's interest to provide a rational means of assisting citizens to protect themselves and their families against major economic risks—emphasizes adequacy, the idea that benefits should be sufficient to meet basic needs. By design social insurance returns must vary across income classes and cohorts, providing proportionately larger returns to those at greatest risk while simultaneously providing somewhat larger benefits to those paying more in to a social insurance program. Otherwise the social adequacy goal would not be achieved. This fundamental difference between private and social insurance led Reinhart Hohaus, actuary and Metropolitan Life Insurance executive, to observe in his now classic 1938 article that social insurance responds to society's need to provide basic protection for the citizenry. He commented that just "as private insurance would collapse if it stressed considerations of adequacy more than those of equity, so will social insurance fail to remain undisturbed if considerations of equity are allowed to predominate over those of adequacy" (Hohaus 1960).

With the exception of the state-by-state enactment of workman's (now called worker's) compensation laws, social insurance programs made little headway during the first third of the twentieth century. But in the context of the economic collapse of the 1930s, the Social Security Act of 1935 was passed. Ironically, Old Age Insurance, the program we have come to know as Social Security, was neither large nor initially very popular because it required collecting a new payroll tax and did not promise to pay out benefits until the early 1940s. In fact, Social Security did not emerge as the dominant source of public old-age income protection until passage of the 1950 amendments to the Social Security Act. But even before that, beginning in 1939 when survivors and selected dependent protections were added to OAI, a pattern of incremental expansion of Social Security was established with the addition of disability insurance in 1956, Medicare in 1965, real benefit increases in the late 1960s and early 1970s, and the automatic cost-of-living adjustment in 1972 (Berkowitz 1991).

This pattern of incremental expansion came to an end in the mid-1970s as the nation's politics changed and as Social Security began to face financing problems brought on by short-term economic downturns in the mid-1970s and early 1980s and by changing demographics. Financing amendments followed in 1977 and 1983, and today it is once again clear that legislation will be needed to address a projected shortfall. But, in marked contrast to these earlier periods, for the first time since the implementation of the program, serious consideration is being given to proposals to privatize and/or means-test OASDI, approaches that would change the nature of "Social Security as we know it," departing radically from the principles that have guided the program since its inception.

Indeed, even when Social Security was under financial stress during the early years of the Reagan administration, no one took seriously proposals to privatize the program. They existed (see Ferrara 1983) but were largely ignored, for they were seen as outside the boundaries of political feasibility. Neither were they considered useful for addressing the real problems before Social Security. Not surprisingly, the members of the National Commission on Social Security Reform—the commission chaired by Alan Greenspan, which forged a bipartisan compromise that served as the basis for the landmark 1983 Social Security financing amendments—unanimously eschewed privatization and other radical proposals:

The members of the National Commission believe that the Congress, in its deliberations on financing proposals, should not alter the fundamental structure of the Social Security Program or undermine its fundamental principles. The National Commission considered, but rejected proposals to make the Social Security program a voluntary one, or to transform it into a program under which benefits are a product exclusively of contributions paid, or to convert it into a fully-funded program, or to change it to a program under which benefits are conditioned on the showing of financial need. (National Commission on Social Security Reform 1983:2-2)

PRIVATIZATION PROPOSALS: EMERGENCE AND TIES TO GENERATIONAL EQUITY THEMES

But since the mid-1990s there has been a virtual explosion of privatization proposals; and they are being taken very seriously. Political activist and author Sam Beard started a national campaign for privatization, suggesting his proposal can create a hundred million millionaires (Beard 1996). The CEO of State Street Bank has put forth his ideas about why privatizing Social Security would be beneficial to all concerned (Carter and Shipman 1996). The Cato Institute—a libertarian think tank—has initiated a major Social Security privatization project, urging that the United States adopt a version of Chile's privatized social security model. Chile's social security program was privatized when its system really *was* bankrupt. Moreover, Chile had a large federal budget surplus, and under General Pinochet its military dictatorship mandated an 18 percent pay raise and other incentives for workers who agreed to shift to the new privatized alternative (Williamson and Hochman 1995). The World Bank (1994), too, has become a forceful proponent of privatizing Social Security systems.

More concretely, Senator Bob Kerrey and former Senator John Danforth (R-Mo.) proposed large reductions (roughly 43 percent on average) in Social Security benefits for tomorrow's retirees to address the OASDI financing problem and to facilitate shifting a portion of workers' OASDI payroll tax contribution into a 1.5 percent contribution for private retirement accounts. Teaming up with former Senator Simpson (R-Wyo.), Kerrey next submitted a bill that would partially privatize Social Security. Perhaps most significantly, the January 1997 report of the 1994–96 Advisory Council on Social Security kicked off spirited debate about the future of Social Security. Rather than presenting one Social Security reform option as in the past, this council split into three factions, each with its own set of recommendations. Moreover, for the first time the advocates of privatizing the program have succeeded in assuring that serious consideration will be given to privatization proposals—an outcome that guarantees complex and heated deliberations (see Advisory Council 1997).

One proposal would maintain the basic commitments and structure of Social Security. It calls for a number of minor changes and serious consideration of one major change, investing 40 percent of the growing Social Security trust fund assets in the stock market via the equivalent of a passively managed index fund. The other two proposals call for the partial privatization of Social Security and the creation of individual IRA-like accounts—fundamental alterations of the program that are sure to generate much controversy. The most radical proposal calls for gradually transforming Social Security into a two-tier scheme with the first level providing a low flat-rate benefit ($410) to all recipients and a second tier based on diverting payroll tax contributions to mandatory IRA-like accounts.

No doubt many factors contribute to the growing prominence of privatization proposals. They include a more conservative political environment, growing concern about the financial pressures that will occur as baby boomers reach retirement age, diminution of faith in institutions (especially government), a booming stock market, the interest of the financial sector in attracting more investors, anxiety about the future of the economy, increased economic inequality, a new Social Security financing problem, and declining confidence in the program.

Although many factors have played a role in the emergence of privatization proposals, the idea would most likely not have moved into the mainstream were it not for the way in which it has been possible to use the generational equity framing of the Social Security policy debate to split support for the traditional social insurance approach and to mobilize support for the privatization alternative. The generational equity theme has been effectively seized upon as a means of justifying reductions in the social welfare sector, especially expenditures directed at the old. A major goal for those seeking to shrink the social welfare function of government is to reduce public support for the hugely popular Social Security and Medicare programs—which together expended $587 billion in 1997.

Writing in 1983 in the Cato Institute's journal, Stuart Butler and Peter Germanis (1983:552) put forth an instructive strategy for doing just that. They call for "guerrilla warfare against both the current Social Security system and the coalition that supports it." They outline a strategy designed to highlight program weaknesses and to split off constituencies supportive of Social Security, especially the young. For example, by defining Social Security as unfair—that is, by emphasizing declining rates of return to the young as opposed to protections provided over the course of life or by contending that too much is being directed at the old at the expense of the young—the generational equity argument serves to decrease public commitment to Social Security. Equally important, by defining most elderly persons as not fully deserving of governmental largesse, the generational equity theme helps delegitimize elderly persons as deserving of public support—defining them instead as "greedy geezers" (see Fairlie 1988) and as a generation that is, as one article suggests, "Consuming Our Children" (see Chakravarty and Weisman 1988).

ASSESSING PRIVATIZATION PROPOSALS

For better or for worse, privatization proposals are now ensconced as an important part of the Social Security financing debate. Hence, all concerned must come to terms with their implications. Using the two Advisory Council private account proposals and the more traditional proposal as examples, we suggest that contemporary debate about the future of Social Security should proceed with the following understandings:

- We are facing a financing problem, not a crisis.
- Privatization does not address the Social Security financing problem.
- Important areas of agreement exist, despite some strong disagreements.
- Privatization shifts risks from the government to individuals.
- Privatization creates winners and losers.
- The Advisory Council report does not exhaust the list of alternatives for reform.
- Conflicting values are at the core of the debate.

THE FINANCING PROBLEM IS MANAGEABLE

Though an excellent political strategy for those seeking to shrink the public sector, the alarmist view that Social Security is going "belly-up" is wrong on several counts. Even if no policy changes were made, after 2029 anticipated revenues would still be sufficient to meet about three-quarters of the program's promises according to Social Security's Board of Trustees (1997). Given the nation's sixty-year tradition of making periodic adjustments to keep the system in projected balance seventy-five years into the future, it is reasonable to assume that a portion of the projected gap would be made up by moderate benefit reductions and payroll tax increases well in advance of 2029. No doubt this represents a real financing problem and should be addressed soon, but the timing and magnitude of the problem hardly calls for pressing the panic button in 1998 (see Ball and Bethell 1997; Myers 1997; Steuerle 1997; Quinn and Mitchell 1996).

It is important to note that nothing about Social Security's financing problems cries out for privatization as a solution. If anything, privatization proposals complicate program financing and make the goal of achieving actuarial balance more difficult. Privatization would generally require both a large rollback of the traditional Social Security benefit package and additional taxes to establish individual "savings" accounts. If a portion of current Social Security benefits are diverted to IRA-like private accounts, new revenues must be found to finance Social Security pensions to all current and many future recipients. For at least the first several decades privatization would make it more difficult to finance Social Security.

AREAS OF AGREEMENT EXIST

In spite of the splits in the Advisory Council, the members unanimously agreed that there is a financing problem, that it can be addressed, and that it should be done sooner rather than later. They also agreed unanimously that some redistribution to low-income persons should be maintained in any Social Security program, that means-testing Social Security is a bad idea, that full protection of the cost-of-living adjustment is essential to the economic well-being of beneficiaries, and that any "sacrifice in bringing the system into balance should be widely shared and not borne entirely by current and future workers and their employers." All three plans improve the rate of return for future beneficiaries through some form of investment of the growing Social Security trust fund assets in the private sector. All three call for increased tax revenues or their equivalent. All three would continue a mandatory and universal retirement, disability, and survivors program.

Council majorities supported extending coverage to all new state and local workers; reducing benefits by roughly 3 percent through a technical change in the benefit formula; taxing Social Security benefits in roughly the same manner as income from contributory defined-benefit plans; and adjusting the COLA to more accurately reflect changes in the cost of living. And there was majority support for a proposal to accelerate the planned increase in the normal retirement age to 67, moving it up to 2011 instead of 2022, and thereafter to index it to changes in life expectancy. Taken together, such changes would address roughly two-thirds of the projected financing problem—arguably a pretty substantial down payment on the projected shortfall.

DISAGREEMENTS

Of course, it is the differences between the plans that generate the greatest controversy. The proposal that would basically maintain the existing program—the Maintain Benefits plan—is supported by six of the thirteen members of the council, including Robert Ball, a former commissioner of Social Security, and the labor representatives among others. Whereas this proposal calls for giving strong consideration to gradually investing 40 percent of trust fund assets in the stock market via something along the lines of a passively managed index fund, it does not call for the creation of individual IRA-like accounts. Because the government bears the risk, it insulates individuals and their families from poor investments and market fluctuations. If government investment in index funds yields a real rate of return of 7 percent over the next thirty-five years, the Maintain Benefits plan would help ease the burden of providing for the retirement of the boomers—significantly decreasing by roughly 35 percent the need to cut benefits or generate additional federal revenues through tax increases. But if the stock market experiences an extended period of decline or stagnation, the plan would compound the problem of paying for the boomers (see Advisory Council 1997; National Academy of Social Insurance 1996).

The more moderate of the two partial privatization schemes—the Individual Accounts (IA) plan—is supported by two members, including the council's chairman, Edward Gramlich. The IA plan would establish small, defined contribution accounts for each worker by mandating a new contribution—arguably an indirect tax increase—of 1.6 percent of covered payroll to individual investment accounts. Workers would have a few investment options, but far fewer than envisioned in the third plan. The administrative costs of the individual accounts would be relatively low because the individual accounts would be publicly managed. Benefit reductions, especially for middle- and high-income workers, would help bring the public portion of the revised Social Security program into long-run actuarial balance. "The combination of the reduced growth in benefits, the increased age of eligibility for full retirement benefits, and the proceeds of the individual accounts would leave total benefits on average at about the levels of present law for all income groups" (Advisory Council 1997:28).

The most radical privatization proposal—the Personal Security Accounts (PSA) plan—calls for a partial privatization of Social Security and is supported by five members, including Sylvester Schieber, an executive with a benefits consultant company, and Caroline Weaver, an economist at the American Enterprise Institute. It calls for gradually transforming Social Security into a two-tier scheme; the first tier would provide a low flat-rate benefit ($410 in today's dollars), and the second tier would be based on contributions made to mandatory IRA-like accounts. Additionally, the value of disability benefits would be reduced and retirement eligibility ages increased. Five percent of the current payroll tax would be diverted into these privately held and managed defined contribution accounts. Those with high earnings and those who make better investment decisions (or are just plain "lucky") would end up with larger second-tier benefits. This proposal would be financed by a seventy-two-year "transition" payroll tax of 1.52 percent and by borrowing $1.9 trillion dollars from general revenues, to be repaid using the projected excess of tax revenues between 2035 and 2075 (Advisory Council 1997).

SHIFTING RISKS: WINNERS AND LOSERS

Privatization—especially large-scale privatization such as that proposed under the PSA plan—may be a bad idea. But it is not necessarily so for everyone—at least if we assume that the most well off do not have a stake in promoting the well-being of the rest of society. Affluent workers would likely do better under privatization plans—at least insofar as they do not experience serious declines in their earning capacities during middle age. Such workers would be well provided for even if the stock market were to stagnate or decline just prior to their retirement. But the biggest winners would be the banks, mutual funds, and investment companies who stand to benefit from the millions of transactions and trillions of dollars in private-sector investment that would follow even a small partial privatization.

It may be economically rational for the affluent to accept the risks associated with privatization. But not so for most middle- and low-income persons (Williamson 1997a). The primary risks are market risk, investment risk, inflation risk, and political risk.

Privatization places low- and moderate-income workers at significant political risk. As Social Security is currently structured, low-income workers get a better return than high-wage workers on their contributions,[1] a factor that keeps millions of the elderly out of poverty during their retirement years. With privatization, upper-middle-income and high-income wage workers would, as voters, have less reason to maintain the purchasing power of the basic benefit that low-income workers are especially dependent upon. Hence, in separating out the interests of higher-income workers from the public portion of the program, privatization schemes set the stage for substantial erosion of political support for the program's redistributive role—an outcome that would further increase the economic and social distance between rich and poor.

Middle- and low-income workers would face especially serious market risks. Long-run returns on stock market investments have generally been quite favorable. But no promises can be made about what will happen to an individual's nest egg in the few years, months, or even days before retirement. This is one of many reasons that privatization would be particularly problematic for middle- and low-income women (Williamson 1997b).

Low- and even many middle-income workers cannot afford good investment advice. They are more likely to make poor investment decisions—for example, investing too conservatively during early working years or taking unacceptably high risks just prior to retirement. And after retirement, beneficiaries would receive much less protection against inflation under the Schieber plan, yet another example of how privatization plans often shift risk from government to the individual. The affluent are better positioned to seek financial advice and to tolerate such risks, but the impact on low- and middle-income retired persons could end up being devastating.

MANY POLICY OPTIONS EXIST

When the focus of Social Security reform moves toward the legislative process, policymakers and the public would be well advised to look beyond these three plans. Certainly, the "consensus" recommendations in the Advisory Council report provide a good starting point, although each should be carefully assessed especially in terms of their costs and benefits for different population groups. But other options must be (and are being) considered.

For example, economist Michael Boskin argues that the consumer price index overstates inflation by perhaps 1 to 1.5 percent (U.S. Senate Committee on Finance 1996). The Boskin commission suggests that the CPI does not provide an accurate basis of measuring changes in overall living standards because it does not account for improvements in quality or the changing purchasing habits of Americans (e.g., buying in discount stores and purchasing substitute goods (e.g., oranges) when the price of another good (e.g., grapefruits) rises. Senator Moynihan calls for a 1.1 percent reduction in annual COLAs. The advantage—namely a quick and fair fix to roughly 70 percent of the projected deficit—is obvious. The danger is that a new approach to approximating changes in the cost of living would substantially understate the effects of inflation, thereby undermining a major feature of the program—the assurance that the purchasing power of benefits, once received, will not decline no matter how long one lives.[2]

Yet other benefit reforms could introduce onetime reductions in the COLA, slight reductions in the value of initial benefits, or selective increases in the age of eligibility for full benefits—all of which are cuts, but none of which undermine the basic premises of the program.

There are options on the revenue side as well, such as the scheduling of a small payroll tax increase (such as 0.5%) thirty or forty years from now. Another revenue-raising approach would require the employer to pay the Social Security payroll tax on all wages that are paid; this would address 65 percent of the projected financing problem. A more modest tax-ceiling approach would restore and maintain the proportion of wages covered by the payroll tax at the previous 90 percent level by 2000; this would address about 14 percent of the projected problem. Other proposals would reduce the fringe benefits exemptions from payroll taxation. As fringe benefits have grown, the proportion of total compensation (cash earnings and fringes) subject to payroll taxation has shrunk. At the extreme, subjecting 90 percent of all cash and fringe benefit compensation to the payroll tax would address roughly 45 percent of the projected financing problem (Bipartisan Commission on Entitlement and Tax Reform 1995). Similarly, Edith Fierst (1997), a member of the Advisory Council, notes that Social Security's actuaries estimate that taxing "the cost of employer-provided group health and life insurance . . . as though it were cash compensation" would address roughly one-third of the predicted shortfall. The burden of this change would fall primarily on higher-income workers, who generally receive relatively and absolutely larger amounts of their total compensation in the form of nontaxable fringe benefits.

IMPORTANT VALUES ARE AT STAKE

The tendency to promote narrow notions of generational equity and to reduce Social Security policy discussion to a mere accounting exercise that focuses on the financial cost of the program overlooks its value as a source of national social cohesion and as an expression of the contributions and obligations of each member of the national community. It has stood as a symbol of the kinds of programs that the federal government has been able to do well.

Substantial ideological differences bound contemporary Social Security debate. But even so, many of Social Security's staunchest defenders have focused on technical changes to the relative neglect of the profound debate that is taking place between two very different value systems: the community-enhancing values of the program's defenders versus the libertarian values of its critics, the latter calling for shrinking the size of the government as well as shifting risk burdens and responsibility from the national community to the individual. This debate is fundamentally about our sense of responsibility to each other; about the basic protection that all working Amercians should be assured of for themselves and their families in old age, disability, or upon the death of a loved one; about the mix of public and private efforts we should encourage to assure that security. And this debate is also about the real impact of various possible changes upon the well-being of individuals and families.

Certainly, all Americans should be encouraged to save. But by shifting much of the risk from government onto individuals, privatization would undermine the basic retirement, disability, and life insurance protections available to all Americans—an outcome that would be unfortunate at a time when the economic transformation of the American economy is rendering employment and living standards less secure. Indeed, as we have discussed, there is nothing about the current financing problem of Social Security that requires such radical and unprecedented change. And there is much to argue for addressing the financing problems in a way that assures our children and theirs the basic protections of this program, which for sixty years has served as an expression of the nation's concern for each member of the national community.

The moral basis of Social Security is the assumption that we, as a people, have a stake in the well-being of our family and neighbors. This idea stands in stark contrast to the highly individualistic notion that is conveyed by the generational equity theme and in related proposals to privatize the program. It is a value that, along with Social Security, is worth preserving and promoting.

NOTES

1. Consistent with the social insurance goal of providing a floor of protection for all Americans, the Social Security benefit formula provides proportionately higher benefits to workers who have worked consistently at lower-paying jobs. It replaces about 58 percent of average monthly earnings for persons retiring at age 65 with yearly earnings equal to one-half of average wages, compared to about 28 percent for workers whose earnings equaled the maximum subject to payroll taxation. So although higher-income workers receive larger monthly benefits than low- and middle-income workers, those monthly benefits replace a smaller proportion of their preretirement earnings.

2. See Stewart and Pavalone (1996) for evidence that the current CPI underestimates increases in the cost of living for those age 62 and over. The problem gets

worse for the very old. Also see Baker (1996) and Madrick (1997) for critical assessment of the conclusions reached by the U.S. Senate Committee on Finance (1996).

REFERENCES

Advisory Council on Social Security. 1997. *Report of the 1994–1996 Advisory Council on Social Security.* Vol. 1, *Findings and Recommendations.* Washington, D.C.: U.S. Government Printing Office.

Baker, Dean. 1996. *Getting the Price Right: A Methodologically Consistent Consumer Price Index: 1953–94.* Washington, D.C.: Economic Policy Institute, April 12.

Ball, Robert M., with T. N. Bethell. 1997. "Bridging the Centuries: The Case for Traditional Social Security." Pp. 259–294 in *Social Security in the 21st Century,* edited by Eric R. Kingson and James H. Schulz. New York: Oxford University Press.

Beard, Samuel. 1996. *Restoring Hope in America.* San Francisco: ICS Press.

Berkowitz, Edward D. 1991. *America's Welfare State: From Roosevelt to Reagan.* Baltimore, Md.: Johns Hopkins University Press.

Bipartisan Commission on Entitlement and Tax Reform. 1995. *Final Report to the President.* Washington, D.C.: U.S. Government Printing Office.

Board of Trustees of the Federal Old Age and Survivors Insurance and Disability Insurance Trust Funds. 1997. *1997 Annual Report.* Washington, D.C.: U.S. Government Printing Office.

Butler, Stuart, and Peter Germanis. 1983. "Achieving Social Security Reform: A Leninist Strategy." *Cato Journal* 3 (2): 547–556.

Carter, Marshall N., and William G. Shipman. 1996. *Promises to Keep: Saving Social Security's Dream.* Washington, D.C.: Regnery Publishing.

Chakravarty, Subrata N., with Katherine Weisman. 1988. "Consuming Our Children?" *Forbes* (November 14): 222–232.

Fairlie, Henry. 1998. "Talkin' 'bout My Generation." *New Republic* (March 28): 19–22.

Ferrara, Peter J. 1983. "The Prospect of Real Reform." *Cato Journal* 3 (2): 609–621.

Ferrara, Peter J. 1995. "A Private Option for Social Security." Pp. 205–213 in *Social Security: Time for a Change,* edited by Kevin Stephenson. Greenwich, Conn.: JAI Press.

Fierst, Edith U. 1997. "Supplemental Statement." Pp. 135–154 in *Report of the 1994–1996 Advisory Council on Social Security,* vol. 1, *Findings and Recommendations,* edited by the Advisory Council on Social Security. Washington, D.C.: U.S. Government Printing Office.

Hohaus, Reinhart A. 1960. "Equity, Adequacy, and Related Factors in Old-Age

Security." Pp. 61–63 in *Social Security Programs, Problems, and Policies*, edited by William Haber and Wilbur J. Cohen. Homewood, Ill.: Richard D. Irwin.

Kingdon, John W. 1995. *Agenda, Alternatives, and Public Policies*. New York: Harper Collins.

Kingson, Eric R., and James H. Schulz. 1997. "Should Social Security Be Means-Tested?" Pp. 259–294 in *Social Security in the 21st Century*, edited by Eric R. Kingson and James H. Schulz. New York: Oxford University Press.

Kotlikoff, Laurence J. 1992. *Generational Accounting*. New York: Free Press.

Madrick, Jeffrey. 1997. "The Cost of Living: A New Myth." *New York Review of Books* (March): 6868–6872.

Myers, Robert J. 1997. "Will Social Security Be There for Me?" Pp. 208–216 in *Social Security in the 21st Century*, edited by Eric R. Kingson and James H. Schulz. New York: Oxford University Press.

National Academy of Social Insurance. 1996. *Social Insurance Update*. (December 1): 1–9.

National Commission on Social Security Reform. 1983. *Report of the National Commission on Social Security Reform*. Washington, D.C.: U.S. Government Printing Office.

Quinn, Joseph F., and Olivia J. Mitchell. 1996. "Social Security on the Table." *American Prospect*. (May–June): 76–81.

Steuerle, C. Eugene. 1997. "Social Security in the Twenty-first Century: The Need for Change." Pp. 241–294 in *Social Security in the 21st Century*, edited by Eric R. Kingson and James H. Schulz. New York: Oxford University Press.

Stewart, Kenneth J., and Joseph Pavalone. 1996. "Experimental Consumer Price Index for Americans 62 Years of Age and Older." Pp. 4–7 in *CPI Detailed Report*, data for April. Washington, D.C.: U.S. Department of Labor, Bureau of Labor Statistics.

U.S. Department of Health and Human Services. 1996. *Income of the Population 55 and Over*. January. Washington, D.C.: Social Security Administration, Office of Research and Statistics.

U.S. Senate. 1995. *Privatization of the Social Security Old Age and Survivors Insurance Program*. Hearings before the Subcommittee on Social Security and Family Protection of the Committee on Finance, 104th Congress, 1st session on S. 824, August 2. Washington, D.C.: U.S. Government Printing Office.

U.S. Senate Committee on Finance. 1996. *Toward a More Accurate Measure of the Cost of Living: Final Report to the Senate Finance Committee from the Advisory Commission to Study the Consumer Price Index*. December 4. Washington, D.C.: U.S. Government Printing Office.

Williamson, John B. 1997a. "A Critique of the Case for Privatizing Social Security."

The Gerontologist 37:561–571.

Williamson, John B. 1997b. "Should Women Support the Privatization of Social Security?" *Challenge* 40 (July–August): 97–108.

Williamson, John B., and Gilberto Hochman. 1995. "Innovative Old-Age Security Models for Developing Nations: Chile and Brazil." *Journal of Aging Studies* 9:245–262.

Williamson, John B., and Fred C. Pampel. 1993. *Old-Age Security in Comparative Perspective*. New York: Oxford University Press.

World Bank. 1994. *Averting the Old-Age Crisis*. New York: Oxford University Press.

PART IV

Voices from Generation X

CHAPTER TWELVE

Third Millennium Declaration

Third Millennium

Third Millennium is a nonprofit educational and advocacy organization whose primary goal is to build consensus around solutions to America's national debt, Social Security, health care, environmental, and educational crises. Members of the organization emphasize the importance of long-term planning to deal with the changing demographics in American society, and they also encourage young people to become active in local community service projects.

In this article Third Millennium suggests that America's youth are in danger of deep-rooted cynicism. Members of the organization warn that a generational war is possible if the current economic problems are not addressed. They argue that deficit spending must end and that Social Security is little more than a fiscally unsound generational scam. They suggest that Social Security cannot remain intact indefinitely and that it is time for the American government to consider alternative retirement systems.

PREAMBLE

We stand at the edge of a new millennium. The superpower confrontation, which brought fear of the apocalypse into the lives of three generations, is over. We live in the richest, freest, and most powerful country the world has ever seen. Most excellent.

But we fear for the future.

Political and social time bombs threaten our fragile successes at home and abroad. Like Wile E. Coyote waiting for a 20-ton Acme anvil to fall on his head, our generation labors in the expanding shadow of a monstrous national debt. Racial, sexual, and economic divisions have made fellow citizens brutal enemies. Our cities have fallen into a shameful state where ordinary acts of daily life have become painful struggles.

For too long, we as a nation have failed to exercise self-control. We've trashed the ethic of individual responsibility. We've exploited racial and sexual differences for political gains. Those in power have practiced fiscal child abuse, mortgaging our future and the futures of those to come. Meanwhile, the engine of democracy has stalled, paralyzed by fringe issues.

It is time to take responsibility. The grave problems facing our country— economic stagnation, social fragmentation, and the deterioration of the environment—demand solutions that transcend partisanship. We believe it is the challenge of our generation to move the country beyond partisan stagnation and focus on the real challenges at hand.

Those of us offering this declaration don't pretend to represent our entire generation. We recognize our generation's intense individualism as one of its strengths. The post–baby boom generation, born after 1960, is far too diverse to let one group represent it all. But we believe young people must initiate change. Our role in serving our country must be to stop the dumping of toxic policies on future generations.

The writers of this statement come from a wide array of backgrounds, careers, and political persuasions, and not every one of us subscribes to every last letter in this statement. We are drawn together, however, by the belief that we can't let our differences—real as they are—excuse further inaction. Conservative, liberal, or none of the above, we unite in the sentiment that the time to act is now.

We look to President Abraham Lincoln, who, at another time when division threatened to destroy the country, pleaded for change: "The dogmas of the quiet past are inadequate to the stormy present. The occasion is piled high with difficulty, and we must rise with the occasion. As our case is new, so must we act anew."

Divisive issues such as abortion and the death penalty must recede to the background. It is up to us to direct our energies to the problems that threaten the future of our nation.

Our generation is often derided for its cynicism. We grew up amidst the betrayals of Vietnam, Watergate, and the savings and loan scandal. We are witness to the highest divorce rate ever. We see neighborhoods across America battle law-lessness, drug abuse, dysfunctional families, and substandard school systems. At the same time, divisive right-wing tactics fuel our country's worst fears and hatreds, while impotent left-wing dogma transforms us into a society of victims and dependents.

But if our common experience has jaded us, it has also added urgency to our outlook. We seek no sympathy and we ask for no handout. We know solving our problems will be tough, and we reject demagogues who tell us they can be solved without breaking a sweat. We must make the sacrifices necessary to address the dire problems facing our country.

To the new generation in power, we say: If you are ready to make the tough choices, we will support you. If you are ready to fight, we will join you. If you are ready to lead, we might in fact follow you. But if not, move out of the way.

The last thing we want is a generational war. We present this statement in the sincere hope that members of our generation—whatever their politics—can together chart a new direction for the country, and that members of all gener-ations can embrace it.

OUR IMPERILED FUTURE

THE NATIONAL DEBT: TAXATION WITHOUT REPRESENTATION

In December 1773, a group of American colonists chanted "No taxation without representation" as they dumped a shipload of tea into Boston Harbor.

Today, a heavy burden is once again being placed on the unrepresented. Just as King George III levied stiff duties with little regard to the effects they would have on American colonists, our democratically elected leaders are forcing unrepre-sented future generations to shoulder the burden of trillions of dollars in debt.

As we approach the new millennium, our generation stares down the barrel of a $4.4 trillion debt that threatens to destroy our future. . . .

On a purely practical level, laying such a heavy burden on future generations is reckless economic policy. In an historical context it is "taxation without rep-resentation," and as we were so aptly taught, "That's not fair."

Unless we meet this problem squarely now, our generation faces the prospect of economic meltdown. At best, the costs of servicing the mushrooming national debt will drain more and more of our national resources. This means a future of economically devastating taxation and minimal government services. Disarmed by the burden of debt, our generation will be impotent to help our poor, clean up our environment, or even build a productive life for our families.

The root of the problem.

During the tremendous boom of the last fifty years, the United States became the greatest economic and military power in the world. Seemingly, our country had unlimited resources. We could support any friend and oppose any foe. We could rebuild Europe, craft a "Great Society," and promise to put a man on the moon in ten years—and actually do it.

But the time when the United States had boundless resources is gone. The United States is no longer the world's largest creditor nation; we are the world's largest debtor. We are no longer challenging ourselves to commit great acts of national heroics; instead, we are robbing our children in order to indulge ourselves in the luxuries of a time gone by.

Sometime during the last half-century, the ethic of self-reliance and diligence that helped America prosper gave way to one of irresponsibility and dependence. We increasingly looked to government alone to meet our needs and solve our problems.

Our political leaders responded by pushing the spending button harder. In a frenzy for votes, they expanded government, failed to cut inefficient programs, and embarked upon the largest spending spree the world had ever seen. "Don't worry, be happy" was their song.

Well, it's definitely time to worry. But we as a nation still refuse to own up to our responsibilities. Even now, we plan not to reduce the debt but to add to it.

Blinded by a current world problem or a short-term economic crisis, we choose to add to the debt, completely discounting the problems and crises future generations will face. By most accounts the complicated world of the future will be filled with crises and problems that, even without a debt, will stretch our ingenuity and drain our resources. . . .

What can be done.

Deficit spending must end by 1999. We must begin paying off the debt by the year 2000.

America needs a wake-up call: the mounting national debt imperils our future. We must stop invoicing future generations for today's spending sprees. Everything must be put on the table: defense, entitlements, farm subsidies, and, as a last resort, tax increases aimed at debt reduction.

To end deficit spending, we need to

- *Change our attitude toward government....* The American people ... must reaffirm our commitment to individual responsibility and stop demanding that government alone solve all our problems.
- *Allow no new net spending.* New programs may be necessary, but they must be offset by equal reductions in existing programs.
- *Limit entitlement spending.* An increasingly large part of the federal budget is "entitlement spending"—that is, programs in which costs grow each year without congressional review. To tackle the deficit, these programs must be restrained. The most obvious place to start is with "middle-class entitlements," such as Social Security and Medicare, that benefit well-off retirees regardless of need. By charging middle- and upper-class retirees for their health insurance, for example, we would save $6 billion a year.
- *Fund programs that work.* No new program should be implemented, nor any existing program be reauthorized, until it includes specific, measurable goals and a schedule for evaluating its effectiveness.
- *Combat waste, fraud, and abuse.* In 1989, the government's own auditing agency, the General Accounting Office, found over $150 billion in waste, fraud, and mismanagement in the federal budget....
- *Streamline government.* The public sector has become the least efficient sector of the economy—and one of the fastest growing. To get more value for each tax dollar, we must change the incentives that drive government....

In the long term, the mushrooming debt will undercut our ability to invest in our future—severely limiting our ability to address critical social, international, and environmental problems.

Social Security: The invisible debt.
Social Security is a generational scam—fiscally unsound and generationally inequitable.

Today's retirees get their benefits directly from the paychecks of working Americans, the majority of whom are less affluent than those they support. Every month, approximately 500,000 millionaires receive a Social Security check. Payments are financed by a payroll tax that is five times higher for today's workers than it was for their grandparents.

Worse still, the Social Security fund is going bankrupt. The U.S. Social Security Administration projects that the Social Security fund could be broke as early as 2020. Even an optimistic scenario projects insolvency no later than 2036. So while today's retirees will get back everything they paid to Social Security (taxes plus interest) in just six and a half years, tomorrow's elderly will get little or nothing back.

Twenty-five years from today—with relatively fewer workers and an increasing number of retirees—we will face a terrible choice: default on our obligations to retirees or raise payroll taxes to as high as 40 percent.

America needs a new contract, fiscally sound, generationally fair, and sure to protect those who need our government's help.

We advocate the following reforms of the Social Security system:

- *Raise the retirement age.* If 65 was the appropriate retirement age in 1940, today, because of rising life expectancies, it should be at least 70. The government should phase in the increased retirement age over the next ten years.
- *Stop paying the greens fees for well-heeled retirees.* Social Security benefits should be based on need. We recognize the promise made to previous generations, and we are willing to honor it. Thus, we agree that everyone should get back everything they personally put into the Social Security system—plus interest. Beyond that, benefits must go only to the needy.
- *End the "surplus" scam.* In 1983, Congress and President Reagan said they would raise payroll taxes to amass surpluses for when the baby boomers retire. They raised taxes, then spent the surplus.

Finally, we recognize that even with these changes, the system is unlikely to remain viable forever. Therefore, we encourage our government to consider serious alternative retirement systems that can eventually replace Social Security.

OUR DIVIDED SOCIETY

AMERICA'S URBAN NIGHTMARE: OUR GENERATION'S GREATEST CHALLENGE

Throughout our lifetimes, the nation's urban centers have increasingly come to resemble war-torn Third World nations.

America's impotence in this crisis has left millions of young people poor, illiterate, imprisoned, and desperate. Some now suggest we "write off" a generation—our generation—and start over.

In some respects the situation has improved since the early 1960s. More urban young people are going to college than ever before. Thousands of inner-city families have broken free of the country's urban despair, building lives of opportunity for themselves and their children.

But, tragically, the latest trends indicate complete social breakdown. Murder is the leading cause of death among urban youth, followed closely by suicide. The vast majority of inner-city children are born into broken families. . . . Economic opportunity has all but disappeared as high tax rates, mediocre schools, uncontrolled crime, and simple racism have fueled the exodus of businesses from our nation's cities.

Despite the reality of a future that offers few resources for bold programs, we believe ameliorating the problems of the inner cities should be a top priority. But we refuse to paper over these complex problems with mere dollars parceled out from Washington.

We draw a lesson from the community activists in our own generation: it is time we turned to the small, entrepreneurial community programs for our lead. Although we don't pretend to have all the answers, we believe our nation can no longer afford to tinker at the margins. We must attack all aspects of the problem simultaneously. Most importantly, we must shift the focus from programs that create dependency to programs that create opportunity.

Crime.
America's crime epidemic is our generation's Vietnam—but today's conflict is even more deadly. During the past three years, more Americans have been murdered on our streets than were killed in the sixteen years of the Vietnam War.

As in Vietnam, most casualties of this war come from poor families. A college education, a good job, and a suburban apartment are our generation's version of a draft deferment.

It is time to bring our generation's best young people onto the battlefield. We vigorously support a police corps that delivers 200,000 new police officers to the streets. . . .

But simply hiring more police is not enough. We must develop a comprehensive strategy to fight the violent crime epidemic. . . .

Criminal justice reform should not focus on the death penalty, but on toughening the sentencing laws and ending the abuse of the parole system. We must also disarm the enemy by restricting access to handguns and other deadly weapons.

Economic revitalization.

Any solution to the problem of the inner cities that does not address the root causes of economic hardship is doomed to failure. Central to any efforts aimed at rebuilding our cities is strong, sustained economic growth.

Overall, the key elements of this growth are alleviating the tax burden in the poorest neighborhoods, vigorously enforcing antidiscrimination laws (especially in lending), improving educational opportunities, and offering residents of the cities opportunities to gain a personal and financial stake in the future. Tenant ownership of public housing is a bold step in the right direction.

Education.

America's urban school systems are among the worst in the industrial world, running with all the efficiency of the old Soviet economy. It's time to bring perestroika to the American school system.

We advocate the following structural reforms:

- *Lengthen the school year.* No business could succeed if it were closed three months a year, and neither can our schools.
- *Stop trapping poor children in second-rate schools.* We call for a genuine public/private school choice program that will enable the children of poor families to attend the same schools as the wealthy.
- *Make schools safe.* You can't learn geometry when you're dodging bullets.
- *Invest in young children.* Because a child's most formative years are ages 0 to 5, it is imperative that our schools develop early-intervention, preschool programs for the underprivileged.
- *Get back to the basics.* The school curriculum must once again be centered on the three "R's," which were the hallmark of our parents' educations.
- *Use technology. . . .* Technology can help bridge the gap between rich and poor school districts.
- *Get the best teachers possible.* That means doing away with outdated teaching certificates and allowing professionals into the classrooms. We can no longer afford to allow teachers' unions to prevent some of our nation's best minds from teaching our most neglected children.

As with many urban problems discussed here, the failing education system is not confined to the inner cities. But the trend is clear: whenever the nation moves in the wrong direction, the poor are hardest hit. It is here we must act most forcefully.

Welfare reform.

The current approach to welfare is a failure because it fosters dependency and penalizes progress. We believe these principles should guide our efforts:

- *Reward self-help.* The poor who are working or furthering their education should get the highest priority.
- *Consolidate and streamline federal and state efforts.* On the federal level, only one agency should be responsible for public assistance funds. Small, community-based, entrepreneurial programs should administer the funds.
- *Require community service.* Adults receiving public assistance should be required to either perform community service, improve their education, or actively seek employment.

Families.

Children need and deserve a mother and a father. We will do whatever we can to support single-parent families, but we find it unacceptable that another generation of children seems destined to pay the price for its parents' irresponsibility.

From America's churches, temples, and mosques to our schools, from Washington to Hollywood, we must renew our emphasis on responsible parenting. The reconstruction of the family is particularly important in the cities, where more than two-thirds of children are born to single mothers. Men who abandon their children are guilty of nothing less than criminal neglect. They must be held responsible.

Finally, we believe that any solution to the problems of the inner cities must begin with participation from the communities themselves. . . . This means the federal government should be a catalyst for change, promoting the general welfare rather than attempting to provide it.

HEALING THE WOUNDS OF DIVISION

Nearly thirty years after Congress passed the Civil Rights Act, American society is still marred by the ugly stain of racism and racial divisions.

It is painfully clear that we are still far from the nation Martin Luther King Jr. envisioned when he shared his dream. Despite our nation's efforts to become more sensitive and tolerant, racial hatred still poisons the hearts of many

Americans, as an unhealthy race consciousness has crept into every corner of American life.

And the hate is not just limited to race. Too often, women in our society are still subjected to second-class treatment both in the home and in the workplace. Meanwhile gays face legally sanctioned discrimination.

The fear, hate, and inequality that still exist in our society are a national disgrace.

Yet during our lifetimes, our society has made great progress toward defeating the forces of ignorance and hate. We applaud our parents' generation for having the courage to fight racism and sexism. Thanks to the heroes of the civil rights and women's movements, our generation has grown up without the Jim Crow laws and institutionalized sexism. . . .

But as we have become more aware of racism, the politicization of the issue has created a disturbing effect. Politicians now levy charges of racism not to bring about racial harmony but simply to batter their opponents. Looters cite racial inequality to justify acts of robbery, violence, and even murder. Meanwhile, the media search for a sensational angle to exploit fears and amplify voices of division.

As a result, we have seen the original intent of the civil rights movement distorted. Divisions that may already exist—black versus white, women versus men, gay versus straight—are only heightened by shortsighted people looking for votes or Nielsen ratings.

Since ours is the most racially and ethnically diverse generation in American history, it remains our challenge to reaffirm the strengths of diversity while rejecting the politics of division. . . .

We envision a day when a single American community of diverse individuals represents all of us. We do not want to stifle cultural differences; we only hope to transform *E Pluribus Unum* from a slogan into a way of life.

How do we begin? By reclaiming a basic principle: we are all created equal. Equality is not a public policy option, it is an inalienable right. . . .

OUR ENDANGERED ENVIRONMENT

There is no better measure of society's commitment to future generations than the steps it takes to ensure a clean, healthy environment. And by this measure we are failing the future.

To finance today's indulgences, we are flooding our planet with far more pollutants than it can process. Witness: the United States presently derives nearly

90 percent of its energy from polluting, nonrenewable sources. Our towns, our corporations, and our government continue to dump waste into our air and our drinking water. Meanwhile, we lead the world in per capita trash production, generating more than 180 million tons of solid waste annually—nearly three-quarters of a ton of garbage per person each year. We're dumping the costs of our shortsightedness on future generations.

At best, these practices are wasteful and selfish; at worst, they are an assault on the future. . . .

There is reason for hope, however. Some progress has been made, if only grudgingly, toward environmental sanity in recent years. The United States, for example, has cut emissions of ozone-depleting CFCs by 50 percent since 1986. However, we continue to abuse our environment in a manner that can't be sustained for long.

America must move more forcefully than ever to ensure that we leave future generations a clean environment. We propose action predicated on the conviction that long-term economic growth begins with environmental stability.

By action, we do not mean a new wave of heavy-handed regulations that, experience tells us, do not work. We advocate employing new methods to achieve sustainable growth in the context of market capitalism. What we propose is a rapprochement with the environment.

How can we do this? Here are just a few ideas:

- *Stop giving polluters a free ride.* Individuals and companies must be held accountable for the pollution they produce. The cost of disposing environmentally destructive materials should be paid by the manufacturers and consumers of those materials. . . .
- *End policies that subsidize the destruction of the environment.* The federal government must review the environmental impact of its own policies. For example, the government currently subsidizes farmers to grow water-intensive crops like cotton and rice in the California desert. This program wastes both tax dollars and precious water resources.
- *Reduce reliance on fossil fuels.* The unrestrained burning of fossil fuels is perhaps the most serious threat to a sustainable environment. . . .
- *Encourage consumer responsibility.* . . . By making environment-friendly products profitable, consumer action can be one of the most powerful weapons in the fight for a clean environment.
- *Craft an environmentally friendly tax code.* Through tax credits, the government can provide incentives for companies to use and develop environmentally sound technologies. Tax incentives should also be used to

encourage water conservation, the use of recycled products, and the reduction of air pollution.

• *Improve enforcement of effective environmental regulations....*

In the long run, good environmental policy is good economic policy. America's commitment to environmental sustainability has already created a $130-billion-a-year pollution-control industry. We hope the United States will compete for innovations in environmental products, which will not only create a more sustainable future but also create jobs.

Abusing the environment to fuel our lifestyle today is the clearest example of generational inequity. Much of the environmental destruction has been caused by an unwillingness to make short-term sacrifices for long-term benefits. We can no longer afford such shortsighted action.

Our future hangs in the balance.

CONCLUSION

For we must consider that we shall be a city upon a hill. The eyes of all people are upon us, so that if we shall deal falsely with our God in this work we have undertaken, and cause Him to withdraw His help from us, we shall be made a story and a byword through the world.   *JOHN WINTHROP, 1630*

Our generation is coming of age at the precise moment when the famous prediction of John Winthrop has been fulfilled, and when his warning resonates loudest. For at no time in our nation's history have the eyes of the world been so keenly focused an America.

As the framework of freedom and democracy keeps our nation unified, we watch other countries splinter. And as new nations emerge from the ashes of totalitarianism, they increasingly examine the American model. We are being analyzed constantly for the effectiveness of our democracy, the fairness of our society, and the strength of our values.

John Winthrop called upon the first community of settlers to be an example for the rest of the world. He stressed individual responsibility and long-term planning for both pragmatic and idealistic reasons. We reaffirm Winthrop's conviction: America's efforts to meet our toughest challenges depend on our ability to look inward. Our willingness to meet these challenges will affect not only the future of our nation, but the future of the world.

We draw our lesson from Benjamin Franklin, a community activist for whom public service meant establishing a volunteer fire department and public library as much as it meant being his nation's ambassador to France. People such as Franklin defined the American commitment to liberty and community that has sustained our democracy. And from each small ripple of freedom and commitment, they shaped the framework of individual and community responsibility that has come to form the mighty tide of American democracy.

We hope that individual involvement on the community level will become the defining characteristic of our generation. For it is from our neighborhoods, streets, and homes that we as a nation draw our strength. The difficulties facing us require that we unite behind this ethic.

Therefore, we as a generation, the generation that will come to power in the third millennium, must reaffirm our commitment to individual responsibility—for our actions and to our communities. The future of our country demands no less.

CHAPTER THIRTEEN

Agenda 2000

2030 Center

The 2030 Center is an action tank founded and run by young leaders to conduct research and advocacy about economic issues affecting America's future. The 2030 Center's goals include winning policy reforms that will provide economic opportunity for younger generations, investment in America's future, and stronger social bonds between generations. Hans Riemer is the founder and director of the 2030 Center. Previously, he was an assistant to Arthur S. Flemming, the former secretary of health, education, and welfare and U.S. commissioner of civil rights. He has also been a project assistant at the National Academy of Social Insurance in Washington, D.C.

The 2030 Center's Agenda 2000 promotes the views and the voice of young Americans on important economic issues facing the country today. Members of the organization call for new societal values that emphasize both individual and collective responsibility. They express concern about far-reaching issues including education and job training, workplace opportunities, and the environment. They suggest that Social Security is a prime example of the collective responsibility that Americans have to one another. They assert that the Social Security program can be modernized while continuing a strong commitment to the national community.

Young leaders founded the 2030 Center to engage young people—and everyone else—in a robust and hard-hitting public debate about America's economic future. We want to revive the prospect of a better future for our generation and for generations to come.

With Agenda 2000, we are launching a forum for discussion and debate, and we hope it will challenge everyone to grapple with the magnitude of changes we need to ensure a rebirth of our country's optimism and vision, and build a stronger society. And we hope Agenda 2000 will help us all take responsibility for making those changes happen.

The premise of Agenda 2000 is that the fundamental challenge facing our generation—and all Americans—is that of building an economic system that generates both opportunity and security.

WE ARE ALL IN IT TOGETHER

The generation of young Americans now in our twenties and early thirties is a growing force in this country. Raised in the shadow of the baby boom, we were born into an era marked by crises and diminished hope: the more uncertain stages of the struggle for civil rights, the Vietnam era, and—most signifi-cantly—a deterioration of standards of living that has undermined progress and made issues about incomes, opportunity, race, and family life much more problematic.

Despite being the first generation raised in the Age of Media, we are not well understood. We are targeted as a mass market and endure manufactured labels and imagery that bear only superficial relation to how we work, think, or engage in our communities.

People say that our generation has no "issue" to spark the imagination, that we have no ideas to activate in the democratic process. After a generation of economic decline, however, we can put the pieces together for ourselves.

Young leaders founded the 2030 Center to address the core economic issues that are shaping America's future. We believe that the challenge to our future is to rebuild our economic system so that when the economy grows, Americans move forward together. The economy should reflect the value that we are all in it together. It used to be this way—and America has no future without broadly shared prosperity.

This is not the only challenge that we face. We do not make the mistake of thinking that all of America's most serious problems can be addressed through economic policy. We also need an ethical revolution to reinforce our sense of individual responsibility and collective obligation to fairness and to the future. Values of environmental sustainability, diversity, and equity have to carry more weight in our society.

But our generation has a special insight into the truism that "when the economy goes bad, everything goes bad." . . .

Our America has, at least, the trappings of more prosperity than thirty years ago, particularly when measured by technological progress. And yet, today, many communities are increasingly impoverished, family incomes are stagnating or declining for broad segments of the population, economic polarization is reaching unprecedented heights, our schools are crumbling while students are mortgaging their futures to pay for education.

Given the unfolding realities of our new economy, these trends promise to grow worse if there is no effort to change course. And all the while, the reigning theory is that nothing can be done.

In fact, the message that our generation hears most often is, "You are on your own." The survival-of-the-fittest philosophy that has come to dominate our era is devouring what once was a successful economic system, and it is threatening our social and political systems.

We cannot just "go it alone." Rebuilding an economy that will move all Americans forward together is going to require bringing together government, the private sector, and individuals to set new ground rules, foster stronger values, and invest in our future. And it is going to require flexing political muscle to reclaim our government and our governing philosophy from powerful interests who profit when we believe that nothing can be done and we do not get involved.

America has the vision, the resources, and the history to get this job done. We have produced Agenda 2000 to generate debate about these important ideas and articulate the platform for which we stand. We will use it to help build a stronger voice for young people everywhere.

LOST: THE VALUES THAT BUILD A SOCIETY

. . . Since about 1973 circumstances for most Americans—and young people in particular—have grown steadily worse.

It was not always this way. In the several decades following World War II, the American economy grew at a rapid clip and, most importantly, in a manner that created broadly shared prosperity. [Corporations] invested in long-term growth, gave resources back to local communities, and provided good wages and benefits. They competed on the basis of innovation and efficiency, in a worker-friendly manner. These were the ground rules of growth, and they helped build an economy that created increasing opportunity from generation to generation.

Then, values changed—for the worse. Today, while the economy grows, wages are falling and benefits are disappearing. The degree of economic inequality in our society, once broadly acceptable, has become intolerable—and it is growing worse. The sense of individual and collective responsibility that once guided the economy has been overtaken by a philosophy that, basically, "whatever happens, happens"; there is nothing that can be done about our problems of economic polarization and insecurity, and there are no boundaries defining right and wrong.

As a result, companies compete by driving basic standards for people downward, and most people are being denied the chance to participate in the rewards of economic growth. America is devolving into a state of economic Darwinism.

This value system threatens to overtake our political culture as well. Today, at great risk to our future, we are abandoning public solutions to public problems. Rather than strive for broad-based change, young people are being told to just "go it alone."

The effort to persuade Generation X to pull out of Social Security and replace the program with individual investment accounts is a prime example. This debate symbolizes a clear division between a direction that promotes survival of the fittest—the philosophy dominating our economy—and one that promotes the interests of the broader community—the philosophy that underpins our political and religious institutions. Replacing Social Security with individual accounts will undermine our values, downsize our national community, and further distance people from one another.

We have witnessed clearly and definitively the power of the market system. In the lifetime of our generation, socialist and centrally planned economies and the societies that they support have stumbled and even fallen. The American economy, guided by a mix of market principles and social values, has proven most capable of simultaneously supporting strong communities and economic prosperity.

Today, we are losing that mix. The idea that we are all in it together has been pushed into the wings as the importance of public values and collective action has diminished. . . .

America needs an economic agenda, both public and private, that reflects our values—in which we are not simply growing but growing together.

THE NUMBERS CRUNCH

An economy that creates increasing security and opportunity is one of the strongest generational legacies. Today, deteriorating circumstances for young people coupled with the failure of public policies to keep pace with change, are reversing America's generational progress.

Decreased earnings.
[Real] earnings for young adults have been falling for nearly twenty-five years. Not growing more slowly but falling. For example, real median weekly earnings for men ages 20–34 have declined about 32 percent since 1973.[1] This earnings decline has affected young people at all education levels.

From 1989 to 1995—years of heralded economic growth—earnings for college graduates with one to five years of experience on the job fell nearly 10 percent.[2] This marks the first time ever that a generation of college graduates has entered the workforce and experienced lower earnings than a previous generation of college graduates.

Economic problems are much more severe for high-school graduates. . . .

In 1995, entry-level earnings for young men with a high-school education were 28 percent lower than they were in 1979. For young women, they were almost 19 percent lower.[3] In 1993, a typical young male high-school graduate earned as much money—in real dollars—as a male high-school dropout earned twenty years earlier.

Circumstances are not much better for young families. Even though dual incomes are more common today than ever before, young families have experienced persistent income declines. The struggle to raise children on failing incomes has been compounded by simultaneously increasing costs for basic services and benefits that families need; the cost of child care has increased 23 percent over the past seven years,[4] while one in three 21- to 24-year-old and one in four 25- to 34-year-old adults have no health insurance.[5]

Diminished opportunity.
In the new global, information-age economy, "knowledge" is a more significant factor of basic economic opportunity than it has ever been. Access to higher education and lifetime training is necessary for decent job opportunity—and for a strong economy that is competitive in the global economy.

Public policies, however, are not building a new American institution of education to meet the challenges of tomorrow and create broad opportunity in this new context; in fact, we have in many ways moved backward in recent years.

Tuition rates at public four-year colleges have increased nearly 9 percent a year over the past 15 years, for a total of more than 250 percent.[6] This is 3.6 times the annual rate of inflation and 2.5 times more than annual earnings have grown for the median working family.[7]

These tuition increases create barriers for a generation scrambling to prepare for the economic realities of tomorrow. Most significantly, the poorest 25 percent of families are actually enrolling their kids in college at a lower rate than they were 15 years ago.[8] . . .

The balance of student aid has also shifted from grants to loans. . . . The average college graduate now has more than $10,000 in debt, and debt is increasing dramatically with each passing year.[9] High costs are also causing many young people to drop out of school before completion. . . .

At the same time, we must face up to the fact that a college education cannot be the sole route to economic opportunity. Only about 25 percent of high-school graduates earn a bachelor's degree today.[10] If, through better policies, we manage to double the number of college graduates, one-half of high-school graduates would still have no college degree.

In other words, college is no panacea. Education policy must ensure that there are no unfair barriers to higher education, particularly by race or income. But education and training are only a partial remedy: if we are going to make a real difference in economic opportunity and earnings growth for this and future generations, we must focus national debate on what is happening in the workplace and with trends towards earnings inequality. This is the only way to harmonize the interests of the college- and non-college-educated members of our generation and society. . . .

[Our generation was raised in an era of bitter political and social division—it is all we have known. While young people are leading a movement to connect communities through initiatives like community service, political debate must focus on real problems that transcend divisions if we are going to produce change.]

A NATION DIVIDED

By economics . . .

America's economic and social system is bound to produce some degree of disparity—mobility and inequality are flip sides of the same coin. Over the past twenty-five years, however, the degree of disparity has gradually shifted from, broadly speaking, natural and inevitable to unnatural and dangerous.

From 1947 to 1973, when the economy grew, Americans moved forward together. The annual income of members of every quintile of the population (by income) grew at approximately the same rate, 2.6 percent. In contrast, since 1973, the bottom 40 percent of the population has experienced falling real family incomes while the top 40 percent has continued to register positive growth rates, increasing higher up on the ladder.[11]

By another measure, in 1970, according to Census Bureau statistics, the top 5 percent of families' average income was about 11.5 times more than the bottom 20 percent of families. By 1994, the divide increased 19 times.[12] . . .

Many politicians and pundits treat this vast polarization as the "unavoidable" consequence of globalization—a problem that, since "nothing can be done," does not merit imaginative investigation. In other words, since they do not know quite what to do, or are unwilling to take a stand, they do not talk about the issue at all. Instead, they turn to simplistic and divisive debate about problems that have more to do with the effects of economic polarization than the cause. For example, the long-term economic problems that our generation hears most about are the federal debt and the aging of the baby boom generation.

But the ongoing trend of economic gains accumulating at the top instead of across the population will, if it continues, have a more drastic effect upon the economic and social circumstances of future generations than repaying the federal debt or financing the retirement of the baby boomers—which already are serious enough.[13] It is alarming, then, that growing economic disparity has not entered political debate as a long-term problem with serious consequences for our society.

. . . And race . . .

Debate about race and the inner cities is even further off course. The ongoing transformation from a middle-class manufacturing economy to an economically polarized, information-based society has dramatically affected local communities in America's cities. The exodus from the inner cities of both well-paying jobs and the middle class in general, along with the economic and social resources that go with them, is leaving behind a core community, composed predominantly of minority populations, that is increasingly isolated from resources and opportunities.[14]

Political debate has offered few meaningful solutions to reverse this trend. Debate about promoting opportunity in the inner cities is frequently confined to discussion of welfare programs, while underlying economic problems—earnings inequality, access to training, investment capital, transportation—are ignored. . . .

If racial division continues to overwhelm discussion about promoting opportunity—while we rapidly shift into a new economy that is closing traditional doors to advancement—America may face a crisis of race that we will not be able to remedy through tolerance or legislation. While many leaders look for ways to dismantle affirmative action—leaving nothing in its place—we are steadily moving towards two separate societies.

...And age...

"Generational conflict" is one of the most telling examples of our country's growing divisiveness as well as the effectiveness with which special interests use the media to manipulate public discussion. The debate over real, but manageable, problems with Social Security has degenerated into false prophecies of impending warfare between the generations. The vapid notion that young people should "rise up" against the elderly contributes nothing to creating solutions while it most certainly undermines the strength of our society.

Indeed, our generation's public identity has been soured by the seemingly endless parade of Gen-X "spokespersons" who have used television to promote their careers, foment generational warfare, and champion a legislative agenda more driven by special interests than the public good. Just as "grassroots" citizen movements have been replaced by "Astroturf" lobbying campaigns directed by highly paid political operatives, today the "voice" of Generation X is all too often brought to you by Corporate America.

The great loss of the generational political movement is that it largely has been co-opted by special interests that are using the voice of our generation to advocate their own narrow agenda—which is invariably little more than replacing Social Security with individual investment accounts, a policy of survival of the fittest.

When circumstances have grown more difficult for young people, we are being misled to place blame on an easy target—the elderly—instead of a true cause—the economy. And America is pushed further towards privatizing public problems in an area where the stakes are literally life and death for our most vulnerable populations.

... Will not stand!

Americans will build a better future when we unite behind a national purpose, drive special interests from the table, and build from common concerns. In such historic moments of urgency, we have relied on this profound sense of interdependence to create public education, civil rights, and Social Security—to take but a few examples. It is the way of our future....

RECLAIMING OUR FUTURE

When young adults returned from the battle fronts of World War II, they were greeted with a national effort to create a better future. This was a time of vast public investments: the GI Bill and the interstate highway construction program, the largest human capital and physical infrastructure investments in our country's history, are two prime examples. Programs such as these provided young Americans with opportunities as vital as those that they had fought to preserve for all Americans—the promise of a better future. . . .

The postwar investment agenda transformed a generation of Americans and, by them, a nation. . . .

INVESTING IN THE ECONOMY

[As in the past,] America needs an economic agenda for the future. We need an investment strategy based on fueling the engines of economic growth: an educated citizenry, modern infrastructure, extensive research and development.

Education and training.
We need to renew our commitment to public education and then reach further still. Constant experimentation—charter schools and open enrollment for K–12 are a good start—and greatly expanded resources for early childhood, elementary, and secondary education are essential to our future.

A core value of our society is that each and every child should have the chance to succeed—or fail—on the basis of his or her own merits and hard work. . . .

Today, public schools work well for the majority of the population; at the same time, however, our educational system and its vast disparities fail millions of children—particularly people of color—in substandard schools. If we stay the current course, these children, through no fault of their own, will have little opportunity to succeed in our new, knowledge-based labor market.

Public–private education and training partnerships must be part of the template for restoring broad economic opportunity and vitality to America. In recent years, forward-thinking local governments, through their public schools and community colleges, have been developing effective partnerships with corporations, to the benefit of both the companies and the local communities. . . .

The private sector alone, however, cannot begin to provide the comprehensive and effective education and social infrastructure that we need for the new knowledge-based economy. . . .

[We need increased public investment. And we] need leadership for education that the whole society can get behind.

Infrastructure.
In the 1950s, President Eisenhower led the country in a massive infrastructure campaign, integrating the nation with a vast system of interstate highways. Despite assertions that government should "get out" of the economy, public investments in infrastructure of this sort—the canals, the railroads—have spurred development and growth throughout America's history.

It is time once again to plan and build for our future—to adapt an old model to a new context. The communications and information infrastructure will be the bridges and canals of the next century, essential to the continued success of our economy and society. Recent efforts to link every classroom and library to the Internet are an excellent start. But this is only the beginning.

Researching and developing our future: Long-term, sustainable growth.
Research is one of the most important investments in the future that we can make. Environmental technologies, particularly alternative energy, promote long-term environmental health. "Applied research" provides businesses and corporations with models they need to improve efficiency and build better products. Research grants to universities allow the academic community to develop innovative, groundbreaking ideas. . . .

The government . . . has the capacity to look far into the future and pursue basic lines of research and matters of understanding that can pay large dividends to society.[15] Long-term investment for the public good—the public perspective—is crucial to our economic advancement.

But investing in technology is about more than just long-term growth. It is, quite simply, about whether, over the long term, we can sustain economic growth at all.

Today, we consume and waste natural resources—topsoil, forests, energy, water, minerals—at a rate that cannot be sustained over the lifetime of our generation, much less for future generations. . . .

Intelligent investment in sustainable environmental technology will increase economic growth, create healthy communities, and improve the quality of life for everyone. America needs a concerted agenda with visionary leadership to invest in building the environmentally friendly economy we will need for the next millennium.

STRENGTHENING COMMUNITIES

Over the past ten years, service entrepreneurs have created organizations that are taking innovative approaches to strengthening communities through volunteerism. A small army of young people, and people of all generations, have rallied to rebuild neighborhoods and communities one at a time.

Investing in the service movement—and educating a new generation of community leaders—is a public- and private-sector responsibility. . . .

While we labor for change in our neighborhoods and our cities, . . . our generation's efforts to strengthen communities through service are being counteracted by declining government financial support for social services and by a hostile corporate climate.

As the economy has ceased to provide broadly shared prosperity, public programs that protect against economic risks and promote economic opportunity have become more central to the strength of our society.

These program areas must be at the top of our agenda if we are going to improve the day-to-day circumstances of broad segments of our population, particularly the most vulnerable.

Social Security.
Social Security protects and expands opportunities for millions of people and strengthens communities that might otherwise fall behind. It has substantially ended what was once one of our most vexing public problems, the poverty of the old. Social Security is one of the most effective initiatives the government has ever undertaken, and it is one of the best examples of how we are all in it together.

Substantially weakening Social Security—which many so-called "generational equity" proponents advocate—will only push us further towards an atomistic society in which individuals go it alone. It is precisely the ascendance of this philosophy that is undermining our communities today.

Many analysts would have us believe that Social Security is but one step from the precipice. While it faces obvious financing challenges resulting from changing demographics, the problems are nowhere near as severe as is often reported.[16] America's challenge with Social Security is to modernize the program while maintaining a strong commitment to the national community—and the collective resources that help build it.

Child care.
. . . We must find innovative and comprehensive ways to help families afford quality child care.

Child care is one of the largest expenses for working families with children, and expanding access can go a long way towards improving education and enhancing economic security. The recent devolution of responsibility for welfare programs to the states increases the need for a national approach to ensuring access to child care and helping families successfully leave welfare. Substandard child care programs simply cost too much to families and to our society.

Health care.
Health care is one of the most serious problems we face today. While we spend more on health care than any other country in the world, tens of millions of people have no health security—including millions of children.

Affordable, quality health care is critically important to the well-being of individuals, families, and communities. Today, many working families, often young and with children, are forced to go without health care in all but emergency circumstances. The nation will take a great stride forward when every family is assured of continuous, quality health coverage. While it may seem paradoxical, extending coverage to the entire population is one of the few plausible mechanisms for holding health care costs down.

Medicare and Medicaid are currently projected to increase in costs at an unsustainable rate. These projections assume cost increases, parallel to health care costs generally, that are totally unsustainable. If all health spending should increase at this rate, by the year 2030 Medicare and Medicaid will consume the federal budget while health care generally will consume 25 percent of the economy and nearly 100 percent of the median four-person family's income.[17]

The entire health care system needs fundamental reform, and the guiding principle must be creating broad-based risk pools that bring everyone—healthy, sick, young, old, rich, poor—together.

Building America's cities.
Over the past several decades, a continuous exodus of capital, good jobs, and people has weakened America's cities and sent many communities into a downward spiral. The erosion of economic opportunity for broad segments of the population over the past generation has particularly impacted state and local governments, reducing their resources while increasing the demand for their services. And it has left millions trapped in an economic prison that breeds crime and violence, counterproductive behavior, and hopelessness.

We need to plan for the long-term futures of our cities. Public and private partnerships are a critical force for change; at the same time, there is nothing that can replace the resources of government and its ability to provide the tools that businesses and people need to create opportunity. While many social policies will improve circumstances dramatically for the most vulnerable communities in America's cities—particularly health care and child care—a vibrant and productive economy will be the most effective resource for social change, and the U.S. economy will come closer to reaching its potential.

Communities need access to capital to enable the growth of existing businesses and the creation of new ones. Companies need incentives to locate and invest in urban communities—and they need quality infrastructure once they move in. And people need the basic resources of any market economy—education, training, job placement, nondiscrimination. Together, these elements of an economic agenda for America's cities can provide an important catalyst for long-term change.

REBUILDING DEMOCRACY

Achieving meaningful change in our economy will require changing the relations of power in our political and economic system. Principles of democracy—of equality between participants—have eroded in government and in the workplace. For employers and politicians, young people are particularly expendable.

In government.
With the decline of political parties and other grassroots citizen organizations, politicians are increasingly dependent upon using television to educate voters about their positions on issues. The average cost of winning a seat in the U.S. House of Representatives has increased by more than 1,092 percent over the past twenty years. . . .

The influence of money on the political process helps explain why government has failed to create economic policies that foster broadly shared prosperity. . . .

On nearly every issue that concerns young people—whether jobs and the economy, education, health care, Social Security, environmental technology—powerful interests are financing sophisticated campaigns to quash change, maintain structural disparities, and siphon our nation's resources upward. . . .

We need to make our political leaders independent from special interests. . . . Any progress we make for our democracy against the money machine will pay dividends across the entire spectrum of issues that matter most.

In the workplace.

... In our economy, earnings for people with decent and even high levels of skill have fallen at a breathtaking pace.

The overriding explanation has less to do with economics than with politics—the exercise of power both in government and in the workplace.

Collective bargaining through labor unions and other progressive workplace arrangements is the only force in our "winner-take-all" economy that enables working people to stand up for their rights. Unions give employees the power to negotiate for wages, benefits, and safety standards.

Labor laws are much weaker today than they were in years past. Compounding this problem, many people now in the workforce—particularly immigrants and women—do not have a history with unions and are more hesitant to organize. While a lack of bargaining power hits them hardest, standards are falling across the board, for everyone.

By 1996, only 5.5 percent of workers ages 18–24 and 12.0 percent of workers ages 25–34 were union members, down from 9.1 and 19.6 percent in 1980.[18] This decline—just as with earnings trends generally—is considerably more steep than for other age groups.

Building an economy that promotes broadly shared prosperity is going to require developing new arrangements between employers and employees that build employees' autonomy, their stake in the enterprise, and their productivity. The challenge is to promote labor market flexibility as well as strong standards for working people. Policies that promote responsible corporate practices must come to the center of the agenda for our political leadership, while the labor laws that have undermined the rights of working people to organize their own unions must be tossed from the books.

If labor has a future, it must have a new face and it must organize industries that have been neglected. Unions will have to reach out to new constituencies like working women and, particularly, people of color—the working population of America's future.

REBUILDING THE BUDGET TO INVEST IN THE FUTURE

It is time to initiate real budgetary reform to free up resources for purposes that can build our future. As well, we need to begin thinking more broadly about how to structure the budget to protect investments that grow our economy and strengthen our society.

As we transition to the next millennium, a central political goal must be to put the future in the federal budget.

Subsidizing the past.

As long as the budget deficit is a central fixture of political debate, the kind of vigorous and visionary policymaking that we need in order to build a better future remains off the table. In today's budgetary climate, there is no room for waste.

Nevertheless, large amounts of our resources are given away to special interests through unnecessary and inefficient corporate subsidies—"corporate welfare." Mainstream estimates place the cost of unneeded subsidies upward of $150 billion over five years.[19]

The bulk of them support industries with heavy investments in the ways of the past, such as agriculture and natural resource extraction—timber production, mining, and fossil fuels. These industries do not produce many jobs for our current workforce and certainly will not for the next generation. Many subsidies encourage activities that damage the environment or export American jobs overseas.

Our common assets as citizens of this country—public lands, the oceans, the sky—should be properly accounted for in our economy and their value shared by the people—in precisely the same way that the cost of degradation is shared. Doing so will create a great pool of resources to invest in the industries of the future and our communities and put us on a path towards more sustainable growth.

Securing the future.

Because of the current structure of the federal budget, investment resources are largely drawn from nondefense discretionary spending. All twelve appropriations in this category add up to less than the defense budget alone. Nevertheless, every year they bear the brunt of deficit reduction efforts, while industry subsidies and military spending are absent from national debate.

The federal government must radically alter its current approach to structuring the budget. Today, the future is not counted in the federal budget. To distinguish investments from current consumption, we should look at creating an "investment" category. . . .

An investment budget would provide a clear representation of the value that America places on the future. Such a budget would help clarify issues of fiscal responsibility. For young people, an investment budget can provide a benchmark to evaluate government priorities and their impact on future generations. Many states have such a budget, and at the national level it could help restore fiscal responsibility. . . .

MOVING FORWARD TOGETHER

The generation of Americans now in our twenties and early thirties is preparing to assume the mantle of leadership for the future. We will take America to a
higher level.

To realize this mission, we must use government as a tool to shape America's
economic progress. That is how America builds strong communities.

We can already see outlines of the economy that we will live with—for much
of our lives—if we do not change course. It does not provide adequate opportunity or security. Many communities are unable to contribute to economic
prosperity or share its rewards.

Change is possible. The balance shifts towards people who participate.

As we approach the year 2000, there is a battle for us to fight, through our
organizations, in the media, in the workplace. The 2030 Center will help lay the
groundwork—through forums, articles, research projects, advocacy campaigns, conversation with our colleagues and classmates and neighbors.

Our challenge is to bring the economy—and the values with which we guide
it—to the center of a national debate about America's future. That is how, in a
new era, we will create a better society.

REFERENCES

1. U.S. Department of Labor. Bureau of Labor Statistics. *Median usual weekly
earnings of full-time wage and salary workers, by age and sex, May 1973–78.*
Washington, D.C.: U.S. Government Printing Office, 1997. U.S. Department of Labor.
Bureau of Labor Statistics. *Median usual weekly earnings of full-time wage and salary
workers, by sex, age, race, and Hispanic origin, quarterly averages (not seasonally
adjusted), 1979–96.* Washington, D.C.: U.S. Government Printing Office, 1997.

2. Mishel, Lawrence, Jared Bernstein, and John Schmitt. *The State of Working
America, 1996–1997.* Economic Policy Institute Series. Armonk: M. E. Sharpe, 1997.

3. Ibid.

4. U.S. House of Representatives. *Green Book: Background Material and Data on
Programs Within the Jurisdiction of the Committee on Ways and Means.* Washington,
D.C.: U.S. Government Printing Office, 1996, chart 10-1.

5. Employee Benefit Research Institute. "Sources of Health Insurance and
Characteristics of the Uninsured: Analysis of the March 1996 Current Population
Survey." *EBRI Issue Brief,* No. 179, November 1996.

6. Wessel, David. "The Outlook: Rising Cost of College Interests the Politicians." *Wall Street Journal*, December 30, 1996.

7. U.S. Department of Commerce. Bureau of the Census. Current Population Reports, various dates. *Historical Income Tables—Persons*. P-7 Series. Washington D.C.: U.S. Government Printing Office.

8. Wessel, David. "The Outlook: Rising Cost of College Interests the Politicians." *Wall Street Journal*, December 30, 1996.

9. Information provided by the College Entrance Examination Board, Washington, D.C.

10. U.S. Department of Education. National Center for Education Statistics. *The Condition of Education 1996*. Washington, D.C.: U.S. Government Printing Office, 1996.

11. Krugman, Paul. "The Spiral of Inequality." *Mother Jones*, November–December 1996.

12. Mishel, Lawrence, Jared Bernstein, and John Schmitt. *The State of Working America, 1996–1997*. Economic Policy Institute Series. Armonk: M. E. Sharpe, 1997. Bagby, Meredith. *Annual Report of the United States of America*. New York: McGraw-Hill, 1997.

13. Baker, Dean. Draft of forthcoming paper, "The Long-Term Economic and Fiscal Consequences of Earnings Inequality." Economic Policy Institute, 1997.

14. Wilson, William Julius. *The Truly Disadvantaged*. Chicago: University of Chicago Press, 1987.

15. Broad, William J. "G.O.P. Budget Cuts Would Fall Hard on Civilian Science: Basic Research at Risk." *New York Times*, April 22, 1995.

16. According to the Social Security Trustees, if no changes are made, by the year 2030 the Social Security program will have, from FICA contributions, 75 percent of the revenues that it needs to pay benefits. This assumption obviously depends upon the idea that nothing will be done to fix the shortfall. See http://www.ssa.gov.

17. Baker, Dean. *Robbing the Cradle: A Critical Assessment of Generational Accounting*. Washington, D.C.: Economic Policy Institute, 1995.

18. U.S. Department of Labor. Bureau of Labor Statistics. *Union affiliation of employed wage and salary workers by selected characteristics*. Washington, D.C.: U.S. Government Printing Office, 1997.

19. This estimate is based on a reading of several sources. For a more detailed analysis consider: Cuff, Courtney, and Gawain Kripke, eds. *Green Scissors 1997*. Washington, D.C.: Friends of the Earth, 1997. Shapiro, Robert J. "Cut-and-Invest: A Budget Strategy for the New Economy." *Progressive Policy Institute*, No. 23. Washington, D.C.: Progressive Policy Institute, March 1995. Information from the Stop Corporate Welfare Coalition, Washington, D.C.

GPSR Authorized Representative: Easy Access System Europe, Mustamäe tee 50, 10621 Tallinn, Estonia, gpsr.requests@easproject.com

www.ingramcontent.com/pod-product-compliance
Lightning Source LLC
Chambersburg PA
CBHW032122020426
42334CB00016B/1038